# WORLD CUP

Packed with essential information, *World Cup 90* is the indispensable pocket companion for anyone interested in this year's tournament – whether they will be following the competition on television or actually going to Italy. It includes:

* the Draw for the First Round of matches with a relevant map
* an analysis of all the teams competing
* information concerning the leading players
* a special section about Italy, its squad, its grounds and its manager
* two sections of stunning action photographs
* information about the past thirteen tournaments including interesting statistics

**AT HOME OR AWAY, THE ESSENTIAL GUIDE TO WORLD CUP 90**

# Acknowledgements

I should like to thank the following who have given me information or ideas I've been able to use: BRIAN GLANVILLE of the *Sunday Times*, TIM GUTCH, GEERT MINNEN in Brussels, SINCLAIR ROAD, ANTONIO DI MONTPELIANO, GERRY FOLEY, ERNEST HECHT, DINO LANATI, ROBERT LIPSCOMB in Paris, MATTHEW GUY, ANDRO LINKLATER, BO CHRISTOPHERSSON in Varberg, MICHAEL THOMPSON-NOEL of the *Financial Times*, JOHN GILL, KLAUS FLUEGGE, KEN PRITCHARD, DEREK JANES, ALDO OREZZI, JOHN MOYNIHAN of the *Independent on Sunday*, LIONELLO WHEELER, KEITH NEIMEYER, DAVID MILLER, GEOFFREY GREEN, BRIAN MOORE, ROGER PRING, CHRISTIAN TYLER, ROBERTO CIANFANELLI, HARRY TATTERSALL, ANDREW SCHULLER, JACK ROLLIN of the *Sunday Telegraph*, KEIR RADNEDGE OF World Soccer, and my father, HAROLD EVANS. JULIET BRIGHTMORE helped me select the photographs, LUCY OGDEN and CAROLINE PLAISTED have been very helpful editors, DAMIAN CONLIN has been very meticulous, and overseeing the whole project has been the wise eye of ELIZABETH ROY.

*About the author:*
Philip Evans has written three novels – *Next Time You'll Wake Up Dead*, *The Bodyguard Man*, and *Playing the Wild Card*, the last two available from Coronet Books. He has also written books about football, several short stories, and has contributed articles to the *Sunday Times*, the *Observer* and the *Financial Times*.

*Photograph credits*
All Sport, Colorsport, Hulton Picture Company, Popperfoto, Sport and General, Syndication International, Bob Thomas. Back cover photographs: Colorsport

# WORLD CUP 90

---

# Philip Evans

Hodder and Stoughton

*For Chris and Adam*

Text copyright © 1973, 1990
Philip Evans
This new edition first published
in Great Britain in 1990

The right of Philip Evans to be identified as the author of this work has been asserted by him in accordance with the Copyright, Designs and Patents Act 1988.

This book is sold subject to the condition that it shall not, by way of trade or otherwise, be lent, re-sold, hired out or otherwise circulated without the publisher's prior consent in any form of binding or cover other than that in which it is published and without a similar condition including this condition being imposed on the subsequent purchaser.

No part of this publication may be reproduced or transmitted in any form or by any means, electronically or mechanically, including photocopying, recording or any information storage or retrieval system, without either the prior permission in writing from the publisher or a licence, permitting restricted copying. In the United Kingdom such licences are issued by the Copyright Licensing Agency, 33–34 Alfred Place, London WC1E 7DP.

**British Library C.I.P.**

Evans, Philip, *1943 Apr. 4–*
  World Cup 1990.
  1. Association football.
  Competitions. World Cup
  (Football championship) I.
  Title
  796.334668

ISBN 0-340-51735-2

Printed and bound in Great Britain for Hodder and Stoughton Paperbacks, a division of Hodder and Stoughton Limited, Mill Road, Dunton Green, Sevenoaks, Kent TN13 2YA. (Editorial Office: 47 Bedford Square, London WC1B 3DP) by Cox and Wyman Ltd, Reading, Berks.

# CONTENTS

| | |
|---|---:|
| **Prologue** | 6 |
| 1  A look at previous tournaments (1930–1958) | 8 |
| 2  The Brazilian triumph continues – despite a rude interruption by England | 31 |
| 3  Holland Finalists on two occasions | 62 |
| 4  Italy triumph for the third time | 88 |
| 5  The hand of Diego | 108 |
| 6  Some statistics | 130 |
| 7  Summary of matches in World Cup Finals 1930–1986 | 139 |
| 8  The teams who will be competing | 141 |
| 9  Leading players in the tournament | 169 |
| 10  Italy – the record, the manager, and the players | 185 |
| 11  Complete First Round Draw | 189 |

# PROLOGUE

Although Italy acted as Hosts to the 1968 edition of the European Nations Championships, in which it was victorious, as well as to the 1980 edition of the same competition, the country has always been eager to host another edition of the World Cup finals, which it first looked after in 1934. The footballing authorities, therefore, entered its name to FIFA on 21 July 1978 as being possible Hosts, soon after the finish of the eleventh edition held in Argentina, in which Italy finished fourth. It was a proposal that received full backing from the Government in October 1983, since Italy had been victorious on the last occasion that the finals were played in Europe, beating West Germany 3–1 in the 1982 Final held in Madrid. On 19 May 1984 FIFA duly assigned it the right to act as Hosts to the 1990 edition, choosing Italy in preference to the Soviet Union.

On 10 June 1987, Italy (Winners in 1982) defeated Argentina (Winners in 1978) 3–1 in an entertaining match in Zurich to commemorate the 'start' of the 1990 tournament. Perhaps not since the mid-Thirties, when Italy triumphed in the World Cups of 1934 and 1938 and also won the 1936 Olympic Games under the magisterial guidance of Vittorio Pozzo, has the game inside the country been more celebrated. It was a popularity fittingly recorded when Italian clubs finished as finalists in all three competitions in the various European Cups at the end of the 1988–89 season, partly thanks to their imported players. Milan, helped by the Dutch trio of Ruud Gullit, Marco Van Basten and Franz Rijkaard, finished as winners in the European Cup, Sampdoria, given tremendous aid by Toninho Cerezo of Brazil and Victor of Spain, finished as finalists in the Cup Winners' Cup and Napoli, with the mercurial Maradona of Argentina as well as Careca and Alemao of Brazil, won the UEFA Cup.

The 1990 edition of the tournament will be considerably larger and more prolonged than was that of 1934, which saw the 16 qualifiers play 17 matches on a knock-out basis. (There were 17 rather than 15 since Germany beat Austria to finish Third, and

## Prologue

Italy's drawn quarter-final with Spain had to be replayed since the theme of the penalty shoot-out had not yet been brought into practice.) The first matches took place on 27 May in Rome, Trieste, Genoa, Florence, Turin, Bologna, Naples and Milan, and the Final between Italy and Czechoslovakia took place on 10 June in Rome. The 1990 tournament, however, will be considerably more ponderous. Before we reach a similar knock-out tournament, the 24 qualifiers will play in six sections of four teams, a filter of 36 matches (in some of which strategy will play a leading part in deciding the 16 most successful teams on points and goal-difference) – providing a final total of 52 games. The opening match between the Holders, Argentina, and Cameroon will take place on 8 June 1990 and the Final not until 8 July.

Eight million extra tourists are expected in 1990, making the authorities desperate to ensure that the tournament proceeds without a hitch. If it does the authorities estimate that for the following two or three years tourism will flourish but if not it will take at least ten years to repair the damage. If only two new stadiums have been constructed (in Torino and in Bari), then the ten other stadiums have all been refurbished, many of them being all-seater. This will be the first major sporting competition in which special provision at each stadium has been made for those handicapped only able to drive special cars and for those in wheelchairs. Since Italians have always followed football with an almost religious passion, and the addiction of their sporting press to hyperbole and invective is second to none, empty seats should be a rarity.

As Italian club sides have remained in the forefront of European Cup competitions, all the stadiums have been looked after in a fitting manner by the appropriate authorities, and for this competition the grounds chosen to host games have been able to benefit from massive Government funding. Billions of *lire* have been spent to ensure that from the point of view of spectators this will be the most sumptuous of all World Cup final competitions.

# 1 A LOOK AT PREVIOUS TOURNAMENTS (1930–1958)

The idea of this book is to provide a readable and interesting guide to what we all may hope to see from what will be the fourteenth World Cup Final tournament to be held in Italy in June and July. But before looking at some of the teams and players who may be taking part, let us look at the past tournaments.

One reason lies in the fascination with the past and the need to recognise that the great players of the past might have been truly great – whatever their date of birth! The other reason is entirely more prosaic: that of looking at power-balances. For instance, most people readily admit that the recent teams from Brazil and West Germany have had the players and methods to most excite coaches and spectators everywhere; and we must not leave out the Holland team of the past few years. But before the war Italy won the trophy twice as well, of course, as being the 1982 winners; and throughout the history of the tournament there have been strong teams from both Europe and South America.

We might point out at the start that 'the World Cup' was something of a misnomer; that its proper name during the years for which it was competed was 'the Jules Rimet Trophy'. The principle of an international tournament was agreed in 1920 by FIFA – Federation of International Footballing Associations – and although it was ten years before the first tournament came to be played, the guiding light behind the idea, and the man who most worked to get the tournament going was Jules Rimet, President of the French Football Federation. Thus the attractive gold trophy – won outright in 1970 by the Brazil team – came to be given his name. And the new trophy, won for the first time in 1974 by West Germany, was entitled the 'FIFA World Cup'.

A sense of history might help us to remember why the achievement of British and Irish football has often been so mediocre – when seen in international terms. The fact is that by 1930 – the year of the first tournament – the four British countries had

# World Cups 1930–1958

withdrawn their associations from FIFA and were thus ineligible to compete. In 1938, it seemed the rule might be waived and, indeed, England were invited to play the rôle of guest team – once Austria had been overrun by the Nazis. But the offer was refused, and it was not until the first post-war tournament came to be played in Brazil in 1950, that any British teams took part. Even on that occasion, the seeming obstinacy and pig-headedness of the administrators had its way! The British Home International Championships preceding the Finals was recognised by FIFA as a qualifying group, in which the first *two* teams could go to Brazil (in recent years the four home countries have been very fortunate to get more than one place – the only glaring exception being that of the 1958 Final tournaments: when all *four* home countries qualified!) The Scots, amazingly, decided that if they did not win the title – they would not go to Brazil! The argument is one of those nonsensical ones that ignores the large element of chance in sport – of whatever kind. The Scots lost 1–0 to England at Hampden – and like Achilles sulking in his tent, stayed at home to lick the communal wound.

But this loss of twenty years – playing against the opposition with the will to win – was something badly missed by the four countries. If Britain gave modern football to the world then the world soon caught up with, and overtook, us in terms of skill, ball-control and tactics. Internationals played as 'friendlies' were all very well but who can forget the way England players – including Finney and Matthews – were received when they returned from Brazil in 1950 – where they had ignominiously been defeated by a team from the USA? And the lessons they were shown three years later by the brilliant teams who came from Hungary. Let alone the failure of England to qualify for the Final tournaments of 1974 and 1978!

We have to face the fact that – as in many things – the pupil has begun to outstrip the master; and forced him to get back to basic principles himself. Sport – as most things – goes round in cycles, and if it is any country's turn to get back and brush up the basic techniques – those will stand them in good stead in years to come.

# Final Stages
## 1930
### Semi-Finals
ARGENTINA 6, UNITED STATES 1 (1-0)
ARGENTINA: Botasso; Della Torre, Paternoster; Evaristo, J., Monti, Orlandini; Peucelle, Scopelli, Stabile, Ferreira (capt.), Evaristo, M.
USA: Douglas; Wood, Moorhouse; Gallacher, Tracey, Auld; Brown, Gonsalvez, Patenaude, Florie (capt.), McGhee.
SCORERS: Monti, Scopelli, Stabile (2), Peucelle (2) for Argentina; Brown for USA.
URUGUAY 6, YUGOSLAVIA 1 (3-1)
URUGUAY: Ballesteros; Nasazzi (capt.), Mascheroni; Andrade, Fernandez, Gestido; Dorado, Scarone, Anselmo, Cea, Iriarte.
YUGOSLAVIA: Yavocic; Ivkovic (capt.), Mihailovic; Arsenievic, Stefanovic, Djokic; Tirnanic, Marianovic, Beck, Vujadinovic, Seculic.
SCORERS: Cea (3), Anselmo (2), Iriarte for Uruguay; Seculic for Yugoslavia.

### Final
URUGUAY 4, ARGENTINA 2 (1-2)
URUGUAY: Ballesteros; Nasazzi (capt.), Mascheroni; Andrade, Fernandez, Gestido; Dorado, Scarone, Castro, Cea, Iriarte.
ARGENTINA: Botasso; Della Torre, Paternoster; Evaristo, J., Monti, Suarez; Peucelle, Varailo, Stabile, Ferreira (capt.), Evaristo, M.
SCORERS: Dorado, Cea, Iriarte, Castro for Uruguay; Peucelle, Stabile for Argentina.

## 1934
### Semi-Finals
CZECHOSLOVAKIA 3, GERMANY 1 (1-0). *Rome*
CZECHOSLOVAKIA: Planika (capt.); Burger, Ctyroky; Kostalek, Cambal, Krcil; Junek, Svoboda, Sobotka, Nejedly, Puc.

GERMANY: Kress; Haringer, Busch; Zielinski, Szepan (capt.), Bender; Lehner, Siffling, Conen, Noack, Kobierski.
SCORERS: Nejedly (2), Krcil for Czechoslovakia; Noack for Germany.
ITALY 1, AUSTRIA 0 (1–0). *Milan*
ITALY: Combi (capt.); Monzeglio, Allemandi; Ferraris IV, Monti, Bertolini; Guaita, Meazza, Schiavio, Ferrari, Orsi.
AUSTRIA: Platzer; Cisar, Sesztar; Wagner, Smistik (capt.), Urbanek; Zischek, Bican, Sindelar, Schall, Viertel.
SCORER: Guaita for Italy.

## Third Place Match
GERMANY 3, AUSTRIA 2 (3–1). *Naples*
GERMANY: Jakob; Janes, Busch; Zielinski, Muensenberg, Bender; Lehner, Siffling, Conen, Szepan (capt.), Heidemann.
AUSTRIA: Platzer; Cisar, Sesztar; Wagner, Smistik (capt.), Urbanek; Zischek, Braun, Bican, Horwath, Viertel.
SCORERS: Lehner (2), Conen for Germany; Horwath, Seszta for Austria.

## Final
ITALY 2, CZECHOSLOVAKIA 1 (0–0) (1–1) after extra time. *Rome*
ITALY: Combi (capt.); Monzeglio, Allemandi; Ferraris IV, Monti, Bertolini; Guiata, Meazza, Schiavio, Ferrari, Orsi.
CZECHOSLOVAKIA: Planika (capt.); Zenisek, Ctyroky; Kostalek, Cambal, Krcil; Junek, Svoboda, Sobotka, Nejedly, Puc.
SCORERS: Orsi, Schiavio for Italy; Puc for Czechoslovakia.

# 1938
## Semi-Finals
ITALY 2, BRAZIL 1 (2–0). *Marseilles*
ITALY: Olivieri; Foni, Rava; Serantoni, Andreolo, Locatelli; Biavati, Meazza (capt.), Piola, Ferrari, Colaussi.
BRAZIL: Walter; Domingas Da Guia, Machados; Zeze, Martin (capt.), Alfonsinho; Lopex, Luisinho, Peracio, Romeo, Patesko.
SCORERS: Colaussi, Meazza (penalty) for Italy; Romeo for Brazil.

HUNGARY 5, SWEDEN 1 (3-1). *Paris, Colombes*
HUNGARY: Szabo; Koranyi, Biro; Szalay, Turai, Lazar; Sas, Szengeller, Sarosi (capt.), Toldi, Titkos.
SWEDEN: Abrahamson; Eriksson, Kjellgren; Almgren, Jacobsson, Svanstroem; Wetterstroem, Keller (capt.), Andersson H., Jonasson, Nyberg.
SCORERS: Szengeller (3), Titkos, Sarosi for Hungary; Nyberg for Sweden.

## Third Place Match
BRAZIL 4, SWEDEN 2 (1-2). *Bordeaux*
BRAZIL: Batatoes; Domingas Da Guia, Machados; Zeze, Brandao, Alfonsinho; Roberto, Romeo, Leonidas (capt.), Peracio, Patesko.
SWEDEN: Abrahamson; Eriksson, Nilssen; Almgren, Linderholm, Svanstroem (capt.); Berssen, Andersson H., Jonasson, Andersson, A., Nyberg.
SCORERS: Jonasson, Nyberg for Sweden; Romeo, Leonidas (2), Peracio for Brazil.

## Final
ITALY 4, HUNGARY 2 (3-1). *Paris, Colombes*
ITALY: Olivieri; Foni, Rava; Serantoni, Andreolo, Locatelli; Biavati, Meazza (capt.), Piola, Ferrari, Colaussi.
HUNGARY: Szabo; Polgar, Biro; Szalay, Szucs, Lazar; Sas, Vincze, Sarosi (capt.), Szengeller, Titkos.
SCORERS: Colaussi (2), Piola (2) for Italy; Titkos, Sarosi for Hungary.

# World Cup 1950 – held in Brazil

Twenty years had elapsed since the tournament was last held in South America, and the problems thrown up had not, it appeared, been diluted. Thirteen teams had competed in 1930; the tally in 1950 would be no larger. The Indians qualified, but would not come; Scotland, as we have seen, fatuously stayed out; the Austrians were going through one of their frequent bouts of diffidence, and felt their team not strong enough (even though they had just beaten Italy – who would play); Hungary, like the Russians, remained in Cold War isolation; the French, knocked out in their qualifying group, and then reprieved, felt the journey too long and arduous; and the Argentinians had squabbled with the Brazilian Federation. As for West Germany, they were still barred from FIFA.

Thirteen teams, then; and the gaps made nonsense of the new pool system, which would apply not merely to the four qualifying groups, but also to the final group – competed in by the four winners. The Uruguayans, for example, had only to play one jog-trot of a game to be through to the final pool – a victory by eight goals to none over Bolivia. Little wonder that they seemed more fresh and zestful in the late stages of the tournament.

The massive Maracana stadium in Rio de Janeiro was still being built when the tournament started – and when it finished. Brazil featured there in the opening match, beating Mexico by four clear goals in front of a happily partisan crowd of 155,000 (the Maracana would hold 200,000). Two of their goals came from Ademir – yet another of those incredible ball-playing inside forwards that the Brazilians had a penchant for producing. Like the Uruguayans in 1930, the Italians in 1934, the Brazilians had prepared with military thoroughness – an air of celibacy and special diets reigned supreme. They would qualify for the final pool – but not before drawing against Switzerland with a mischosen team, and having to fight hard against a Yugoslavian side.

Co-favourites with Brazil were – England! Appearing for the first time in the competition, with some devastating form behind them, the English had to be fancied. Whatever the balance of power suggested, eyes turned interestedly towards them. They had yet to find a centre-forward to replace Lawton, but Matthews was there, Finney was there, Mortensen was there, Mannion was there; and these were players whose skill was legendary. They scraped through their first game against Chile, finding the heat and humidity so oppressive that they took oxygen at half-time. And then came the shock of the tournament – possibly one of the greatest shocks in the history of international football – as England went down by just the one goal to the United States.

A number of the American players had stayed up into the early hours of the morning; several of them expected a cricket score and indicated as much to British journalists. In the event, it was eight minutes before half-time when Gaetjens headed in Bahr's cross (or was it a miskicked shot?); and that, whatever the English forwards would do in the second half, remained the only goal of the match. The victory of Chile over the Americans a few days later and by five goals to two emphasised England's shame. And although Matthews and Milburn were brought in for the final English game against Spain, although many felt the English deserved at least a draw, the die was cast. England were out of a tournament whose previous editions they had ignored, one for which they had been heavily favoured.

Into the final pool along with Spain, Brazil and Uruguay went Sweden. They had won the 1948 Olympic tournament with a team that included Gren, Nordhal and Liedholm – all, alas, now playing in Italy and blocked from selection. What irony, then, that in their first game the Swedes should play the Italians and win by the odd goal in five! A draw against the other team in their pool, Paraguay, and Sweden went through.

Little good it was to do them, with Brazil now turning on all the fireworks. In their first game the Brazilians beat Sweden 7–1; in their second, Spain by 6–1. Their trio of inside forwards – Jair, Ademir and Zizinho – seemed uncontrollable: professional counterparts of those countless boys who juggle footballs on the Copacabana beach from sunrise to sunset. Brazil, it seemed, would handsomely win the title.

The challenge came from Uruguay, held to a draw by Spain, victors over Sweden (who would in turn defeat the Spanish with that perverse logic that accompanies these affairs). If the Brazilians had Jair, Ademir and Zizinho – the Uruguayans had Juan Schiaffino, as thin as a piece of paper, a player of enormous technical skills that would later be appreciated by European audiences when he found his way into the cauldron of Italian league football, once described by Tommy Docherty as the best player he ever had to face.

But for all Schiaffino's skills, the Uruguayans were the first to admit that they were unable to match the Brazilians in terms of pure technique. Tactical expertise was needed, and tactical expertise was used. Hard as they might try, the Brazilian forwards seldom seemed able to penetrate the light-blue defensive barrier thrown up by the Uruguayan defence, the dark mastery of Maspoli in the opposing goal. No score at half-time.

Two minutes after the interval, the Maracana erupted as Friaça closed in from the wing, shot – and scored. But the Uruguayans had made their point, knew that they were able to cope with the 'superteam' that opposed them. Schiaffino it was who put them ahead, ghosting through the centre to knock in a cross. And ten minutes before the end, Ghiggia, the Uruguayan left-wing, cut in, beat his fullback to score.

The 'right team' had lost; Uruguay had won a match of breath-taking quality and the tournament for a second time after an interval of twenty years.

# 1950 – Final Stages

## Final Pool

URUGUAY 2, SPAIN 2 (1–2). *São Paulo*

URUGUAY: Maspoli; Gonzales, M., Tejera; Gonzales, W., Varela (capt.), Andrade; Ghiggia, Perez, Miguez, Schiaffino, Vidal.

SPAIN: Ramallets; Alonzo, Gonzalvo II; Gonzalvo III, Parra, Puchades; Basora, Igoa, Zarra, Molowny, Gainza.
SCORERS: Ghiggia, Varela for Uruguay; Basora (2) for Spain.

BRAZIL 7, SWEDEN 1 (3-1). *Rio*

BRAZIL: Barbosa; Augusto (capt.), Juvenal; Bauer, Danilo, Bigode; Maneca, Zizinho, Ademir, Jair, Chico.
SWEDEN: Svensson; Samuelsson, Nilsson, E.; Andersson, Nordahl, K., Gard; Sundqvist, Palmer, Jeppson, Skoglund, Nilsson, S.
SCORERS: Ademir (4), Chico (2), Maneca for Brazil; Andersson (penalty) for Sweden.

URUGUAY 3, SWEDEN 2 (1-2). *São Paulo*

URUGUAY: Paz; Gonzales, M., Tejera; Gambetta, Varela (capt.), Andrade; Ghiggia, Perez, Miguez, Schiaffino, Vidal.
SWEDEN: Svensson; Samuelsson, Nilsson, E.; Andersson, Johansson, Gard; Johnsson, Palmer, Melberg, Skoglund, Sundqvist.
SCORERS: Palmer, Sundqvist for Sweden; Ghiggia, Miguez (2) for Uruguay.

BRAZIL 6, SPAIN 1 (3-0). *Rio*

BRAZIL: Barbosa; Augusto (capt.), Juvenal; Bauer, Danilo, Bigode; Friaça, Zizinho, Ademir, Jair, Chico.
SPAIN: Eizaguirre; Alonzo, Gonzalvo II; Gonzalvo III, Parra, Puchades; Basora, Igoa, Zarra, Panizo, Gainza.
SCORERS: Jair (2), Chico (2), Zizinho, Parra (own goal) for Brazil; Igoa for Spain.

SWEDEN 3, SPAIN 1 (2-0). *São Paulo*

SWEDEN: Svensson; Samuelsson, Nilsson, E.; Andersson, Johansson, Gard; Sundqvist, Mellberg, Rydell, Palmer, Johnsson.
SPAIN: Eizaguirre; Asensi, Alonzo; Silva, Parra, Puchades; Basora, Fernandez, Zarra, Panizo, Juncosa.

SCORERS: Johansson, Mellberg, Palmer for Sweden; Zarra for Spain.

URUGUAY 2, BRAZIL 1 (0–0). *Rio*

URUGUAY: Maspoli; Gonzales, M., Tejera; Gambetta, Varela (capt.), Andrade; Ghiggia, Perez, Miguez, Schiaffino, Moran.
BRAZIL: Barbosa; Augusto (capt.), Juvenal; Bauer, Danilo, Bigode; Friaça, Zizinho, Ademir, Jair, Chico.
SCORERS: Friaça for Brazil; Schiaffino, Ghiggia for Uruguay.

## Final Positions

|         | P | W | D | L | F  | A  | Pts |
|---------|---|---|---|---|----|----|-----|
| Uruguay | 3 | 2 | 1 | 0 | 7  | 5  | 5   |
| Brazil  | 3 | 2 | 0 | 1 | 14 | 4  | 4   |
| Sweden  | 3 | 1 | 0 | 2 | 6  | 11 | 2   |
| Spain   | 3 | 0 | 1 | 2 | 4  | 11 | 1   |

(Goals: F, A)

# World Cup 1954 – held in Switzerland

And here was another instance of the 'wrong' team coming through to take the trophy, when Germany won their first World Cup and the brilliant Hungarians were denied their right. Bizarre organisation in which two teams from each group were 'seeded', leaving the supposedly stronger teams apart in the early stages; and the presence of a handful of really formidable teams in Hungary, Brazil, Germany, Uruguay and Austria – both these ensured that in later years this would come to be known as the last of the 'open' tournaments, the last in which teams seemed more concerned to score, than to prevent, goals.

England were there, shaky after a hammering administered at the hands of the Hungarians only a couple of weeks earlier when their winter defeat at Wembley had been exposed as no fluke. In Budapest they lost 7–1, a disorganised rabble in front of brilliant passing and shooting. History was on their side, Matthews, Wright and Finney in it; but few gave them any chance. And Scotland were also there – having repeated one part of their rôle from 1950 by losing to England; this time, however, having the courage to enter in spite of their lack of confidence.

Uruguay were strong, entering their first European tournament, unbeaten to date. Schiaffino was still there; they had splendid new wingers in Abbadie and Borges; a powerful stopper in Santamaria, later to be the bulwark of Real Madrid's invincible side. The Brazilians were slightly fancied despite being involved in a period of neurotic assessment. Their game, they felt, was too ingenious; so they closed the defence with care, came down hard on flair unless it could be harnessed to teamwork. They would wait until 1958 before perfecting the balance, but in their first game of the tournament – a 5–0 drubbing of Mexico – they introduced two great backs in the Santoses (no relation), a fine distributor in Didì, a unique winger in Julinho – a man of violent pace, superb balance, close control and with a rocket of a shot.

In *their* first game, the Uruguayans beat the Czechs 2–0; then annihilated Scotland by seven clear goals, Borges and Abbadie getting five between them. The Scottish campaign had not been helped by dissension off the pitch and the resignation, after the first defeat at the hands of Austria, of Andy Beattie, the team manager; but the Uruguayans looked good, Schiaffino in regal form. Through to join them in the Quarter-finals went Yugoslavia – who had held Brazil to a 1–1 draw in a memorable match in which their goalkeeper Beara (a former ballet dancer) had performed prodigies in defence and Zebec had given evidence of his all-round skill; England, drawing 4–4 with Belgium first time out before beating Switzerland 2–0; the Swiss, thanks to a played-off game against the Italians, who had been strangely static; Brazil;

# World Cups 1930-1958

Austria, who defeated the Czechs 5-0 with their talented half-back Ocwirk emerging as one of the players of the tournament; Germany and Hungary.

This last pair provided most of the news. The Hungarians went out in their first game, drubbed Korea 9-0; then were forced to play the Germans, the latter not having been seeded. The wily German coach, Sepp Herberger, cleverly decided to throw away this match, banked on winning the play-off against Turkey (which he did) and fielded a team largely composed of reserves. The Hungarians came through 8-3, the Germans had not given away any secrets; but most important, it was in this game that Puskas was injured, that a vital part of the Hungarian machine was put out of action.

The Hungarians had won the 1952 Olympiad; in Hidegkuti they had a deep-lying centre-forward of great verve and authority, a man who could make and score brilliant goals; at inside forward they had Kocsis and Puskas, the former a little man with the neck of a bull who could leap great heights to head a ball, the latter with a hammer of a left foot; and in the half-back line they had an excellent exemplar in Boszik, always driving forward with speed, ingenuity and strength. With four players of genius and others who were little behind, it was easy to see why the Hungarians were widely considered favourites to win the tournament.

Two things upset them. First, the injury to Puskas, who would play again only in the Final and at half-speed. The other was what came to be known as the 'Battle of Berne', a disgraceful Quarter-final tie which pitted them against the Brazilians. Hungary won the game 4-2 after being two up in the first eight minutes, after giving away a penalty, after themselves scoring from one, after Nilton Santos and Boszik had been sent off for fighting in a match that seemed more suited to a boxing ring. After the game the Brazilians invaded the Hungarian dressing-room, went berserk and came close to inflicting further serious injury on the Hungarian players. Hungary went through to the Semi-finals where they would play an unforgettable game against Uruguay, victors over an England team that fought hard, laid siege to the Uruguayan goal without really capitalising on their approach play (where Matthews was outstanding) and was let down by Merrick, the goalkeeper.

The other Semi-final would be between Austria who beat Switzerland 7–5 after having trailed 2–4 at half-time; and Germany, ploughing on with force and thoroughness against the talented Yugoslavs. In the event, the Germans 'came good' when it mattered. They scored twice from penalties in their 6–1 win, now seemed ominously hard to beat.

The Hungary–Uruguay game, even without Puskas, was a gem. Two-nil up with fifteen minutes to go, the Hungarians seemed through – until the Uruguayans counter-attacked. Schiaffino put Hohberg through, the move was repeated three minutes before the end, and extra time was on. It nearly began without Hohberg himself, who had been forced to retire 'injured' after having been overwhelmed by delighted team mates. But recover he did, to burst through early in the first period of extra time and smack in a shot – that came back off a post. In retrospect, it can be seen as the turning point; for Kocsis twice in the second period rose to head home crosses; and Hungary were through.

A Puskas far from fit, too chubby round the middle and with a sore ankle, returned for the Final. Great player though he was, the Hungarians had managed well without him, and might have done better to discard him (as Alf Ramsey would prefer Roger Hunt to Jimmy Greaves twelve years later, sacrificing rare gifts to teamwork, and win). Yet again, the Hungarians went off like a train, two goals up in eight minutes, seemingly well on the way to a victory that awaited them.

What mattered most, perhaps, was the swiftness of the German reply. Three minutes later they had drawn back a goal through Morlock; then Rahn drove home a corner; at the other end Turek remained in stupendous form between the goalposts; Rahn got the goal that would be the winner; Puskas scored – only to be given offside; and the invincible Hungarians had been beaten.

They had been beaten by a better team on the day; by the punishment of earlier games against South Americans; by a certain amount of internal dissension to do with the injury to Puskas. Yet they remained the best team that Europe had seen to date, possibly the best team that Europe has yet seen. And it took

# World Cups 1930–1958

an almost equally brilliant team from the other side of the world and four years later, to push them into the light shadows; the amazing Brazilians of the Sweden tournament, and their latest wonder-boy – Pelé.

# 1954 – Final Stages

## Quarter-Finals

GERMANY 2, YUGOSLAVIA 0 (1–0). *Geneva*

GERMANY: Turek; Laband, Kohlmeyer; Eckel, Liebrich, Mai; Rahn, Morlock, Walter, O., Walter, F. (capt.), Schaefer.
YUGOSLAVIA: Beara; Stankovic, Crnkovic; Cjaicowski I., Horvat, Boskov; Milutinovic, Mitic (capt.), Vukas, Bobek, Zebec.
SCORERS: Horvat (own goal), Rahn for Germany.

HUNGARY 4, BRAZIL 2 (2–1). *Berne*

HUNGARY: Grosics; Buzansky, Lantos; Boszik (capt.), Lorant, Zakarias; Toth, M., Kocsis, Hidegkuti, Czibor, Toth, J.
BRAZIL: Castilho; Santos, D., Santos, N.; Brandaozinho, Pinheiro (capt.), Bauer; Julinho, Didì, Indio, Tozzi, Maurinho.
SCORERS: Hidegkuti (2), Kocsis, Lantos (penalty) for Hungary; Santos, D. (penalty), Julinho for Brazil.

AUSTRIA 7, SWITZERLAND 5 (2–4). *Lausanne*

AUSTRIA: Schmied; Hanappi, Barschandt; Ocwirk (capt.), Happel, Koller; Koerner, R., Wagner, Stojaspal, Probst, Koerner, A.
SWITZERLAND: Parlier; Neury, Kernen; Eggimann, Bocquet (capt.), Casali; Antenen, Vonlanthen, Hugi, Ballaman, Fatton.
SCORERS: Ballaman (2), Hugi (2), Hanappi (own goal) for Switzerland; Koerner, A. (2), Ocwirk, Wagner (3), Probst for Austria.

URUGUAY 4, ENGLAND 2 (2-1). *Basel*

URUGUAY: Maspoli; Santamaria, Martinez; Andrade, Varela (capt.), Cruz; Abbadie, Ambrois, Miguez, Schiaffino, Borges.
ENGLAND: Merrick; Staniforth, Byrne; McGarry, Wright (capt.), Dickinson; Matthews, Broadis, Lofthouse, Wilshaw, Finney.
SCORERS: Borges, Varela, Schiaffino, Ambrois for Uruguay; Lofthouse, Finney for England.

## Semi-Finals

GERMANY 6, AUSTRIA 1 (1-0). *Basel*

GERMANY: Turek; Posipal, Kohlmeyer; Eckel, Liebrich, Mai; Rahn, Morlock, Walter, O., Walter, F. (capt.), Schaefer.
AUSTRIA: Zeman; Hanappi, Schleger; Ocwirk (capt.), Happel, Koller; Koerner, R., Wagner, Stojaspal, Probst, Koerner, A.
SCORERS: Schaefer, Morlock, Walter, F. (2 penalties), Walter, O. (2) for Germany; Probst for Austria.

HUNGARY 4, URUGUAY 2 (1-0) (2-2) after extra time. *Lausanne*

HUNGARY: Grosics; Buzansky, Lantos; Boszik (capt.), Lorant, Zakarias; Budai, Kocsis, Palotas, Hidegkuti, Czibor.
URUGUAY: Maspoli; Santamaria, Martinez; Andrade (capt.), Carballo, Cruz; Souto, Ambrois, Schiaffino, Hohberg, Borges.
SCORERS: Czibor, Hidegkuti, Kocsis (2) for Hungary; Hohberg (2) for Uruguay.

## Third Place Match

AUSTRIA 3, URUGUAY 1 (1-1). *Zurich*

AUSTRIA: Schmied; Hanappi, Barschandt; Ocwirk (capt.), Kollman, Koller; Koener, R., Wagner, Dienst, Stojaspal, Probst.

URUGUAY: Maspoli; Santamaria, Martinez; Andrade (capt.), Carballo, Cruz; Abbadie, Hohberg, Mendez, Schiaffino, Borges.
SCORERS: Stojaspal (penalty), Cruz (own goal), Ocwirk for Austria; Hohberg for Uruguay.

## Final

GERMANY 3, HUNGARY 2 (2-2). *Berne*

GERMANY: Turek; Posipal, Kohlmeyer; Eckel, Liebrich, Mai; Rahn, Morlock, Walter, O., Walter, F. (capt.), Schaefer.
HUNGARY: Grosics; Buzansky, Lantos; Boszik, Lorant (capt.), Zakarias; Czibor, Kocsis, Hidegkuti, Puskas, Toth, J.
SCORERS: Puskas, Czibor for Hungary; Morlock, Rahn (2) for Germany.

# World Cup 1958 – held in Sweden

The Brazilians came and conquered – came to Sweden as one of the favourites (thanks to the on-paper banality of much of the opposition), conquered with an extraordinary demonstration of prowess and skill in the Final. The backstage people concerned, for the first time, harnessed the natural talent of the players, made the team's play really effective. In 1950 the players had been allowed to express themselves too freely; in 1954, they had been too restrained. Now the blend was right.

Yet the truth remains, that like the Hungarians before them but to a lesser degree, the Brazilians proved that great teams – so called – depend essentially upon the coming-together in one period of time of a clutch of great players. Didì was in evidence again, full of lithe passes, famous for his 'falling leaf' shot – struck with the outside of the foot and fading distressingly in mid-flight;

the Santoses were playing still at fullback; and in the forward line were two new geniuses in Garrincha and the new black prodigy, Pelé. And there was Zagalo, a player who covered vast tracts of ground at electric pace, one with lungs of leather and an astute footballing brain. The components were there, and the world waited to see whether they could be put together.

All four British teams competed; the Welsh and Irish for the first time. The former had a fine goalkeeper in Kelsey, the majestic John Charles, a clever inside-forward in Allchurch, an impish winger in Cliff Jones. The latter had Danny Blanchflower and Jimmy McIlroy, but the Munich air disaster had deprived them of Blanchflower's brother, Jackie, a commanding centre-back. Both teams thrived on the intimate atmosphere they created off the field, devoid of the paranoia and bitching that had surrounded English team selection.

To be fair to England, they had suffered terribly from Munich. The accident deprived them of Duncan Edwards, their brilliant left-half; Tommy Taylor, a dangerous centre-forward; and Roger Byrne, a resourceful back. Players such as these could not be replaced overnight, admittedly; but some of the selection was bizarre in the extreme. Lofthouse was left at home, when his experience might have been invaluable; and Bobby Charlton, whose amazing swerve and lethal shooting had delighted everyone in the previous three months, was taken – only to be left on the touchlines for the whole tournament. Courage, it seemed, was lacking – the courage that often wins matches and tournaments.

The Scots had eliminated Spain but lost 4–0 to England in Glasgow. Few held out for them much hope of success. The Hungarians had lost too many of their star players in the aftermath of the 1956 Revolution, and such as remained were long in the tooth. Argentina competed, but without its much-famed 'Trio of Death' in the inside forward positions – Maschio, Angelillo and Sivori – all playing with Italian clubs and ignored. And the Germans seemed weak, despite the continued and cunning presence of Herberger, the coach.

The Russians competed for the first time, having won the 1956 Olympiad in Australia. They had the amazing Yachin in goal, kept

# World Cups 1930–1958

themselves to themselves, and would play the sturdy sort of game that one has come to expect from them in recent years – functionalism with just the occasional flash of forward and midfield genius.

Playing at home, the Swedes called upon several of their stars based in Italy – the elegant Liedholm, tall and commanding in midfield; Nacka Skoglund, a hero of their 1950 World Cup team; Gustavsson, a commanding centre-back; and Kurt Hamrin, an electric little outside-right. To begin with, their supporters were pessimistic, but pessimism soon changed to optimism.

No one anticipated much from the French, yet they were to be the revelation of the tournament. In their first game, they walked through Paraguay 7–3, three of the goals coming from Juste Fontaine, who had come to the tournament not expecting to gain a place. He would score thirteen goals in all – a record that will not easily be beaten. And alongside Fontaine was Kopa – small, strong, beautifully-balanced with fine control and the ability to give a defence-splitting pass.

Group IV was the focal point – Brazil, Russia, England and Austria. The Brazilians beat the other two, drew a goalless game against England, who also drew with Russia and Austria. To a play-off, and the Russians came through by the one goal. If only Tom Finney had not been injured in the first game of the tournament. If only.

The Irish drew against the Germans, beat the Czechs, lost to Argentina – who finished bottom of the pool! They came through after a play-off against Czechoslovakia, by the odd goal in three, with McParland scoring his second goal of the game in the first period of extra time. Courage, in their case, had paid off.

The Scots drew with Yugoslavia, went down to both France and Paraguay. Better news from the Welsh, who went to a play-off in their pool against the Hungarians – and won 2–1 after trailing at half-time. The victory would put them through against Brazil, and few gave them much hope.

That especially after the 'real' Brazil had played for the first time in the third game of their qualifying group. Out had gone Jose Altafini, nicknamed 'Mazzola' for his resemblance to the great

post-war Italian inside-forward; a man who would play for Italy in
the 1962 finals, who at the age of thirty-four would score against
Derby County in the Semi-final of the 1972–73 European Cup
trophy goals that were *par excellence*, those of a venomous striker.
And in would come Garrincha and Pelé.

Both were to have an extraordinary effect on the 1958 competition, an extraordinary effect on players and spectators throughout
the world. Garrincha and Pelé – two of the great instinctive players
of the age, of any age. The former was a winger who had all the
powers of Matthews – the vicious swerve that took him outside the
full-back, the ability to accelerate into astonishing speed from a
standing start. Despite – perhaps because of – a curiously twisted
knee, a legacy from birth, his ball-control was exceptional. And
Pelé, at seventeen, his head pointed like a coconut, with all his
legendary skills already there for all to see – the ability to 'kill' a ball
on thigh or chest, to shoot ferociously from impossible angles, to
head a ball with a power that reminded people of Lawton or
Kocsis.

So what chance Wales, against players such as these? In
the event, much. If only John Charles had been fit to play, the
one Welshman who could have put pressure on the Brazilian
defence. As it was, the Welsh defence played superbly; and Pelé
was later to describe the one goal of the match as the most
important he had ever scored. And there's over a thousand to
choose from!

Into the Semi-finals with Brazil went France, Germany,
Sweden. The Germans churned on, their ageing team and cunning management able to find answers to all the questions posed
by the Yugoslavs. Sweden went through with Hamrin on venomous form – stockings rolled down, small and compact, hard to
stop once he began to find his stride, scorer of the first goal against
the Russians, maker of the second.

And there was France – the team no one was prepared to take
seriously, even though they had won their qualifying group and
scored eleven goals in the process. Against the Irish, Fontaine
scored twice more to re-emphasise his effectiveness. Tired and
depleted by injuries, the Irish had no cause for complaint. Their

effort, like that of the Welsh, had been brave and dignified.

In the Semi-finals, it was the turn of the French to suffer at the hands of Brazil. The score was still 1–1 when Jonquet, the elegant French centre-half was forced to retire in the thirty-seventh minute: a retirement that was to prove fatal as Pelé scored a hat trick and Brazil ran out winners 5–2. France would have consolation later, when they would defeat Germany in the match to decide third place by six goals to three, four coming from the incessant Fontaine.

Germany had proved no match for Sweden. The raucousness of German chanting at international matches is legendary, but in Sweden the German supporters found their match. As the Swedes progressed from round to round, so grew the noise of their fans, nationalist to the extreme. And so on the field, the Germans could find no answers to the wiles of Liedholm in midfield, the venom of Hamrin as he cut in from the wing. They would unearth a potentially great defender in Schnellinger, a powerful midfield player in Szymaniak – but the Germans knew that they deserved to be out.

In the Final, the Swedish crowd was silenced by FIFA. An official had attended the Semi-final game, put a stop to organised cheering . . . and a Swedish crowd deprived of its cheerleaders would scarcely cheer at all. Just the once, as Liedholm put Sweden ahead after four minutes. 'When the Brazilians are a goal down,' had said George Raynor, Sweden's Yorkshire coach, 'they panic all over the show.' But Raynor must have been thinking of the overtrained 1954 Brazilians or the dazzling unpredictables of 1950.

Twice, it was Garrincha; twice he swerved maniacally past Swedish defenders and centred; twice Vavà rushed in to score. And ten minutes after half-time it was Pelé's turn. Trapping a long centre on his thigh, he hooked it over his head, slashed it into the net. He would score Brazil's fifth goal with his head after Zagalo had torn through for the fourth. And though Sweden would get a second goal, that would be that.

The crowd applauded as the Brazilians did two laps of honour, first with their own flag, then with that of the Swedes. Their supporters chanted '*samba, samba*'. And the world knew that it had seen a new style of football.

# 1958 – Final Stages

## Quarter-Finals

FRANCE 4, IRELAND 0 (1–0). *Norrkoping*

FRANCE: Abbes; Kaelbel, Lerond; Penverne, Jonquet, Marcel; Wisnieski, Fontaine, Kopa, Piantoni, Vincent.
IRELAND: Gregg; Keith, McMichael; Blanchflower, Cunningham, Cush; Bingham, Casey, Scott, McIlroy, McParland.
SCORERS: Wisnieski, Fontaine (2), Piantoni for France.

GERMANY 1, YUGOSLAVIA 0 (1–0). *Malmo*

GERMANY: Herkenrath; Stollenwerk, Juskowiak; Eckel, Erhardt, Szymaniak; Rahn, Walter, Seeler, Schmidt, Schaefer.
YUGOSLAVIA: Krivocuka; Sijakovic, Crnkovic; Krstic, Zebec, Boskov; Petakovik, Veselinovic, Milutinovic, Ognjanovic, Rajkov.
SCORER: Rahn for Germany.

SWEDEN 2, RUSSIA 0 (0–0). *Stockholm*

SWEDEN: Svensson; Bergmark, Axbom; Boerjesson, Gustavsson, Parling; Hamrin, Gren, Simonsson, Liedholm, Skoglund.
RUSSIA: Yachin; Kessarev, Kuznetsov; Voinov, Krijevski, Tsarev; Ivanov, A., Ivanov, V., Simonian, Salnikov, Ilyin.
SCORERS: Hamrin, Simonsson for Sweden.

BRAZIL 1 WALES 0 (0–0). *Gothenburg*

BRAZIL: Gilmar; De Sordi, Santos, N.; Zito, Bellini, Orlando; Garrincha, Didì, Mazzola, Pelé, Zagalo.

WALES: Kelsey; Williams, Hopkins; Sullivan, Charles, M., Bowen; Medwin, Hewitt, Webster, Allchurch, Jones.
SCORER: Pelé for Brazil.


## Semi-Finals

BRAZIL 5, FRANCE 2 (2–1). *Stockholm*

BRAZIL: Gilmar; De Sordi, Santos, N.; Zito, Bellini, Orlando; Garrincha, Didì, Vavà, Pelé, Zagalo.
FRANCE: Abbes; Kaelbel, Lerond; Penverne, Jonquet, Marcel; Wisnieski, Fontaine, Kopa, Piantoni, Vincent.
SCORERS: Vavà, Didì, Pelé (3) for Brazil; Fontaine, Piantoni for France.

SWEDEN 3, GERMANY 1 (1–1). *Gothenburg*

SWEDEN: Svensson; Bergmark, Axbom; Boerjesson, Gustavsson, Parling; Hamrin, Gren, Simonsson, Liedholm, Skoglund.
GERMANY: Herkenrath; Stollenwerk, Juskowiak; Eckel, Erhardt, Szymaniak; Rahn, Walter, Seller, Schaefer, Cieslarczyk.
SCORERS: Schaefer for Germany; Skoglund, Gren, Hamrin for Sweden.


## Third Place Match

FRANCE 6, GERMANY 3 (0–0). *Gothenburg*

FRANCE: Abbes; Kaelberl, Lerond; Penverne, Lafont, Marcel; Wisnieski, Douis, Kopa, Fontaine, Vincent.
GERMANY: Kwiatowski; Stollenwerk, Erhardt; Schnellinger, Wewers, Szymaniak; Rahn, Sturm, Kelbassa, Schaefer, Cieslarczyk.

SCORERS: Fontaine (4), Kopa, penalty, Douis for France; Cieslarczyk, Rahn, Schaefer for Germany.

# Final

BRAZIL 5, SWEDEN 2 (2–1). *Stockholm*

BRAZIL: Gilmar; Santos, D., Santos, N.; Zito, Bellini, Orlando; Garrincha, Didì, Vavà, Pelé, Zagalo.
SWEDEN: Svensson; Bergmark, Axbom; Boerjesson, Gustavsson, Parling; Hamrin, Gren, Simonsson, Liedholm, Skoglund.
SCORERS: Liedholm, Simonsson for Sweden; Vavà (2), Pelé (2), Zagalo for Brazil.

# 2 THE BRAZILIAN TRIUMPH CONTINUES – DESPITE A RUDE INTERRUPTION BY ENGLAND

## World Cup 1962 – held in Chile

It should, perhaps, have been held in Argentina. But if Chile had recently had earthquakes, then the general antipathy towards Argentina in footballing circles had not lessened. And as a spokesman for the Chilean claim put it, they needed the World Cup '*because* we have nothing'. Cunning logic indeed; and the Chileans set about building a new stadium in Santiago to house a hysterical populace. (Cynics pointed out Chile had won nothing since the Pacific War in the middle of the nineteenth century.)

Brazil were the favourites, inevitably. They had two new centre-backs; and that was all. Garrincha, Zagalo, Didì and Pelé were still there – though the last would play only two games before being replaced by another exciting striker in Amarildo. And taken seriously with the Brazilians were the Russians – who on a recent South American tour had beaten Argentina, Uruguay and Chile.

England had played well on their way to Chile, beating Peru 4–0 in Lima. In Greaves and Charlton they had world class forwards; in Bobby Moore, a debutant in Lima, a defender of poise. But the self-confidence was not there, the forwards would fail time and again to find a way through the packed defences that would make a nonsense of the early part of the competition.

Italy arrived with Gianni Rivera in their ranks, arguably one of the really gifted players Europe has seen since the end of the war. Eighteen then, a precision passer of the ball and with a perfect sense of balance he would play one good game before being dropped. The Italians also brought with them a host of *Oriundi* –

foreigners of Italian extraction – such as Altafini, Sormani, Maschio and Sivori. A strong team on paper, but football matches are not won on paper – and the Italian campaign would be catastrophic.

After a goalless draw against Germany, the Italians found themselves involved in yet another of those World Cup 'battles' when they came to play Chile in Santiago. At the root of the trouble were some silly newspaper articles written by Italian journalists, critical of the organisation of the tournament, critical of the squalor of Santiago, critical of the morals of Chilean womanhood. From the start of the game the Chileans spat at the Italians, fouled them viciously. Ironic, therefore, that the two players sent off in the game should both have been Italian; while a left hook thrown by Sanchez, the Chilean winger – one that broke Maschio's nose – went unseen by the referee. Two-nil to Chile, and the Italians were effectively out of the tournament.

Germany won that second group, with Schnellinger powerful in defence, Seeler powerful in attack, Szymaniak destroying everything in midfield. They had come up with a useful inside-forward in Helmut Haller, who would find fame in Italy in later years and compete in two further World Cups. And the Chileans, inevitably, came through.

In group III, Brazil beat Mexico 2–0; were held to a goalless draw by the unfancied Czechs – a game in which Pelé pulled a muscle, and was lost to the rest of the tournament; then beat Spain, with Amarildo – Pelé's replacement – getting both goals in a 2–1 victory. The Czechs went through even though they had lost one of their games, drawn another.

In group I, the Russians won a violent yet exciting game against Yugoslavia 2–0; then were involved in an extraordinary match against the Columbians, who after being 3–0 down in the first fifteen minutes took the final score to 4–4. Yachin in goal had a sad game, sad enough for some commentators to prophesy the end of the greatest goalkeeper of modern times. Premature indeed, if only for Yachin's fine displays in England four years later. Yugoslavia would go through to the Quarter-finals with Russia, their little inside-forward, Sekularac, one of the men of the tournament.

## World Cups 1962–1970

And so to group IV, where the Hungarians looked a fine side. In Florian Albert they had unearthed a centre-forward of high gifts, another who would do marvellously in 1966. And in Solymosi, the right-half, they had a player of relaxed quality. These two were highly responsible for the 2–1 defeat of the English side in the first game; the 6–1 thrashing administered to Bulgaria in the second.

As for England, they played good football – with Bobby Charlton on great form – to beat the Argentinians 3–1. Alan Peacock made his debut, and a fine one. But in the final game against the Bulgarians, the English could find no way through a massed defence, had to be content with a goalless draw. They were through, but few would dare to class them with the Hungarians.

In the event, they met – and were beaten by – Brazil. The 3–1 scoreline seemed slightly unjust; but Garrincha was in devastating form, seemingly having added to his vast repertoire of tricks the ability to head a ball viciously. And though Hitchens equalised for England before half-time, two mistakes by Springett in goal gave goals to Vavà and Amarildo after the interval.

No surprise, that result, but surprises elsewhere. Chile, for example, came through against Russia – with Yachin still inexplicably tense in goal, and the crowd manic in its joy. Not for the first or last time, the 'home' team had confounded early prognostication.

And Hungary went out. For eighty of the ninety minutes against the Czechs Hungary attacked, inflicting serious damage on the Czech crossbar and posts. Nothing, it seemed, would ever be a few millimetres farther in the right direction; and though Solymosi and Albert did everything that was asked of them, their team ever trailed to an early, thirteenth-minute goal from the Czech inside-forward, Scherer.

In the last Quarter-final tie, the Yugoslavs put out the Germans. Only four minutes of the game remained when Galic, the inside-left, dribbled his way through the German defence and passed to Radakovic – head bandaged after a collision – to score. But the Germans could have had little reason for complaint. In Sekularac, the Yugoslavs had one of the best midfield players of the tournament; in Soskic a strong, agile goalkeeper; in Markovic, a commanding centre-back, who on the day would outplay the formidable Uwe Seeler.

In the Semi-finals, it was the turn of Chile to fall before the devastating Garrincha. He scored the first of four Brazilian goals with a fierce left-foot shot, the second with another of his newfound trampoline-like headers. And though the Chileans hit back with a goal before half-time from Toro, two further goals – this time from Vavà – in the second half, and only a penalty in return, put the Brazilians through.

Not, however, without tremblings. In the second half of the game Garrincha himself was expelled for kicking retaliatorily at a Chilean opponent; and then suffered the indignity of having his head cut open by a bottle thrown from the crowd as he was leaving the pitch. In the event, the injury was not serious, the threat of suspension from the Final very real. It was said, however, that the President of Brazil had listened to the game on headphones during Mass; that he had appealed personally to the disciplinary committee on Garrincha's behalf. The brilliant winger would play in the Final after receiving a caution.

The opposition to Brazil would be provided by the Czechs, victors in the other Semi-final against Yugoslavia. As in the Quarter-final, the Czechs had much less of the play; but this time took their chances well, scoring three goals, conceding one. Masopust controlled the midfield; the other two half-backs, Pluskal and Popluhar, sealed up the middle of the defence with rugged authority; Kvasniak ambled round in the forward line prompting and guiding. And the weary Yugoslavs were left to lose the match for third place, by the one goal and against a Chilean side again whipped on by a partisan crowd.

As in 1958, Brazil gave away the first goal of the Final – Masopust scoring in the fourteenth minute after having run on to an exquisite through-pass from Scherer; as in 1958, the team's reaction was swift and interesting. It was Pelé's replacement, Amarildo, who scored, running almost to the left-hand goal line with the ball, screwing an extraordinary shot past Schroiff, the

Czech goalkeeper, who had positioned himself perfectly at the near post to narrow the angle.

One-one, then, at half-time; and when Brazil scored again in the sixty-ninth minute, good goal though it was, it came against the run of the play. Amarildo it was who collected a pass from Zito, cut past a defender and crossed for Zito himself to charge in and head just under the bar. Thus was the slightly one-paced elegance of Masopust and Kvasniak rewarded; and salt was further rubbed into the wound twelve minutes from time when Djalma Santos hooked a centre high into the Czech penalty area, Schroiff lost its flight against the glare of the sun, lost it when it hit the ground, and Vavà snapped in to score, 3–1, seemingly a convincing win; but Garrincha had been well controlled, Didì had been obscure.

Brazil had won the Cup for the second time, but with little of the flair that they had shown in Sweden. True, Pelé had been absent for the important games, and Pelé might have made a considerable difference. The Brazilians, however, had been forced to use Zagalo as a deep-lying winger, and the 4-2-4 formation of 1958 had wilted into the 4-3-3 of 1962, would even tempt people to think of four midfield players and only two genuine strikers.

More serious, it had been a disappointing tournament. The great Puskas, taking time off from scoring goals for his new club, Real Madrid, said of the football he had seen that it was 'war'. The qualifying games had provided a string of disappointments, defensive skill had been at a premium. The tournament in Sweden had provided 119 goals, that in Chile thirty less; and where Fontaine had scored so freely in 1958, the highest figure that any individual goalscorer would reach in Chile was four.

# 1962 – Final Stages

## Quarter-Finals

YUGOSLAVIA 1, GERMANY 0 (0–0). *Santiago*

YUGOSLAVIA: Soskic; Durkovic, Jusufi; Radakovic, Markovic, Popovic; Kovacevic, Sekularac, Jerkovic, Galic, Skoblar.
GERMANY: Fahrian; Novak, Schnellinger; Schultz, Erhardt, Giesemann; Haller, Szymaniak, Seeler, Brulls, Schaefer.
SCORER: Radakovic for Yugoslavia.

BRAZIL 3, ENGLAND 1 (1–1). *Viña del Mar*

BRAZIL: Gilmar; Santos D., Mauro, Zozimo, Santos, N.; Zito, Didì; Garrincha, Vavà, Amarildo, Zagalo.
ENGLAND: Springett; Armfield, Wilson; Moore, Norman, Flowers; Douglas, Greaves, Hitchens, Haynes, Charlton.
SCORERS: Garrincha (2), Vavà for Brazil; Hitchens for England.

CHILE 2, RUSSIA 1 (2–1). *Arica*

CHILE: Escutti; Eyzaguirre, Contreras, Sanchez, R., Navarro; Toro, Rojas; Ramirez, Landa, Tobar, Sanchez, L.
RUSSIA: Yachin; Tchokelli, Ostrovski; Voronin, Maslenkin, Netto; Chislenko, Ivanov, Ponedelnik, Mamikin, Meshki.
SCORERS: Sanchez, L., Rojas for Chile; Chislenko for Russia.

CZECHOSLOVAKIA 1, HUNGARY 0 (1–0). *Rancagua*

CZECHOSLOVAKIA: Schroiff; Lala, Novak; Pluskal, Popluhar, Masopust; Pospichal, Scherer, Kvasniak, Kadraba, Jelinek.
HUNGARY: Grosics; Matrai, Sarosi; Solymosi, Meszoly, Sipos; Sandor, Rakosi, Albert, Tichy, Fenyvesi.
SCORER: Scherer for Czechoslovakia.

# Semi-Finals

BRAZIL 4, CHILE 2 (2–1). *Santiago*

BRAZIL: Gilmar; Santos, D., Mauro, Zozimo, Santos, N.; Zito, Didì; Garrincha, Vavà, Amarildo, Zagalo.
CHILE: Escutti; Eyzaguirre, Contreras, Sanchez, R., Rodriguez; Toro, Rojas; Ramirez, Landa, Tobar, Sanchez, L.
SCORERS: Garrincha (2), Vavà (2), for Brazil; Toro, Sanchez, L. (penalty) for Chile.

CZECHOSLOVAKIA 3, YUGOSLAVIA 1 (0–0). *Vina del Mar*

CZECHOSLOVAKIA: Schroiff; Lala, Novak; Pluskal, Popluhar, Masopust; Pospichal, Scherer, Kvasniak, Kadraba, Jelinek.
YUGOSLAVIA: Soskic; Durkovic, Jusufi; Radakovic, Markovic, Popovic; Sujakovic, Sekularac, Jerkovic, Galic, Skoblar.
SCORERS: Kadraba, Scherer (2), for Czechoslovakia; Jerkovic for Yugoslavia.

# Third Place Match

CHILE: Godoy; Eyzaguirre, Cruz, Sanchez, R., Rodriguez; Toro, Rojas; Ramirez, Campos, Tobar, Sanchez, L.
YUGOSLAVIA: Soskic; Durkovic, Svinjarevic; Radakovic, Markovic, Popovic; Kovacevic, Sekularac, Jerkovic, Galic, Skoblar.
SCORER: Rojas for Chile.

# Final

BRAZIL 3, CZECHOSLOVAKIA 1 (1–1). *Santiago*

BRAZIL: Gilmar; Santos, D., Mauro, Zozimo, Santos, N.; Zito, Didì; Garrincha, Vavà, Amarildo, Zagalo.

CZECHOSLOVAKIA: Schroiff; Tichy, Novak; Pluskal, Popluhar, Masopust; Pospichal, Scherer, Kvasniak, Kadraba, Jelinek.
SCORERS: Masopust for Czechoslovakia; Amarildo, Zito, Vavà for Brazil.

# World Cup 1966 – held in England

When he took over from Walter Winterbottom the managership of the English national side, Alf Ramsey promised that England would win the 1966 tournament. They did and he did; for there had been fewer stronger examples in the history of the game of 'the players' manager'. It was Nobby Stiles who said it after England had beaten Germany in the Final. '*You* did it, Alf,' he cried tearfully. 'We'd have been nothing without you.'

England had to be favourites, given home advantage, given a successful Scandinavian tour just before the series began. On paper they had a fine goalkeeper in Banks, a potential match-winner in Greaves, a gifted and well-drilled defence. But in midfield they relied on Bobby Charlton, always known as a striker. In the event Charlton would play superbly in the Semi-final; be decisive in the Final. But those days were ahead.

Eyes also turned inevitably towards Brazil during their Scandinavian tour. But it was clear that the great days were passed. If Pelé was still there, threatening as ever, there were many questions that received unsatisfactory answers. Who would fill in for Zagalo, with his tireless and effective running? Who was there to replace the immaculate Didì? Was Garrincha sufficiently recovered from a car crash and a series of serious knee operations? In fact, so strange an amalgam was the Brazilian party between unproven young players and older hands that they brought with them the very two defenders they had omitted on grounds of old age four years earlier – Bellini and Orlando.

Russia still had Yachin, still lacked the spark that makes triumphant teams. The Italians had three stylish inside-forwards

# World Cups 1962–1970

in Mazzola, Rivera and Bulgarelli, an accomplished goal-scoring back in the giant Facchetti. They had beaten Argentina 3–0 just before the competition opened. But they also had a reputation for playing below form away from home. And the Argentinians that day had fielded something of a reserve side.

The Germans still had the indomitable Seeler up front, the indestructible Schnellinger in defence. It was known that they lacked a good goalkeeper, but had unearthed a fine young attacking wing-half in Beckenbauer, still had Helmut Haller to give guidance in midfield, and in Wolfgang Overath possessed another midfield player of the highest skill and fierce ability to read the patterns of a game.

The Brazilians were undoubtedly drawn in the toughest group – against Bulgaria, Hungary and Portugal. They won the opening game, against the first of these three, lost the other two. Against the Bulgarians both goals came from freekicks, a cannonball from Pelé, a 'banana' shot from Garrincha; and Pelé spent much of the match trying to avoid scything tackles.

The Brazilians then came across Hungary, losers to Portugal in their first game thanks to some desperately inefficient goalkeeping. (More than one authority thought that Hungary would have won this competition had they been served in goal even remotely well.) The Hungarians had Albert, one of their heroes four years previously; they had a fine new forward in Bene, who had played superbly in the winning 1964 Olympic team; they had another hero from 1962 in Meszoly, always prepared to break into attack from behind; and they had Farkas, a deadly finisher close to goal.

Without Pelé, the Brazilians looked feeble indeed. Garrincha looked creaky, the two elder statesmen of the defence – Djalma Santos and Bellini – ominously static. Against fast and tricky running, that Brazilian defence crumbled quickly. Bene swerved and knifed through the middle after three minutes of play to slide the ball home; and although Brazil equalised through the young Tostao just before half-time, their goal came against all justice.

It was in the second half that their fate was sealed. First Albert ran through, slid the ball to Bene on the right, and Farkas rushed in to smack home the volleyed cross – as spectacular a goal as the competition was to see. And then came a penalty, tucked home by Meszoly. The Liverpool crowd rose to the Hungarians, and particularly Albert; the Brazilians went back to camp to plan survival against Portugal.

They did for this match what they might have done earlier – play young men capable of running for ninety minutes. Pelé came back clearly not fit, and was put out of the game early on by a vicious tackle from Morais, one that failed to receive from the too placid English referee the punishment it deserved – expulsion. All those who saw it will never forget the sight of Pelé, his face agonised, lying by the touchline swathed in a blanket.

The game against Hungary had been Brazil's first defeat in a World Cup match since 1954 – when they had been put out in that infamous game – by the Hungarians. The Portugal game showed that they deserved to be out. They had no answers to Albert, Bene and Farkas; now they had no answers to the fast running and powerful shooting of Eusebio. It was the famous coloured player from Mozambique who smashed in a shot in the fourteenth minute – for Manga, the Brazilian goalkeeper to shovel it away into the path of Simoes. A headed goal from Eusebio, then a right-foot shot – and Brazil (despite Rildo's second-half score) were out. They caught the train to Euston complaining – rightly – of inefficient refereeing. But they had proved the point that great teams are made up of great players, that greatness is not bestowed magically from above to those countries who feel they deserve it.

Elsewhere Argentina and West Germany came through from group II, the former gathering a reputation for ruthlessness that would serve to dim appreciation of their undoubted skills. Both teams beat Switzerland and Spain, their game together was drawn. The West Germans looked classy in a 5–0 victory over Switzerland. They still had their own goalkeeping problems; but the defence remained firm, the midfield enterprising. As for Spain, they used their older players initially – and like Brazil came to rue their choice. When they did put out their youngsters, it was against the Germans and too late, despite a spirited performance.

England came through in the first group, desperately unconvincing. Against Uruguay they were unable to pierce the defensive

# World Cups 1962–1970

barrier; against Mexico it took a superb, spectacular shot from long-distance and Bobby Charlton to break the deadlock; against France they looked unconvincing against a team down to ten men for much of the game. The English defence, however, appeared impressive; fortunate indeed to have a goalkeeper of Banks' class in a year of so much bad goalkeeping. The Uruguayans beat France, drew with Mexico, to join them.

Up in the North-east it was nearly all Russia. They disposed of North Korea in the opening game, scoring three goals in the process; then scored just the one goal against a lethargic Italian team bereft of Rivera's skills. As so often Italian caution in team selection and tactics brought its just rewards. But they still had to play North Korea – a game that should have given them little cause for sleeplessness.

In the event, the game was as big a shock as England's defeat at the hands of the Americans sixteen years earlier. Though the Italians lost Bulgarelli in the thirty-fourth minute with strained ligaments (an injury caused by his own foul tackle), they throughout played like ghosts. Pak Doo Ik it was who scored the only goal of the match just before half-time, and when the final whistle came, the Middlesbrough crowd rushed on to the pitch in joy. Who could ever forget the sight of one enormous British sailor tucking a Korean player under each arm and rushing round the pitch like a lunatic. As for the Italians they went home in shame, were pelted with rotten vegetables on arrival at Genoa airport at the dead of night.

Two of the Quarter-finals remain memorable – and for totally differing reasons. The Russians won by the odd goal in three against the Hungarians, manifestly less imaginative, but having in goal a Yachin instead of a Gelei; and at Sheffield the West Germans won 4–0 against a dispirited and disorganised Uruguayan team that had two men sent off and never really tried to stay in the game.

London and Liverpool would see the more fascinating matches. For their game against Argentina at Wembley, England left out the injured Jimmy Greaves (and were perhaps glad to do so, for his form had been disappointing) and brought in Geoff Hurst – whose last game, against Denmark, had been disastrously uninspiring. As so often happens in these things, Hurst turned out to be the match-winner, scoring the only goal of the game thirteen minutes from time; and once forcing Roma, the Argentian goalkeeper, to an acrobatic windmill-like save at point-blank range.

Everything, however, came to be overshadowed in most people's minds by the events just before half-time when Rattin, the South Americans' captain, was sent off by the German referee, Herr Kreitlin, for objecting to the booking of one of his team mates. Rattin himself had been booked for a trip on Bobby Charlton; but though there had been many nasty and cynical Argentinian fouls, that particular one had been by no means the worst. Later the referee claimed to have sent off Rattin 'for the look on his face'. In the event the game was held up for eleven minutes while Rattin refused to move, while the Argentinian coach, Juan Carlos Lorenzo, argued from the touchline, while officials tried to get the game restarted. So the Argentinians lost the most effective player in midfield; and there can be little doubt that had they initially gone out to play as well as they could, the result might have been very different. Certainly England's eleven players made heavy work of the game in the second half against ten opponents bent merely on destructive tactics.

After the game officials moved quickly to protect the referee against the Argentinian reserves, who joined their colleagues to pound on the door of the English dressing-room, to make insinuating gestures and statements to World Cup officials. One of their players urinated on the floor outside the English quarters, their manager rubbed forefinger and thumb meaningfully together, and Alf Ramsey was distressed enough to refer to them as 'animals' in a remark that he later – understandably grudgingly – was forced to withdraw.

England were through, the mundanity of their play masked by events off the ball. And in the Semi-finals they would meet Portugal, winners against the North Koreans in a game as extraordinary as that at Wembley. After their bizarre and heartwarming achievements against the Italians, the Koreans took on Eusebio and his men, nipping about smartly. A goal in the first minute was a fine tonic; two more soon after and the fancied Portuguese were three down.

That was the point at which Eusebio must have realised that Nemesis was staring him in the face. He ran through for one goal, smashed home a penalty after Torres had had his legs taken from underneath him, added two further goals in the second half. Augusto got a fifth, from a corner, and the Koreans were finally forced out, having given vast entertainment, having puzzled everyone as to the nature of their achievement. Everyone knew that for months they had lived in solitary and rigorous confinement. But the quickness with which they had learnt made many people wonder whether future competitions wouldn't deserve greater participation on the part of teams drawn from those countries with little footballing tradition.

Given the magnificent way in which Lancashire – and particularly Liverpool – had supported its games in the competition, Liverpudlians deserved much better than they received from the Russia–Germany Semi-final, little more nor less than a war of attrition. Sabo made a potentially vicious tackle on Beckenbauer – only to come away limping himself; a long-range sliding effort from Schnellinger on Chislenko left that Russian limping. He went off for treatment, returned, lost a ball to Held, chased the German and was rightly sent off by Concetto Lo Bello, the famous Italian referee. Haller it was who scored the first German goal a minute before half-time, just after Schnellinger's tackle; and Beckenbauer curled a shot around the Russian defensive wall for the second. Porkujan replied for Russia, but too late. And although the Russian manager publicly blamed Yachin for the two German goals, the truth was that without him they might have ceded two or three in the first twenty minutes.

The England–Portugal Semi-final provided a pleasant and enthralling contrast. It was in this game that the English really came together to look formidable, the defence strong as ever, Bobby Charlton stupendous in midfield and behind the attack in a performance that must have gone a long way to earning him the award as European Footballer of the Year. Everything he tried, and he tried everything, came off. His swerving runs, long passing, ferocious shooting – all were in evidence. He it was who scored the first goal, after José Pereira had pushed out a shot from Hunt; and just as important, every Portuguese player he passed on the way back to the centre circle stopped to shake his hand.

From first whistle to last the game was played at an electrifying pace, graced by electric skills. There was the battle between Torres and Jack Charlton, two giants in the air; that between Stiles and Eusebio, with the heart and guts of the former matched against the amazing skills of the latter; and there was the battle in midfield between Charlton and the Portuguese captain, Coluna, with his casual talent for passing, his instinctual reading of the game. When Hurst raced through eleven minutes from the end and cut the ball from the by-line for Charlton to hammer in his second goal, that seemed that. But three minutes later Jack Charlton was forced to give away a penalty, taken and scored by Eusebio. And the last few minutes were played out in a frenzy – Stiles making a fine last-ditch tackle on Simoes, Banks going down brilliantly to a vicious shot from Coluna. England were through to the Final; and though Eusebio left the pitch in tears, comforted by his team mates, he would have the consolation (admittedly small) of scoring in Portugal's victory over Russia for the third place match, and thus consolidate his position as the tournament's leading scorer.

The Final would prove as dramatic as the changes in the weather – now brilliant sunshine, now driving rain; certainly the most dramatic Final that the competition has ever seen. It was the Germans who took the lead – in the thirteenth minute after Ray Wilson – normally so cool at fullback – had nonchalantly headed a loose ball down to the feet of Haller, for the German inside-forward to slide the ball past Banks. It was a lead Germany would hold for only six minutes – until Hurst turned in a free-kick taken too swiftly by Bobby Moore.

It was eighteen minutes into the second-half before England took the lead. For much of the match Alan Ball had run Schnellinger ragged – Schnellinger, thought of by many as the best fullback in the world. Time after time Ball had forced him away from his touchline and into the middle, where he had been manifestly less

# World Cups 1962–1970

assured. Now the small, red-haired England 'winger' forced and took a corner. The ball came to Hurst, who shot – only for a German defender to block and Peters to clip the rebound past Tilkowski, the German goalkeeper.

Pressing increasingly towards attack, the Germans were leaving themselves vulnerable in defence. Three minutes from what should have been the end of the game Hurst burst through, passed too shallowly to Charlton – whose shot was tame. And in the last minute, agonisingly, the Germans equalised. The referee deemed Jack Charlton to have obstructed Held (many thought the offence inverted), Emmerich drove the kick powerfully through the England wall, and when Held touched the ball on, Weber – the centre-half – rushed in to score.

Thus to extra-time, with both teams exhausted apart from Alan Ball, seemingly ready to run for many hours yet. Ten minutes into the first period he scampered off down the right wing and crossed precisely – for Hurst to smash a shot against the underside of the crossbar. We can now say that it was probably not a goal. But to establish that fact it took a lot of people many hours of very hard work in cinema laboratories all over the world. At the time the referee conferred with linesman – the Russian Bakhramov – and the most contentious goal of a World Cup Final was allowed.

In the last minutes, with England having hung on bravely, Hurst it was again who ran through a demoralised and static German defence to slash in a fierce shot with his left foot. He had done what no one had done before, scored a hat trick in a Final. And England, though far from being the most stylish or interesting team of the competition, had done what Alf Ramsey had said they would. They would have their critics, and many would complain about the incompetence and lack of sensibility in much of the refereeing. But the competition had been the best organised and best supported of any, and England's games in Semi-final and Final worthy to set with the best in the history of the World Cup tournament.

# 1966 – Final Stages

## Quarter-Finals

ENGLAND 1, ARGENTINA 0 (0–0). *Wembley*

ENGLAND: Banks (Leicester City); Cohen (Fulham), Wilson (Everton); Stiles (Manchester United), Charlton, J. (Leeds United), Moore (West Ham United); Ball (Blackpool), Hurst (West Ham United), Charlton R. (Manchester United), Hunt (Liverpool), Peters (West Ham United).
ARGENTINA: Roma; Ferreiro, Perfumo, Albrecht, Marzolini; Gonzalez, Rattin, Onega; Solari, Artime, Mas.
SCORER: Hurst for England.

WEST GERMANY 4, URUGUAY 0 (1–0). *Sheffield*

WEST GERMANY: Tilkowski; Hottges, Weber, Schultz, Schnellinger; Beckenbauer, Haller, Overath; Seeler, Held, Emmerich.
URUGUAY: Mazurkiewiez; Troche; Ubinas, Gonçalves, Manicera, Caetano; Salva, Rocha, Silva, Cortez, Perez.
SCORERS: Held, Beckenbauer, Seeler, Haller for West Germany.

PORTUGAL 5, NORTH KOREA 3 (2–3). *Everton*

PORTUGAL: José Pereira; Morais, Baptista, Vicente, Hilario; Graça, Coluna, Augusto; Eusebio, Torres, Simoes.
NORTH KOREA: Ri Chan Myung; Rim Yung Sum, Shin Yung Kyoo, Ha Jung Wong, O Yook Kyung; Pak Seung Jin, Jon Seung Hwi; Han Bong Jin, Pak Doo Ik, Li Dong Woon, Yang Sung Kook.
SCORERS: Pak Seung Jin, Yang Sung Kook, Li Dong Woon for North Korea; Eusebio 4 (2 penalties), Augusto for Portugal.

RUSSIA 2, HUNGARY 1 (1–0). *Sunderland*

RUSSIA: Yachin; Ponomarev, Chesternjiev, Voronin, Danilov; Sabo, Khusainov; Chislenko, Banichevski, Malafeev, Porkujan.

HUNGARY: Gelei; Matrai; Kaposzta, Meszoly, Sipos, Szepesi; Nagy, Albert, Rakosi; Bene, Farkas.
SCORERS: Chislenko, Porkujan for Russia; Bene for Hungary.

## Semi-Finals

WEST GERMANY 2, RUSSIA 1 (1-0). *Everton*

WEST GERMANY: Tilkowski; Hottges, Weber, Schultz, Schnellinger; Beckenbauer, Haller, Overath, Seeler, Held, Emmerich.
RUSSIA: Yachin; Ponomarev, Chesternjiev, Voronin, Danilov; Sabo, Khusainov; Chislenko, Banichevski, Malafeev, Porkujan.
SCORERS: Haller, Beckenbauer for Germany; Porkujan for Russia.

ENGLAND 2, PORTUGAL 1 (1-0). *Wembley*

ENGLAND: Banks (Leicester City); Cohen (Fulham), Wilson (Everton); Stiles (Manchester United), Charlton, J. (Leeds United), Moore (West Ham United); Ball (Blackpool), Hurst (West Ham United), Charlton, R. (Manchester United), Hunt (Liverpool), Peters (West Ham United).
PORTUGAL: José Pereira; Festa, Baptista, Carlos, Hilario; Graça, Coluna, Augusto; Eusebio, Torres, Simoes.
SCORERS: Charlton, R. (2) for England; Eusebio (penalty) for Portugal.

## Third Place Match

PORTUGAL 2, RUSSIA 1 (1-1). *Wembley*

PORTUGAL: José Pereira; Festa, Baptista, Carlos, Hilario; Graça, Coluna, Augusto; Eusebio, Torres, Simoes.
RUSSIA: Yachin; Ponomarev, Khurtsilava, Korneev, Danilov;

Voronin, Sichinava; Metreveli, Malafeev, Banichevski, Serebrianikov.
SCORERS: Eusebio (penalty), Torres for Portugal; Malafeev for Russia.

## Final

ENGLAND 4, WEST GERMANY 2 (1-1) (2-2) after extra time. *Wembley*

ENGLAND: Banks; Cohen, Wilson; Stiles, Charlton, J., Moore; Ball, Hurst, Charlton, R., Hunt, Peters.
WEST GERMANY: Tilkowski; Hottges, Schultz; Weber, Schnellinger, Haller; Beckenbauer, Overath, Seeler, Held, Emmerich.
SCORERS: Hurst (3), Peters for England; Haller, Weber for Germany.

# World Cup 1970 – held in Mexico

Given that the tournament tended to be played alternately in Europe and South America, it was inevitable that Mexico would be a venue sooner or later. For many, however, the 'later' would have been preferable. The 1968 Olympiad had shown precisely and agonisingly the problems thrown up in expecting top-class athletes to compete at high altitudes. And few parts of central Mexico were at less than 6–7,000 feet above sea level. The nonchalant could at least pretend that it made life more interesting.

What could have been prevented – and wasn't – was the callous selling-out of the tournament to financial interests. Too many games were played in noonday heat – merely to satisfy European television companies eager to televise games at peak viewing times. England, for example, played their vital group match against Brazil

The last moments of the 1930 Final in which Uruguay beat Argentina 4-2, the scorer being Hector Castro (just to the left of the right-hand upright), who was known as 'El Manco' after his right arm had been amputated at the elbow.

The only goal of the Semi-final in the 1934 World Cup in which Italy beat Austria, scored by Enrico Guiata. Italy went on to win the Final against Czechoslovakia 2-1 after extra time had been played.

Italy triumph again in 1938 by beating Hungary 4-2. Holding the Jules Rimet trophy is their manager, Vittorio Pozzo, and just to *his* left is Silvio Piola, who scored twice in the Final.

The 1950 World Cup and Uruguay's goalkeeper, Roque Maspoli, manages to dive down to the ball before Brazil's forward, Ademir, can reach it. Uruguay won the match 2-1, although Brazil had 'home' advantage, and thus took the title for the second time.

Max Morlock (West Germany) slides the ball under the arms of the advancing Hungarian goalkeeper, Gyula Grosics, to score his side's first goal in the 'unexpected' 3-2 victory in the 1954 Final.

Harry Gregg (Northern Ireland) fails to stop a shot by Uwe Seeler (West Germany), in a group match from the 1958 World Cup which finished in a 2-2 draw.

Kalle Svensson dives to prevent trouble from John Charles during the goalless draw in the 1958 tournament between Sweden and Wales.

From the 1958 Final. The electrifying Garrincha centres for Vavà to strike home Brazil's first, and equalising, goal in the 5-2 defeat of Sweden.

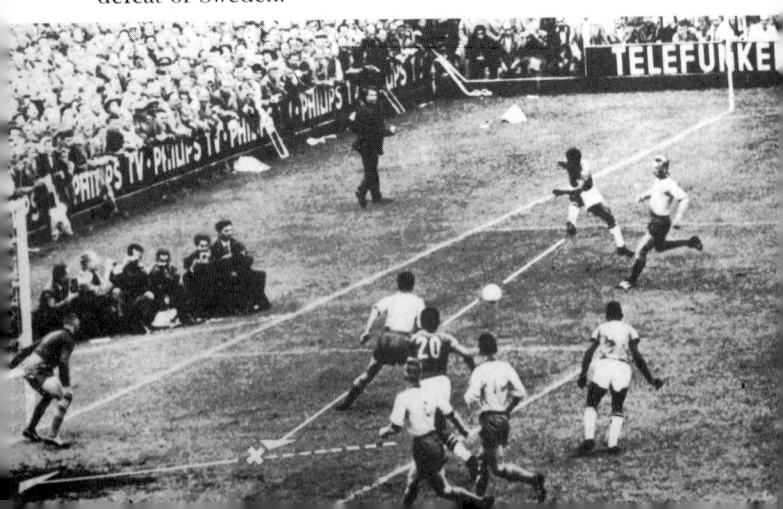

Luis Suarez (Spain) trying to find a way through an uncompromising Czechoslovakian defence during the 1962 World Cup, which his side lost just by the one goal. Czechoslovakia proceeded to the Final.

The Brazilian team before the 1962 Final in which they beat Czechoslovakia 3-1. *Top (left to right):* Djalma Santos, Zito, Gilmar, Mauro, Nilton Santos and Zozimo. *Bottom:* Garrincha, Didi, Vavà, Amarildo and Zagalo.

Brazil against Hungary in 1966 and Jairzinho attempts a header which the Hungarian goalkeeper, Jozsef Gelei, manages to save. It was a memorable match which Hungary won 3-1.

Russia versus Hungary Quarter-final in 1966 which Russia won 2-1. Here Ferenc Bene (second from left) scores Hungary's only goal.

1966 Quarter-final between England and Argentina. Referee Kreitlen orders off Antonio Rattin after he had objected to the 'booking' of a colleague. Play was held up for ten minutes in which time the Argentinians petitioned, argued and at one time appeared ready to leave the field *en masse*.

Third Place match in 1966 between Portugal and Russia. Eusebio (Portugal) forces his way through the Russian defence only to see his shot saved by Lev Yachin. Despite this, Portugal won 2-1 and Eusebio finished as the highest scorer in the tournament.

1966 Final and Wolfgang Weber scores in the final minute of normal time. Also in the picture are Uwe Seeler, George Cohen, Bobby Moore, Ray Wilson, Kurt Schnellinger, Jackie Charlton and Gordon Banks (the goalkeeper).

Geoff Hurst (England) makes sure of victory in the 1966 Final by driving home the fourth goal in England's 4-2 victory over West Germany. The German player is Wolfgang Overath.

# World Cups 1962–1970

at noon, in temperatures of nearly 100 degrees and there was barely an England player who had not lost eight or ten pounds in weight as a result of dehydration.

England's preparations had been thorough enough. The team arrived in Mexico well before the tournament started; good accommodation had been found; supplies of food and drink had been flown out (though the Mexican customs officials appeared un-cooperative at first); the players were even supplied with reading material by Coronet Books, one of the country's leading paperback publishing firms. Leaving Mexico for a short tour, England won handsome victories over Columbia and Ecuador, the defence seemingly as ungenerous as it had been in 1966.

It was after the second of these games, as the team stopped off in Bogota on the way back to Mexico that Bobby Moore, the English captain, was absurdly accused of having stolen a bracelet from a hotel jewellers. Much has been written about this extraordinary incident, that would last for nearly two years, until the 'charges' were finally dropped. The important point to underline is Moore's amazing coolness during the whole affair. In a situation where many players might have cracked under the nervous strain imposed by being unable to fly back to Mexico with the rest of the team, of having to remain in a state of semi-solitary confinement while the matter was tentatively cleared up Moore was simply magnificent. Within days he was to go out and prove to the world that, as in 1966, he remained the best defensive wing-half in modern football.

If England had Moore, then Brazil still had Pelé. The Brazilians had taken, only months before the Finals, the extraordinary step of sacking their manager, the bubbling Joao Saldanha, and replacing him with Mario Zagalo, one of the heroes of 1958 and 1962. No one doubted the Brazilian talent. If they had a goalkeeper of laughable mediocrity in Felix, if their defence seemed unsound – then they had Gerson in midfield and up front Jairzinho and Tostao. The latter had recently undergone eye surgery, but was known to be a formidable foil to Pelé. The first few games would tell all about Brazil.

The West Germans were there also, eager for the chance to

revenge their defeat at the hands of the English four years previously. The bulk of that side remained; they had two incisive wingers in Grabowski and Libuda, a 'new' goalkeeper in Maier, one of the best of the tournament. And that is not meant disparagingly. One of the many contrasts between the 1966 competition and that to be held in Mexico would be the overall improvement in goalkeeping standards. Banks (England), Kavazashvili (Russia), Piot (Belgium), Calderon (Mexico), Albertosi (Italy) and Mazurkiewicz (Uruguay) – all, with Maier, kept goal well in conditions that were far from helpful, ones in which the ball moved fast through the rarefied air, swerving and dipping unexpectedly, ones in which the brightness of the light put a premium on good judgement. We might note here that the fearsome Gerd Muller, who would score most goals in the tournament, came to face only two of the above-mentioned, when Germany played their Semifinal against Italy and their final game against Uruguay.

The Italians came strangely, having qualified with some ease against East Germany and Wales in their preliminary group. In Riva they had a striker of renown, his left foot a terrifying weapon when given the chance to exercise itself. But too often Riva's brilliant goals had camouflaged weaknesses in the defence, lack of understanding in midfield. Mazzola was there for the second time, Rivera for the third – both players of high technical accomplishment, and supposedly unable to play together. The Italians decided in favour of the *staffeta*, a system whereby Mazzola would play the first half of each game, Rivera the second. The latter found it unacceptable, said so loudly, was nearly sent home as punishment, stayed, and in two games at least, would prove that he is one of the world's great intuitive players.

The Russians looked solid as ever, with Kavazashvili a worthy successor in goal to the great Yachin, and Shesternev a sweeper little behind Bobby Moore in terms of technical expertise and tactical acumen. They had an interesting young striker in Bishovets, but would play a type of football that lacked genuine inventiveness. Uruguay were another team strong on paper, again served brilliantly in goal (by Mazurkiewicz, one of the very small clutch of good goalkeepers four years previously), and with some terrifyingly robust defenders. One remembers particularly Montero Castillo in the centre of the field, Ubinas and Ancheta elsewhere. And the joker in the pack had to be Peru, coached for the tournament by Didì, the Brazilian ex-player and perennial hero of 1954, 1958 and 1962. It was known that they had some forwards of dazzling technical gifts, but did they have a team, could they put together a game?

Generally speaking those teams that were expected to come through came through. The first game of the first group – and the tournament – was that between Mexico (the hosts) and Russia. A goalless draw, as with its 1966 counterpart, sounded an ominous warning. But Belgium played some light, waltzing football to beat El Salvador the following day; and when they came to meet Russia, deserved better than the 4–1 defeat that they allowed to be inflicted upon them. Bishovets scored two of those goals, Shesternev marshalled the defence superbly; and it was one of those days when the Russians showed the world just what they could do when prepared to cast off thoughts of weighty preparation and overdrilled tactics. And in the final game of the group, the Mexicans went through against the Belgians 1–0, thanks to a hotly disputed penalty decision, one that seemed to have been not uninfluenced by the frenzy of a vast home crowd. Mexico, unconvincingly, and Russia through, then, from that group.

Group II looked good for both Italy and Uruguay. Israel looked too raw, Sweden – despite the presence of one or two players of high talent, such as Kindvall and Grahn, who played their club football outside Sweden – lacked strength in depth. They it was who first faced Italy, going down to a drive from some long range delivered by the Italian midfield player, Domenghini, who throughout the tournament would play with a ubiquity that perilously ignored the heat of the sun and the rarity of the air. The Uruguayans scraped through 2–0 against Israel, more importantly lost Pedro Rocha, their midfield general after only a few minutes of play. It was an injury that would force the South American team even further back on to their defensive and uncompromising heels, for Rocha would take no further part in the tournament.

The next match brought these two teams together into a goalless draw, with both sets of players full of hostility (both masked and overt). Riva was to claim that from the first Uruguayan defenders had spat at him whenever they were close; which did not excuse his lethargy. More dreary football was to follow, and the results continued to prove evidence of the essentially defensive attitudes that permeated group matches. The Swedes beat the Uruguayans, who went through on a marginally better goal average; and the Italians got through with two goalless draws and that one win. Top of the group with only one goal in three matches: that, surely, couldn't be the stuff of which world champions were made?

Group III was, indubitably, the toughest on paper; and certainly the matches from that group provided some of the most fascinating football. If the English won their first game against Rumania, they did so with some lack of ease, thanks to a goal from Geoff Hurst in the seventieth minute, and despite some sadistic tackling by the Rumanian defenders, a certain Mocanu in particular. If the Brazilians appeared to thrash the Czechs 4–1, it must be remembered that Petras scored the first goal of the match for Czechoslovakia, that they were served with some indifferent goalkeeping, that the third Brazilian goal (scored by Jairzinho) looked suspiciously offside. But Pelé was on superb form, scored an extraordinary goal; Rivelino put another in from a swerving free-kick; Jairzinho scored again, always threatened when he had possession; and Gerson in midfield sprayed accurate passes around with high panache, underlining the thought that so many of the world's finest distributors have been players whose athleticism was far from robust. Gerson, for example, is something of a one-paced player (and that pace never faster than slow-medium) who is a compulsive cigarette smoker. Hardly the stuff of which the textbook heroes are made, but a player of great influence.

Too many people – and particularly in England – have tended to overlook the fact of Gerson's absence when England came to play Brazil. That is not to say that England didn't play thoroughly well, that they did not suggest themselves as one of the two or three best teams of the tournament during that game. It was a classic, worthy to enter the Pantheon of brilliant World Cup games. The English had gone to Mexico in the rôle of villains, with too many people

## World Cups 1962–1970

disgruntled as to the manner of their victory four years earlier; and this animosity was to manifest itself at every turn. The night before the Brazil game a crowd several thousand strong milled round the Hilton Hotel, where they were staying, and contrived to make enough noise to prevent the players getting any sleep. Many admitted afterwards that they had for long minutes and hours simply stood by the windows of their rooms, staring at the crowd below, and at the inability of the Mexican police to deal with the problem.

They then went out at midday, in scorching heat that approached 100 degrees of Fahrenheit and played Brazil off the pitch for long stretches of the game. Mullery played brilliantly, policing Pelé with scrupulous toughness. True, Pelé got away from him in the early minutes of the game after Jairzinho had rounded Cooper on England's left and smacked across a perfect centre; up went Pelé, down came the ball, and down also came Gordon Banks to scoop the ball up with his right wrist – a save that must rank with the very best in the history of the World Cup tournament. Otherwise Pelé was kept moderately quiet; and Moore at the heart of the defence gave further evidence that he was the best defensive player in the world, his timing of the tackle precise, his reading of the game astute, his distribution imaginative.

The only goal of the match (perfect evidence that goals in themselves do not exciting football make) came after fourteen minutes of the second half, after Tostao had teased the left of the English defence and slid the ball across goal for Jairzinho to score. The truth was, however, that if Banks was forced to at least three other saves of high quality, England were given, and missed, a plentitude of chances at the other end. Ball hit the bar, missed another good chance; Astle blazed wide after being put into an attractive position; Hurst might have had a goal, but shot feebly at the crucial moment. If the style is the man, then the style must also be the game; and yet again we were left to ponder that one of the essential weaknesses of the English game was its lack of high technical accomplishment – where the world's best strikers would snap up chances with glee, too often English forwards had not the basic 'killer' instinct that comes hand in hand (or foot to foot) with technical prowess.

The Brazilians went on to beat the Rumanians, again despite the deprivation of Gerson; and, on this occasion, that of Rivelino. England drafted in a handful of 'reserves' for the game against the Czechs, played badly, won through a disputed penalty; and joined Brazil in the Quarter-finals.

In group IV were the mysterious Peruvians. In their first game, they fell behind to Bulgaria, conceded two goals from set pieces; and then in the second half turned on their skills. Many were quick to compare them with the Brazilians in their flamboyance, their brilliant control. In defence they had a sturdy player in Chumpitaz, some imaginative forwards in Gallardo, Sotil, Cubillas and Baylon; and in the space of twenty minutes turned the two-goal deficit into a 3–2 score that would last until the game's finish.

That would prove to be the decisive game in the group. For although they fared poorly against Morocco in their first match, the West Germans seemed certainties for qualification; a thought that was reinforced when they came to play the Bulgarians in turn. Though the East Europeans scored first through Nikodimov (following a free kick), the Germans ran in five goals, three of them going to Muller. Libuda was on venomous form on their right, Muller and Seeler brave and energetic in the middle. In fact Muller would score another hat trick when the Germans came to meet Peru a few days later, marching firmly along the road that would make him the tournament's highest scorer. Despite that 3–1 defeat, Peru would qualify.

No goal Muller scored in the competition was, however, more important than that he slashed home in the Quarter-final tie that followed, when the Germans were drawn against England. It was a game England could, and should, have won. For a team of their defensive prowess to lead by two clear goals and eventually lose by the odd score in five was remarkable. It is too easy to blame Peter Bonetti, drafted into the goalkeeping position after Banks had been forced to withdraw with a stomach complaint of mysterious origin. Banks may well have saved two of the three German goals

---

\* Soon after the Peruvians arrived an earthquake ravaged their country, killing thousands.

# World Cups 1962–1970

to be scored; but there were other, better reasons to explain the collapse.

England's lead came through Mullery – racing through to exchange passes with Lee, sliding the ball out to Newton on the right, smashing home the perfect cross; and Peters – knocking in another fine cross from Newton. That left England two up after five minutes of the second half, and seemingly set for a good win. And then came the substitutions – Grabowski on for Libuda; Bell and Hunter on for Charlton and Peters – that were to prove decisive. While Charlton remained, Beckenbauer, his policeman, stayed quiet; without further patrolling duties, Beckenbauer cut loose, scored the first, important, German goal. Where Cooper had controlled Libuda on the left, he now found Grabowski irrepressible. Although Hurst nearly made the score 3–1 with a fine low header, it was the Germans who came through, Seeler backheading a long cross from Schnellinger.

As in the 1966 Final, the game between the two countries entered extra time, with the crowd noisily pro-German, and England's defence looking increasingly tired. Hurst scored – to be given, mysteriously, offside. And then came the deciding goal – Grabowski winning control on the right, punting over a cross, which Muller tucked away as the ball was nodded down to him. England were out of the competition, after having controlled vast stretches of their games against Brazil and West Germany, after having suggested themselves strongly as possible opposition for Brazil in the Final.

Through into the Semi-finals with Germany would go Italy, Brazil and Uruguay. The last won through in the final moments of extra time in a hard game against the Russians, and with a hotly disputed goal into the bargain. But the Russians had missed too many chances to have reason for bitter complaint.

Brazil went through, now with both Rivelino and Gerson back in the side, and at the expense of Peru to the tune of 4–2. Gallardo scored two goals for the entertaining Peruvians, but they were up against a side that knew their own footballing language and were more adept practitioners.

And Italy went through, stuttering for much of their game

against Mexico, until Gianni Rivera made his appearance at the start of the second half and suggested openings for his compatriots. Riva scored twice, delighting those who knew his prowess and were still waiting patiently for evidence of its existence; and there was a goal from Rivera himself, nice ammunition for those who felt that Italy were squandering his exquisite talents, that there should always have been a place for him in that team, with or without the brave resourceful Sandro Mazzola.

The Semi-final draw – Brazil against Uruguay, Italy against West Germany – promised, and delivered, much. The first of these games pitted the resource of the Brazilian midfield and attack against the misanthropy of the Uruguayan defence, with its squad of muscular central defenders. In the event, it was Uruguay who scored first, through Cubilla (as opposed to Cubillas, the Peruvian), and though Brazil equalised just before half-time through Clodoaldo, the important second goal did not materialise until fourteen minutes before the end, when Jairzinho danced past three defenders on the right and drove the ball home from a sharp angle. A goal from Rivelino in the last second of the game gave the scoreline a lopsided quality that was grossly unfair to the courage and ingenuity of much of the Uruguayan play, still deprived of the skills of the injured – and potentially influential – Pedro Rocha.

But Italy against West Germany – that was really something of a collector's item. It was an interesting comment on the Italian footballing mentality that after a game of thrilling interest, despite the fact that their team had been victorious, many Italian commentators would dismiss it as being something of a circus turn on the grounds that neither of the two defences was good enough. In fact, Italy created much of their good fortune early in the game when a bad tackle by Bertini left the elegant Beckenbauer with an injured arm. He would play much of the game at strolling pace and in some pain, his arm strapped to his chest.

The Italians took the lead after only seven minutes, Boninsegna clearing Riva out of his way to plant a left-footed shot firmly past Maier. Given the Italian penchant for defensive expertise, the Germans must have known that they had a titanic struggle on their hands, and well though they played against the cautious Italians in

## World Cups 1962–1970

the second half, too many chances went begging. Indeed it was not until the third minute of injury time that Schnellinger, the German sweeper (and ironically he served brilliantly in that rôle at club level for AC Milan), came forward to slide the ball home after Grabowski had crossed from the left.

Into extra-time, and on came the nervousness and the mistakes. The Germans went ahead after five minutes through Muller; Burgnich came up to knock in Rivera's free kick; Riva scored a fine goal with that formidable left foot of his – and the first period of extra-time ended with Italy leading 3–2. The Italians were pulled back again soon after the resumption of play, when Muller dived low to head home; and then came the decisive goal, with the talented Boninsegna taking the ball out to the left, leaving his opponent Schulz on his bottom, and crossing for Gianni Rivera to drive the ball precisely into goal. Once again Rivera had missed the first forty-five minutes; once again he had been decisive in the later stages of a game. The Italians were through, not remotely the second best side in the tournament, but undoubtedly one of high technical accomplishment, and in that Semi-final game, having given the lie to those detractors eager to claim that Italian teams always lack fire and spirit.

In the play-off for third place the Germans did what the Italians had failed to do – and beat Uruguay. They did so with a fine goal scored by Overath after a thrilling movement that involved Libuda, Muller and Seeler. There was entertaining action at both ends, with Mazurkiewicz and Walter (the young German goalkeeper) both being forced to fine saves. But a match of technical adroitness could not raise the crowd – which, like the televised world, awaited the Final itself.

Brazil won it, and won it handsomely. They did so with football of assured fluency, they did it by underlining brilliantly, and against the master exponents of defensive football, all the old clichés about attack being the best means of defence. Of the Italians Sandro Mazzola covered vast tracts of ground, played with authority and spirit; Boninsegna showed what a dangerous striker he could be, given even a few metres of space; Facchetti strove manfully against Jairzinho. But much of the marking was sloppy on the one hand, crude on the other; and there was about the team as a whole a curious refusal to play with any real vestige of self-confidence.

It was, fittingly, Pelé who gave the Brazilians the lead after eighteen minutes, heading down Rivelino's cross; if the great man had a comparatively human game, then his presence and brilliance had given the tournament as a whole a fine streak of class. And no one looked more bemused than he when the Italians equalised a few minutes before half-time through Boninsegna and after a silly back-pass by Clodoaldo had left Felix stranded outside the Brazilian goal.

That was delusion indeed, for in the second half the Brazilians made heavy amends. Gerson, who throughout played with a majesty that capitalised on the failure of the Italian midfield, was the scorer of the second of the four Brazilian goals, his left foot curling in a fine shot from distance. Jairzinho it was who scored the third, slipping in a pass from Pelé and setting a new record by virtue of having scored in all six games in which he played; and the Italians were a thoroughly demoralised side by the time Carlos Alberto came through down the right touchline to crash the ball in after an exquisitely weighted pass from Pelé had put him through in the last few minutes of the game.

The Italians brought on Juliano for the ineffectual Bertini; with six minutes to go, bizarrely substituted Rivera for Boninsegna – a move that was staggering in its lack of logic. Had Rivera appeared earlier, in place of the tired Domenghini, one might have seen the point, he might have effected something of a rescue. But the ship had been truly sunk; despite their appearance in the Final the Italians would go home and indulge in the most Machiavellian post-mortems. And by virtue of their third victory, the Brazilians would appropriate the Jules Rimet trophy.

It was a popular victory, a welcome evidence that attacking football and intuitive genius still had their place in a footballing world obsessed by 'work-rate' and (often) skill-less hard running. Winning the tournament in 1966 England had conceded only three goals, scored eleven. Four years later, the Brazilians had triumphed by conceding seven goals and scoring nineteen. Either

England or West Germany – not to mention Uruguay – might have made of the Final more than did the Italians. And it remained true (as it may always remain true) that some of the refereeing left much to be desired. But Ferenc Puskas, and many other great stars of the past, would have approved. The football of the Brazilians was many miles removed from the 'war' that people had gloomily forecast as being the only result of international competition. Above all, the Brazilians made the thing look enjoyable, had helped to restore that enthusiasm without which sport in any form will wither away. More chants of *'samba'*, and the spectacle of the greatest player of that, or any, generation – Pelé – being raised aloft by delighted Brazilian fans.

# 1970 – Final Stages

## Quarter-Finals

WEST GERMANY 3, ENGLAND 2 (0–1) (2–2) after extra time. *Leon*

WEST GERMANY: Maier; Schnellinger, Vogts, Fichtel, Hottges (Schulz); Beckenbauer, Overath, Seeler; Libuda (Grabowski), Muller, Loehr.
ENGLAND: Bonetti (Chelsea); Newton (Everton); Cooper (Leeds United); Mullery (Spurs), Labone (Everton), Moore (West Ham United); Lee (Manchester City), Ball (Everton), Hurst (West Ham United), Charlton (Manchester United) [Bell (Manchester City)], Peters (Spurs) [Hunter (Leeds United)].
SCORERS: Mullery, Peters for England; Beckenbauer, Seeler, Muller for West Germany.

BRAZIL 4, PERU 2 (2–1). *Guadalajara*

BRAZIL: Felix; Carlos Alberto, Brito, Piazza, Marco Antonio; Clodoaldo, Gerson (Paulo Cesar); Jairzinho (Roberto), Tostao, Pelé, Rivelino.

PERU: Rubiños; Campos, Fernandez, Chumpitaz, Fuentes; Mifflin, Challe; Baylon (Sotil), Perico Leon (Eladio Reyes), Cubillas, Gallardo.
SCORERS: Rivelino, Tostao (2), Jairzinho for Brazil; Gallardo, Cubillas for Peru.

ITALY 4, MEXICO 1 (1–1). *Toluca*

ITALY: Albertosi; Burgnich, Cera, Rosato, Facchetti; Bertini, Mazzola (Rivera), De Sisti; Domenghini (Gori), Boninsegna, Riva.
MEXICO: Calderon; Vantolra, Pena, Guzman, Perez; Gonzales (Borja), Pulido, Munguia (Diaz); Valdivia, Fragoso, Padilla.
SCORERS: Domenghini, Riva (2), Rivera for Italy; Gonzales for Mexico.

URUGUAY 1, RUSSIA 0 (0–0) after extra time. *Mexico*

URUGUAY: Mazurkiewicz; Ubinas, Ancheta, Matosas, Mujica; Maneiro, Cortes, Montero Castillo; Cubilla, Fontes (Gomez), Morales (Esparrago).
RUSSIA: Kavazashvili; Dzodzuashvili, Afonin, Khurtsilava (Logofet), Chesternijev; Muntijan, Asatiani (Kiselev), Kaplichni; Evriuzhkinzin, Bychevetz, Khmelnitzki.
SCORER: Esparrago for Uruguay.

# Semi-Finals

ITALY 4, WEST GERMANY 3 (1–0) (1–1) after extra time. *Mexico City*

ITALY: Albertosi; Cera; Burgnich, Bertini, Rosato, (Poletti) Facchetti; Domenghini, Mazzola (Rivera), De Sisti; Boninsegna, Riva.
WEST GERMANY: Maier; Schnellinger; Vogts, Schulz, Beckenbauer, Patzke; Seeler, Overath; Grabowski, Muller, Loehr (Libuda).

SCORERS: Boninsegna, Burgnich, Riva, Rivera, for Italy; Schnellinger, Muller (2) for West Germany.

BRAZIL 3, URUGUAY 1 (1–1). *Guadalajara*

BRAZIL: Felix; Carlos Alberto, Brito, Piazza, Everaldo; Clodoaldo, Gerson; Jairzinho, Tostao, Pelé, Rivelino.
URUGUAY: Mazurkiewicz; Ubinas, Ancheta, Matosas, Mujica; Montero Castillo, Cortes, Fontes; Cubilla, Maneiro (Esparrago), Morales.
SCORERS: Cubilla for Uruguay; Clodoaldo, Jairzinho, Rivelino for Brazil.

## Third Place Match

WEST GERMANY 1, URUGUAY 0 (1–0). *Mexico City*

WEST GERMANY: Walter; Schnellinger (Lorenz); Patzke, Fichtel, Weber, Vogts; Seeler, Overath; Libuda (Loehr), Muller, Held.
URUGUAY: Mazurkiewicz; Ubinas, Ancheta, Matosas, Mujica; Montero Castillo, Cortes, Fontes (Sandoval); Cubilla, Maneiro (Esparrago), Morales.
SCORER: Overath for West Germany.

## Final

BRAZIL 4, ITALY 1 (1–1). *Mexico City*

BRAZIL: Felix; Carlos Alberto, Brito, Piazza, Everaldo; Clodoaldo, Gerson; Jairzinho, Tostao, Pelé, Rivelino.
ITALY: Albertosi; Cera; Burgnich, Bertini (Juliano), Rosato, Facchetti; Domenghini, Mazzola, De Sisti; Boninsegna (Rivera), Riva.
SCORERS: Pelé, Gerson, Jairzinho, Carlos Alberto for Brazil; Boninsegna for Italy.

# 3 HOLLAND FINALISTS ON TWO OCCASIONS

## Victorious West Germany – at last (1974)

Second in the tournament of 1966; third in that of 1970 West Germany finally got their reward in the 1974 World Cup finals. They had received a fillip two years previously when, with Gunther Netzer at the top of his form as a play-maker in midfield, they had won the 1972 edition of the European Nations Championship; and they had received a recent bit of prompting when a club side, Bayern Munich, had won the 1974 edition of the European Champions' Cup.

For the first time since 1950 the format would be changed with the top two teams in each group not moving on to contest the Quarter-finals but to play in two further groups. The winners of these would contest the Final; the teams who would finish second would meet to decide the third and fourth places.

In 1970 it was teams from the Americas who had won four of the eight places for the Quarter-finals and had provided the most convincing winners of any tournament to date, but four years later the boot was very much on the European foot with West Germany being followed home by Holland and Poland. The Holland of Cruyff, of Neeskens, of Van Hanegem in fact could stand comparison with the most commanding of the sides which had won the World Cup for Brazil. And the measure of the superiority shown by European sides was the fact that the only occasion on which a South American team had a victory over a European one was when Brazil defeated East Germany in a match from the Second Round. In truth the South American sides suffered most terribly from their lack of physical preparation – with Uruguay in particular exercising the most lethal form of thuggery; especially when they met Holland in a game in the First Round.

## World Cup 1974

Brazil opened the tournament by playing very defensively against Yugoslavia. True Pelé had chosen not to play; Gerson, Tostao and Clodoaldo had all suffered vital injuries and the only members of the 1970 side left were Rivelino and Jairzinho but the great strength of the team on this occasion seemed to lie in its defence with Leao proving a more than useful goalkeeper, with Luis Pereira proving an excellent central defender and with the blond fullback, Francisco Marinho, surging forward with some useful runs down the left side of the field: 0–0 then with the Yugoslavs being impressive in the second part of the game. Maric had shown that he was a fine goalkeeper, Buljan made several telling interceptions at the back and Acimovic had been most intelligent in suggesting pathways for the attack.

Brazil's next game would also be goalless – but on this occasion against Scotland who had beaten Zaire 2–0 in their first game in the Group. In the first twenty minutes the champions from South America seemed set to tear Scotland apart with their inventive football and skill at taking free-kicks; but gradually Scotland came into the game strongly and as the game progressed the authority of Billy Bremner in midfield became absolute. David Hay became an increasingly important figure alongside him and both men saw scoring chances pass inches wide on the wrong side of the goalpost. With Holton and Buchan totally neutralising the potential threat from Jairzinho; with Lorimer and Morgan having fine games; with Bremner and Hay sealing up the middle of the field by their intelligent use of the ball – many people thought Scotland were desperately unfortunate not to gain a win. Yugoslavia demolished Zaire 9–0 on the same day, so Scotland went into the next game against Yugoslavia needing to win; or hoping against hope that Brazil would win by less than a two-goal margin against Zaire. With the two matches taking place at the same time matters looked promising at half-time, for Brazil had been unable to score more than once; and the Scotland–Yugoslavia game was still goalless. But halfway through the second period a Rivelino left-footed shot screamed into the Zaire goal; and soon after Valdomiro added a third. Worse was to follow as Karasi, who had come on the field only minutes before as a substitute for the Yugoslavians, scored with a header which left Scotland needing two goals in seven minutes. It was not to be, however, for although Jordan scored in the final minute of the game, Scotland were left rueing their failure to score against Brazil and the plain truth that they had taken matters far too easily against Zaire. They would have the small consolation of remaining the only team playing in the tournament to stay unbeaten and the fact that Bremner and McGrain would feature prominently in the lists of the best players who had been on duty in West Germany.

Group I saw the host nation being drawn against Australia, Chile and East Germany: the first occasion on which the two Germanies had played each other since the partition after the last war. Chile had come to the tournament by a curious route. They had been forced to play a deciding eliminator against Russia, had been there and drawn 0–0, then had been given a walk-over to the Finals proper when the Russians had refused to play the return match in Santiago – a refusal which had much more to do with political than sporting reasons, since Chile had recently experienced a right-wing coup! Despite some sinuous dribbling on the part of Caszely, some vigorous defensive work by Figueroa and some sharp bursts of counter-attacking by Ahumada, the West Germans hung on to win by just a single goal. Chile next held East Germany, who had beaten a gallant Australia 2–0, to a 1–1 draw. In their turn West Germany beat Australia 3–0 which, of course, meant that when the two Germanies played their 'inaugural' match the home side were already qualified to play in the Second Round; so it came as little surprise to find the East defeating the West merely by the one goal – a defeat which meant that West Germany would (be able to!) avoid the thrilling Holland team for a further handful of matches.

In truth Holland had enthralled everybody in their opening matches. Teams representing Dutch clubs had featured in five of the previous six editions of the European Cup, and had been victorious on four occasions; and the coach responsible for the pressing football that had gained an enormous reputation all over the world, Rinus Michels, had recently been called back to take charge of the Holland squad. The team contained exciting full-backs in Suurbier and Krol, gifted players in the midfield in Neeskens and Van Hanegem and in attack they possessed in Johan Cruyff one of the two best players in the tournament (the other being Franz Beckenbauer). Certainly their class was immediately apparent in the first game they played, a 2-0 victory against a crude and ruthless Uruguay. Uruguay played as though they were totally deprived of skill and talent; three players were cautioned, Julio Montero Castillo was sent off for aiming a series of knee-high tackles, and only Mazurkiewicz in goal and Rocha in midfield showed any type of form. A 1-1 draw against Bulgaria and a 3-0 defeat by Sweden and it was small wonder that Roberto Porta, the Uruguayan manager, stated just prior to the return of the team to Montevideo, 'This is the worst football we have ever played. It is a national disgrace.'

Sweden had proved to be one of the most interesting of teams in the opening games. They began with two goalless draws against Bulgaria and Holland but in their 3-0 win over the Uruguayans they had showed that they were coming into useful form at just the right time. They possessed one of the better goalkeepers in the tournament in Ronnie Hellstroem, had useful players in midfield in Grahn and Bo Larsson and in Edstroem were served by one of the most skilful of goalscorers. And the two teams to move on to the Second Round, therefore, were Sweden and Holland, who slaughtered Bulgaria 4-1 with two of their goals coming from penalties by Neeskens.

In Group IV we had a riveting start to the second half of the game between Italy and Haiti when the first goal came from ... Haiti! In fact that score by Sanon was the first goal to have been let in by Dino Zoff for 1,143 minutes of international play. It set the football world wondering: were we in for as big an upset as England's defeat in 1950 at the hands of the United States or as Italy's defeat in 1966 at the hands of North Korea? No. Italy pulled themselves together and although the goalkeeper for Haiti, Francillon, made a series of superb saves, the Italians ran out 3-1 winners at the end of the game. A sour footnote to this, for a Haiti defender Ernest Jean-Joseph was found to have taken drugs before the match, was beaten up and sent home in disgrace on the orders of Jean-Claude Duvalier, son of 'Papa Doc'. RIP?

On the same day Poland, the conquerors of England in the qualification group, made their first appearance in the competition when they faced Argentina – and fascinated everybody with the poise of their football. Many members of this team had taken part two years earlier when Poland had been Olympic champions; in Deyna they had one of the most intelligent and skilful of midfield players on view; in the young Zmuda and the tall, blond Gorgon they possessed a pair of effective central defenders; and in Lato and Szarmach they had players who could score smoothly. In fact both struck in the 3–2 win by Poland; and these two scored four goals in the 7–0 triumph over Haiti – with the prowess of Francillon ensuring that the defeat did not enter double figures as he made one crucial save after another. It was small wonder that in the following season he would come to West Germany to play his football as a mercenary.

On the same day Argentina and Italy played out an entertaining 1–1 draw. Despite the presence of 50,000 Italian supporters in the crowd of just under 72,000, the Italians just could not put things right. Although Mazzola played intelligently throughout the game both Riva and Rivera were badly 'off song'; and a vital mistake on the part of the Italian coach, Feruccio Valcarreggi, made the game awkward for Italy when, as a marker for the small, lively, Argentine winger Houseman, he appointed Capello – an attacking midfield player! This move turned Capello into a quasi-fullback; and although Valcarreggi understood his mistake too late, the damage had already been done. Houseman it was who scored for Argentina; and the only manner in which the Italians could score their goal (which fortunately for them made the game a draw) was to force the Argentine centreback, Perfumo, to put the ball into his own net. So they went into their next game against Poland requiring just a draw to pass through to the next round.

Alas, it was not to be. Poland won 2–1 but in truth the Italians were overwhelmed. Mazzola played effectively throughout, Anastasi was incisive in the first-half and Facchetti resolute in the second, but the Poland midfield of Deyna, Kasperczak and Maszczyk was dominant throughout, with the first-named being the

# World Cup 1974

best player on view as well as the scorer of one of the Polish goals. With Argentina beating Haiti 4-1, with Babington continuing his good run of form and despite the heroics of Francillon in the Haiti goal, the Italians finished third in their qualifying group, behind Argentina on goal difference. Small wonder that *La Squadra* found itself being attacked as it left the stadium by its 'supporters'!

East Germany, West Germany, Yugoslavia, Brazil, Holland, Sweden, Poland and Argentina therefore went through to the Second Round. Holland, in their first game, set about the unfortunate Argentina in the manner born, with Cruyff scoring once in each half and with the whole team totally dominating the game. The other goals in the 4-0 victory came from Rep and Krol and, although Suurbier was forced to leave the field injured, the Dutch were extremely fortunate in team selection throughout the championship, having comparatively few injuries, and they were able to choose ten of their team for all seven of the games.

In the same group Brazil defeated East Germany by just the single goal. In the 60th minute they were awarded a free-kick some ten metres outside the East German penalty area, Dirceu broke from the 'wall' at the last moment and allowed a cannonball of a shot from Rivelino to scream through. A fast-moving drive from Rivelino was the first score in their next game against Argentina – a game which Brazil won by 2-1, and the reply soon after by Brindisi was the first goal to be given away in the tournament by Brazil. A header by Jairzinho proved to be the eventual goal, and Brazil moved on to play the Dutch in their final game in the group; there they received a nice, sharp lesson in football skill, for although the introduction of Dirceu on the left side of the midfield had given them a far greater degree of penetration, they were still a team lacking in the highest of talents. In the crucial game their defenders chopped and hacked the Dutch from the outset, encouraging the retribution which their opponents were not slow to deliver. Ze Maria perpetrated a rugby tackle on Cruyff; Neeskens found himself being knocked cold by one of the centre-backs in Mario Marinho then being scythed down by the other, Luis Pereira. For his pains Pereira found himself being sent off. But the two goals in the first period of the second-half were worth waiting for: Neeskens played a free-kick to Cruyff on his right, dashed forward and struck the return over the head of the Brazilian goalkeeper, Leao. And the second was scored by Cruyff driving home a centre by Rensenbrink. It was a memorable day, indeed, for Dutch football which had seemed to say 'The King is Dead, Long Live the King'.

It came as no surprise to learn that the response after the game in Brazil was severe: coffins of the leading players were paraded in the streets and an effigy of Zagalo, the manager, was burnt.

The other group saw matches between West Germany and Yugoslavia, won by the Germans 2–0, and between Poland and Sweden won by the Poles by just the odd goal, scored by the man who would finish as the leading scorer in the tournament, Lato. In the first of these games West Germany for the first time in this tournament used Rainer Bonhof, whose skills with the ball and intelligent running into space gave a new dimension to the play of the European Nations Champions, so that the second half of the game should have seen more than the second goal scored by Gerd Muller. And most noticeable in the other game was the dribbling of Gadocha, the opportunism of Lato, the acrobatics of the goalkeeper Tomaszewski, and the organisation of Deyna. In fact, after losing this encounter it fell to the Swedes to tackle West Germany, a game which they lost 4–2, three of these goals being scored soon after half-time in a three-minute period.

The fortunes of the two teams were reversed at half-time, Sweden going in with a 1–0 lead; but West Germany came back strongly, with Bonhof in particular in glorious form on the right side of their midfield, scoring the second goal that put his side into the lead.

On the same day Poland beat Yugoslavia 2–1 with goals from Deyna and Lato; a score that was repeated three days later when Sweden beat the Yugoslavs but since neither side could hope to progress further, this game turned out to be packed with entertaining and spirited football, with both Maric and Hellstroem given many opportunities to show what excellent goalkeepers they were. (Indeed, many thought that they were the two most gifted goalkeepers in the entire tournament.) And this left the match between

## World Cup 1974

West Germany and Poland to decide which team would take part in the final.

West Germany won by a second-half goal by Gerd Muller, but many felt that the game should not have taken place when it did. A rainstorm had made the pitch unplayable, and although the West German authorities drew off as much water as they could and put the time of the match back, it could have been postponed until the following day. Tomaszewski saved a penalty from Holzenbein, but in the first-half Maier made an incredible double-save from Lato and Gadocha to put heart into the Germans. Beckenbauer was beginning to display authoritative form in defence, and the midfield of Bonhof, Hoeness and Overath gradually stood up to the Polish wiles of Deyna and Kaspercak.

Poland would have the small satisfaction of beating Brazil in the match to determine third and fourth places: a just reward for having entertained so many people with their thrilling football over the previous four weeks. The goal was from Lato, Poland showing itself once more to be thoroughly more imaginative and interesting; Brazil had a strong defence and midfield but a pitifully inadequate attack. It was an uninspiring game.

But the Final, the following day, got off to an electric start when Holland were awarded a penalty by the English referee, Jack Taylor, within the first minute and before any West German had touched the ball! 1–0 to Holland, and for the following twenty-five minutes the Dutch arrogantly rolled the ball about to each other, making pretty patterns, and under no threat whatsoever from the West Germans, who were entirely stunned. Then West Germany were awarded a penalty of their own when Holzenbein was tripped inside the area by Jansen, and when Gerd Muller gave West Germany a 2–1 lead just before half-time the Dutch were really shaken. The crucial issue in the match, however, was the man-to-man marking of Cruyff by the West German fullback, Bertie Vogts. Cruyff was undoubtedly the most gifted attacking player in the tournament, possessing a footballing brain that was lightning fast, and all the attributes of phenomenal players – lovely balance, glorious ball control and an exceptional shot in either foot. With his being so effectively shackled throughout the game, the effect on Holland, in psychological as well as in physical terms, was crucial; and after the West Germans had been awarded a penalty they played with new spirit, Franz Beckenbauer very astutely marshalling his forces in defence. With Rainer Bonhof spurring the midfield, and Grabowski aiding Muller up front, West Germany were able to hang on to that first-half lead and take the tenth edition of the World Cup.

It had been a real mixture of a tournament. Among the matters that had been frowned upon some said that the new formula for the tournament had led to much careless or plain bad football which had seen the eventual champions beaten in an unimportant game from the First Round. But surely no game should be described as being 'unimportant'? And then there had been the fact that while Australia had battled bravely the other two weaker teams, Zaire and Haiti, had conceded 28 goals between them. Elementary arithmetic, here, for without those games and goals you get 69 goals in 32 games which would be by some measure the worst goals per game average. In addition some nations – or rather the players of some nations – had taken to demanding fees for giving interviews and vast sums for succeeding in winning the title.

On the positive side, however, was the firmness and quality of some of the refereeing and many, many moments of memorable footballing skills. If the West German team that had won the European Nations Championship two years previously had played more fluid and imaginative football than the new holders of the World Cup, some of the most memorable football had been played by Sweden, by Poland and by Holland. Especially Holland, who would be in the forefront of the competition four years later.

# 1974 – Final Stages

## Group A

|  | P | W | D | L | F | A | Pts |
|---|---|---|---|---|---|---|---|
| HOLLAND | 3 | 3 | 0 | 0 | 8 | 0 | 6 |
| BRAZIL | 3 | 2 | 0 | 1 | 3 | 3 | 4 |
| EAST GERMANY | 3 | 0 | 1 | 2 | 1 | 4 | 1 |
| ARGENTINA | 3 | 0 | 1 | 2 | 2 | 7 | 1 |

## Group B

| | | | | | | | |
|---|---|---|---|---|---|---|---|
| WEST GERMANY | 3 | 3 | 0 | 0 | 7 | 2 | 6 |
| POLAND | 3 | 2 | 0 | 1 | 3 | 2 | 4 |
| SWEDEN | 3 | 1 | 0 | 2 | 4 | 6 | 2 |
| YUGOSLAVIA | 3 | 0 | 0 | 3 | 2 | 6 | 0 |

## Third Place Match played in Munich

POLAND 1, BRAZIL 0 (1–0) Lato for Poland

POLAND: Tomaszewski; Szymanowski, Gorgon, Musial; Kasperczak (Cmikiewicz), Deyna, Maszczyk; Lato, Szarmach (Kapka), Gadocha.
BRAZIL: Leao; Ze Maria, Alfredo, M. Marinho, F. Marinho; Paulo Cesar Carpeggiani, Rivelino, Ademir da Guia (Mirandinha); Valdomiro, Jairzinho, Dirceu.

## Final played in Munich

WEST GERMANY 2, HOLLAND 1 (2-1) Breitner (pen.), Muller for West Germany and Neeskens (pen.) for Holland

WEST GERMANY: Maier; Vogts, Schwarzenbeck, Beckenbauer, Breitner; Bonhof, Hoeness, Overath; Grabowski, Muller, Holzenbein.
HOLLAND: Jongbloed; Suurbier, Rijsbergen (De Jong), Haan, Krol; Jansen, Neeskens, Van Hanegem; Rep, Cruyff, Rensenbrink (R. Van de Kerkhof).

# Another Home Victory in Argentina (1978)

Never has a political background so affected a World Cup tournament. Before the military junta of General George Videla seized power in 1976, many had been extremely concerned that the 1978 edition of the World Cup had been given to Argentina; but after the coup fears were increased when thousands of people were tortured, imprisoned without trial or simply 'disappeared', never to be heard of again. The junta set up a new body, the Ente Autarquico Mundial to make sure that all preparations for the tournament – including the construction of three new stadia and the remodelling of three others – would be carried out in time. And there can be little doubt that, without the setting up of the EAM and the hard work done by this body, the tournament would probably have been relocated to Brazil, Mexico or Spain. And the corollary of that, of course, was that there was that much more extra pressure on Argentina to win!

The presence of great players obviously helps the prestige of a tournament: and, sadly, the two heroes of the 1974 World Cup chose not to take part. Franz Beckenbauer had, fifteen months previously, signed for New York Cosmos for $2,500,000 and

# World Cup 1978

Johan Cruyff absolutely refused to take part, despite huge offers. These two were not the only absentees. West Germany had to compete without the talents of Gerd Muller, Wolfgang Overath, Paul Breitner, Uli Hoeness and Jurgen Grabowski; and Wim van Hanegem dropped out at the last moment after being informed that he could not count on a regular place in the side. The host country, Argentina, had lost several players from her 1974 side who had moved to play in Europe such as Kempes, Brindisi, Carnevali, Wolff and Heredia, who were now in Spain, and Babington who had moved to West Germany. When it came down to it Cesar-Luis Menotti, nick-named El Flaco (the Thin One) expressed interest in only Kempes, Wolff and Oswaldo Piazza playing at centre-back for the French club of St Etienne. In the event, Wolff could not be released by Real Madrid and the family of Piazza were involved in a road accident, so Kempes was the only man to join the squad.

Scotland were favoured by many. They had had a successful tour of South America in 1977, and in their qualifying group had eliminated the 1976 winners of the European Championship, Czechoslovakia. Even though their final win in the qualifying round had been in part thanks to a penalty that wasn't in their match away against Wales, euphoria was high. WE'RE ON OUR WAY TO RIO trumpeted a headline in a Scottish daily paper with a neat disregard for geography. 'Of course we'll win the World Cup. If I say that it saves you from asking me again,' said the ebullient Scottish manager Ally Macleod, who favoured Hungary were Scotland not to succeed in their mission! (Hungary joined Mexico as being the only two countries not to win any point whatsoever.) He paid a visit to Cordoba in the January of 1978 and was delighted with the accommodation – so the feedback to Scotland's fans was just what they required. But the few realists in their camp had other evidence. Danny McGrain would be ruled out of this World Cup through injury; Gordon McQueen, the first-choice stopper, would receive an injury only a fortnight before the tournament that would rule him out; and much to the surprise of everyone, Andy Gray, the young central striker who was on top form, would not make the selection.

Brazil were favourites to do well, perhaps even to win the tournament. They had dismissed Oswaldo Brandao a year previously and had appointed in his place a young army captain, Claudio Coutinho, who was attempting to 'Europeanise' the Brazilian game by placing the emphasis on stamina and covering each blade of grass on the pitch. A far cry indeed from those days of Pelé, Gerson and Tostao. Coutinho had compounded his strategy by not selecting Francisco Marinho, who had been one of the most-admired fullbacks in the previous tournament as well as that wayward forward, Paulo Cesar.*

Italy, the conquerors of the qualifying group above England – and the only team to qualify on goal difference – were given scant chance of success. The chief play-maker to the team, Giancarlo Antognoni, had been having a desperate season trying to prevent his club side of Fiorentia from being relegated; and for some months had suffered a strain to his right ankle which had required a complete rest. In addition, his wife had a miscarriage only a few days prior to Italy's first game against France. Giacinto Facchetti, the sweeper, was ruled out of football altogether, having been on the receiving end of a tackle from Romeo Benetti. The team had recently recruited a young fullback, Cabrini, who was strong in the tackle and eager to set up counter-attacks; at their training camp, spent just outside Buenos Aires, Enzo Bearzot, the Italian manager, decided that the time had come to be brave and to play Paolo Rossi the young, adroit and courageous forward who had just finished the season in Italy as the chief scorer. With Marco Tardelli settling firmly into his role as a defensive player in midfield Bearzot hoped, above all, to encourage the Italian team to play more open football, completely throw off those defensive shackles which were set firm in the Italian club game and attempt to play more freely. He would have his wish much sooner than he could have expected!

It came after thirty-eight seconds of play in the first of Italy's

---

* Soon after the finish of the tournament Coutinho was to drown in an accident at sea.

# World Cup 1978

games in Group I when Didier Six collected a glorious through pass from the midfield, raced down the left touchline and crossed the ball into the centre for Bernard Lacombe to out-jump the Italian defence and head a simple goal. Thunder-struck the Italians simply knew that they had then to attack and take the game into the French half, to stand any chance of gaining a victory and driven on by the experience of Romeo Benetti, by the fact that Tardelli carried out a masterly shackling job on Michel Platini, by the smooth manner in which Bettega and Rossi formed a partnership in the attack, Italy won the game 2–1. On the same day Argentina had had a 2–1 win over Hungary with two Hungarians, Nyilasi and Toroscik, being sent off for committing ugly fouls at the end of the game. Yet the atmosphere in the River Plate stadium was sour from the start, with a snowstorm of Argentinian favours thrown onto the pitch as the teams came out; tension throughout that could have been cut with a knife.

Four days later Italy had little difficulty in defeating a depleted Hungarian team 3–1 but one of the best matches of the tournament was to take place that same evening in Buenos Aires when Argentina defeated a gallant France by a 2–1 scoreline. It was truly an enthralling spectacle, every minute packed with good football – and atrocious refereeing decisions on the part of the Swiss officials; Jean Dubach, 'gave' Argentina a penalty when the accomplished black sweeper Marius Tresor landed on the ball while challenging Luque in the penalty area and was adjudged to have handled it intentionally. And this in injury time! It was a monstrous decision compounding the fact that the referee had failed to award France a penalty of their own when Six was pulled down in the penalty area. And the same player should have scored, following a glorious run by Platini, but shot wide when he had only the goalkeeper to beat. Lucky, lucky Argentina.

Thus when Argentina met Italy again (following their drawn game in the 1974 tournament) both sides had already qualified for the Second Round. The match was, however, still important, as Argentina very much wished to stay in Buenos Aires and not have to travel to Rosario, over 300 kilometres to the north-east of the capital: which would be their fate if they failed to secure a victory.

There would be no nonsense on this occasion about the refereeing for the choice had fallen to Abraham Klein who made it clear from the first that he would not 'play the gallery'. With the Italians knowing that a draw would suit them – falling back on defensive man-to-man marking and making sudden breaks from defence into attack – the only goal of the game came in the sixty-seventh minute when, after an interchange of passes between Antognoni and Rossi, the latter slid a perfectly placed pass through to Bettega, who screwed his shot past Fillol, the commanding goalkeeper for Argentina. But although it was Bettega who won most of the glory, it should be pointed out that both Benetti and Causio ran their hearts out in midfield, and Gentile (called in as stopper after Cuccureddu had replaced the injured Bellugi) completely marked Kempes out of the game. And in the afternoon of the same day France received some reward when they defeated Hungary 3–1. A curious event happened before the game when France were asked to change their strip because television viewers with black and white sets found it hard to differentiate between the blue of France and the red of Hungary. A sure sign, this, of interests other than simple footballing ones being considered! Even though France were forced to leave the tournament after this win, they made a tournament record that year by being the only country playing to have used all twenty-two of their permitted players, with Marius Tresor the only man to have played in all 270 minutes of their games.

Group II saw West Germany play Poland play Mexico play Tunisia: the easiest of all the four groups. Sadly, it got off to a goalless draw between West Germany and Poland – the fourth occasion in succession that the opening game in the tournament has been something of a 'goalless grimmie'. Deyna was the man of the match directing operations in the midfield with skill and intelligence, and several famous faces from the Polish triumph of four years earlier were there: Gorgon and Zmuda in the middle of the defence and Lato and Szarmach in the attack. Also there was Wlodzimierz Lubanski, who had been put out of the game entirely for two years with an injury he had received in June 1973 when England had played Poland in Warsaw. Was this draw inevitable?

# World Cup 1978

Many people thought so, with both teams ensuring a place for themselves in the last eight.

The following day Tunisia amazed many people by defeating Mexico 3–1. Like many of the unknown teams in the past they possessed a player of absolute class, a slim character in their midfield, Dhiab Tarak, who laid on all three goals for the African side – all scored in the second half, after Mexico had scored from a penalty just before half-time. This was a real test of character, and the group table at the end of the day would show Tunisia standing proudly above West Germany, Poland, and Mexico who had put on a pathetic display. Four days later Tunisia proved their worth against an altogether stronger team by holding Poland to a 1–0 win, totally dominating the second half and being most unfortunate not to gain a draw. Meanwhile Mexico was proving itself the weakest team in the competition by losing 6–0 to West Germany. And as if to add insult to injury, Tunisia next held West Germany to a goalless draw while Poland beat Mexico 3–1, although Tomaszewski in their goal was called upon to save some five close shots from his opponents.

If the real heroes of the first two groups had been teams which would take no further part in the competition the games from the third group seemed more concerned with watching Brazil – the 9–4 favourites before the competition started – try to beat itself and not qualify for the Second Round. It was an unhappy ship. Rivelino was overweight and rebellious; Coutinho had fallen out with Zico, another of the stars; and it was as well that Amaral and Oscar played magnificently at the heart of the defence so that Brazil were the only team playing in this tournament to remain unbeaten, and that Batista and Cerezo produced play of the first order in midfield. They were held to a 1–1 draw by Sweden in the opening game; and then drew 0–0 with Spain in the game which they surely would have lost had not Cardenosa missed a marvellous chance when right in front of the goal. In their third game, however, they beat Austria 1–0. But Austria had already qualified, thanks to two wins against Spain (2–1) and Sweden (1–0) which left these two to play each other and see which team would go through if Brazil slipped up. Spain won this affair 1–0 – but they must have been somewhat forlorn to leave the competition after having showed the most marvellous spirit in defeating Rumania and Yugoslavia in their qualifying games.

Group IV saw Scotland drawn against Iran, Peru and Holland; a draw which Ally Macleod, the Scottish manager, said he 'wanted'. 'That leaves us to go through to the last eight with Holland and after that the players won't need any motivating.' We were never to find out, because although Scotland took an early lead against Peru and completely dominated the first period of the first half, things began to go sadly wrong. Cubillas, Munante and Oblitas at last decided to run at the Scottish defence and gradually started to drive it wild with a succession of one-twos. Finally, the inevitable happened, and in the forty-second minute Peru finally scored through Cueto. A disastrous moment at which to give away a goal. Worse was to follow, however, in the sixty-fourth minute, when Scotland were awarded a penalty after Rioch was brought down by Cubillas. Masson took the kick but it was a truly feeble effort which Quiroga, in the Peruvian goal, found no trouble in saving. That was Scotland's last chance, for Peru totally dominated the last 25 minutes of the game. Cubillas scored twice – and Scotland had a bitter postscript when Willie Johnston their wing-forward, was found to have taken 'pep' pills. So morale for the next match, against Iran, couldn't have been lower.

Maybe that excuse could be used profitably, because the match was one of the very worst there has ever been in the history of the World Cup. Surely Scotland have never played such bad football? The result was a 1-1 draw, with Scotland's score coming from an own goal by Eskandarjan; one of the best Scottish players Martin Buchan was kicked in the face by the man whose role at fullback he had taken in the first match, Willie Donachie; and it could so easily have been another traumatic defeat had not Ghasimpour shot straight at Rough when put through in the first half. No wonder the hundreds of Scottish supporters, who had travelled over 9,000 kilometres to Argentina, began to wail with fury; no wonder that restaurants in Glasgow which in former times had used the name of the Scotland manager in their advertising started to put up signs which read, 'Ally MacLeod does NOT eat here'!

# World Cup 1978

Holland had shown how it could be done by beating Iran 3–0 and when it became the turn of Peru they won 4–1; so when these two sides met it came as no surprise to find them playing very cagily, settling for a 0–0 draw.

Experts often point out that Scotland play terribly against poor teams, handsomely against the good ones. And so it proved when Scotland played Holland in their final match. The team selection was put right at long last, with Souness being played in midfield and proving that he was exactly the right link to get the best out of Dalglish up front. In fact it was Dalglish who volleyed Scotland's equaliser ten minutes after Rensenbrink had given Holland a lead in the thirty-fourth minute with a penalty: the thousandth goal in the history of the World Cup. Scotland got their retribution early in the second half when Gemmill scored a penalty after Krol was adjudged to have fouled Souness, and in the sixty-eighth minute the same player scored what was admitted by some to be the best goal of this World Cup, when he jinked his way through the Dutch defence to score with a hard shot from close range. The Scottish supporters had a bare four minutes of wishful thinking about their appearance in the Second Round before Rep laid their wish to rest, scoring with a screaming shot from 23 metres.

What had gone wrong with Scotland and their hopes? Partly the blame lay in the arrogance with which Scotland had gone to Argentina, having done far too little homework as to the strengths and weaknesses of their opponents; partly it lay in team selection – in the loyalty to Rioch and Masson, who had been dropped by their club sides, in the under-use of Souness; partly it lay in the accommodation which left the players very bored when not depressed; and partly with the players themselves – many of whom simply did not realise how much they had let down their supporters. But these supporters themselves were to blame. 'Bring on the English' they roared when, at one stage in the game against Holland, they seemed to be in with a chance of reaching the last eight.

Group A in the Second Round consisted of Italy, West Germany, Austria and Holland; Group B of Argentina, Poland, Brazil and Peru. Of these, Italy was the only country to have won all its games in the early stages and those wins had been achieved in what many people thought had been the most difficult group, and by a new formula of play: Enzo Bearzot had dragged his players away from the negativity induced by *catenaccio* (man-to-man marking plus a sweeper) and introducing the Total Football which had been played by Holland in the previous World Cup and the West German team in 1972.

In their first game in the Second Round Italy played West Germany, and optimists hoped for an encounter as entertaining as that when they had last met in a World Cup, the 4–3 victory by Italy in a Semi-final in 1970. No chance of that on this occasion: Italy were now regarded as an attacking team and from the first moment West Germany settled down to play a form of *catenaccio* with Rumenigge and Holzenbein on the wings being drawn back to play in midfield and Klaus Fischer left alone in the attack. 0–0 the result (the third goalless draw out of West Germany's four games to date), but Bettega missed two chances from close distance – and the Italian triumphal march had been stopped.

On the same day Holland had a most uplifting 5–1 victory over Austria in Cordoba. The Dutch players showed fresh zest on being away at last from the heights of Mendoza; Holland were able to call upon some talented substitutes in Pieter Wildschut and Erny Brandts, the 22-year-old centre-back; and the injury to Neeskens had given a chance to Arie Haan. Johnny Rep scored two of the goals and Robbie Rensenbrink scored from a penalty and showed that he was coming back into form. A most significant win, this, in psychological terms, as well as being most disheartening for the other teams.

Four days later Holland played West Germany at Cordoba, with the Dutch hyper-keen to reverse the result of the previous World Cup Final. They began their mission miserably, going down after only three minutes to a tap-in by Abramczik, when a thundering free-kick by Bonhof had only been parried by Schrivers, but when they equalised in the twenty-sixth minute it was with a truly memorable shot on the part of Haan, who let fly from roughly 25 metres out. Maier never even touched the ball. It was the first occasion in which he had been beaten in 475 minutes of play in

World Cup games: a new record. West Germany, however, were playing with considerably more character than they had shown in their game against Italy, and took the lead again in the seventieth minute when Dieter Muller headed in a centre; it was only after Holland had taken off Wildschut and substituted that angular forward, Dirk Nanninga, that they were able to get a draw from the game. He it was who helped Rene Van der Kerkhof slice in from the left and put the ball past Maier from a narrow distance.

On the same day in Buenos Aires Italy beat Austria 1–0, thanks to a goal from Rossi scored in the thirteenth minute – after which the team just fell back on defence. Austria showed very little wit or imagination in their play (in fact that goal of Rossi's had followed an unwise back pass from a fullback), and Krankl spent much of the game being the lone ranger of the attack. He it was who scored the decisive goal three days later when Austria beat West Germany 3–2 after volleying the Austrian second goal. A very sad way for Helmut Schön to retire as manager of the West German team: first, third and second in the preceeding editions of the tournament. On the same day Holland came to play Italy in Buenos Aires. Thanks to their 5–1 victory over Austria they knew that all they had to do was to gain a draw. But in the first ten minutes Italy could have scored twice, and in fact they took the lead in the nineteenth minute when Brandts skimmed the ball past Schrivers into the goal – in an attempt to stop Bettega from scoring. As well as giving away an own goal, he damaged the right knee of the goalkeeper, who had to be substituted soon after by Jan Jongbloed, the goalkeeper from the 1974 side who, while still 'cold' made two astonishing saves from Rossi and Benetti. Then the wrestling began: Benetti kicked Haan and fouled Rensenbrink, and in retribution Haan booted Zaccarelli and Rep flattened Benetti. By half-time the names of Rep and Benetti were in the book and it was then that Bearzot made the grave mistake of taking off Franco Causio – who had played skilfully down the right wing – and putting on Claudio Sala. The Italian rhythm went and soon after Brandts atoned for his own goal by swinging his right-foot at the ball while surrounded by Italian players and driving the ball through to score; and in the seventy-seventh minute there came once more one of those thunderous shots from Haan from 32 metres out, which nearly removed the back of the net. Two minutes later Italy substituted Graziani for Benetti in an attempt to score twice in the remaining minutes of the game, but to no avail; and the cruel spate of fouling continued with Haan himself and Cabrini and Tardelli being booked. Holland were through to the Final.

In Group B Brazil at last began to play in the manner hoped for by all their supporters. Away from the difficult playing surface at Mar Del Plata, their first match was at Mendoza, where they beat Peru 3–0 thanks to two goals from Dirceu, one of these being from a free kick which swung inwards at the last moment to leave Quiroga toally helpless. Zico came on as substitute in the seventieth minute and scored from a penalty soon after.

That evening Argentina beat Poland 2–0, thanks largely to a skilful display by Mario Kempès who scored both goals in the fifteenth and seventieth minutes, and rescued another by making a spectacular save off the goal-line after Fillol had been beaten. The penalty was taken by Deyna playing in his hundredth international, but his weak shot was saved – and Poland's last chance went. Although in the first half they had played very well, with Boniek and Adam Nawalka outstanding and although a shot from Lato hit the side-netting early in the second half, it became increasingly one-way traffic, with Argentina spurred on by the baying of the crowds, who seemed much more intense at Rosario than they had been in the larger stadium at Buenos Aires. A real 'pressure-cooker' of a ground.

You think that games between England and Scotland have an electric atmosphere? Forget it. When Argentina play Brazil hatred is a factor that is present even before the ball has been kicked. Four players were booked; others 'left their feet' in many instances showing their studs and Ricardo Villa, who had come on for Ardiles after half-time, was extremely fortunate not to be sent off after committing an over-the-ball foul on Batista, the Brazilian midfield player. It was a truly forgettable goalless draw with little football managing to survive all the spitefulness.

In the afternoon of the same day Poland had beaten Peru 1–0

but truly the score could have been in double figures. Why wasn't it? Thanks to that remarkable goalkeeper, Ramon Quiroga, who made amazing saves all through the game and in the final minutes advanced beyond the halfway line in order to break up the Polish attacks. Truly he deserved the nickname of 'El Loco'! The goal for Poland was scored by Szarmach, the woodwork was hit on two occasions and this feeble effort on the part of Peru can only have served to make all Scotsmen round the world feel most distressed by the memory of Scotland's weak displays.

The final day of this Round saw Brazil beat Poland 3–1. But rather it might be put the other way round because the Polish finishing was truly terrible. Both Lato and Szarmach seemed to have lost that vital edge of speed and thought which had made them so successful four years earlier, and although Leao was at the top of his form it is true to say that he absolutely had to be, because Poland's midfield players played with great authority. The first of Brazil's goals came from a swerving free kick of great power struck by Nelinho and the other two from Roberto. In that evening Argentina beat Peru. Why was the game started three-quarters of an hour after the game between Brazil and Poland had actually finished? Because of 'home' advantage; the argument being that Argentina should play all their games in the evening so that the crowds could attend without disrupting their work. Ridiculous. Be that as it may, Argentina knew that the game had to be won by a clear four goals in order to give her a place in the Final. People will always see this game as being a 'fix', but the fact is that poor Peru were just overrun in the second half, after going in 2–0 down at half-time. In fact they could have scored twice themselves in the first half, when Munante and Oblitas both went near with chances. Kempes and Luque scored twice, with the other goals being scored by Tarantini and Houseman (a much less effective player than he had been in 1974). So it was Argentina versus Holland in the Final.

The day before we saw the match between Brazil and Italy to decide third and fourth places. Both teams possessed supporters and experts who thought that they were the best teams in the competition. Brazil had yet to lose a game, while the Italians, in addition to having beaten Argentina, felt that they had played the best football of the tournament. But, as against Holland, Italy allowed itself to be overtaken after Causio had scored a goal in the thirty-eighth minute. First Nelinho shot powerfully from the right corner and the ball swerved *inwards* to defeat Zoff, and the winning goal came from Dirceu, who swung in a fierce shot from just outside the penalty area. So Brazil retained their record of remaining unbeaten; however they could be considered unfortunate in TWO respects at least – that of playing their first round matches at Mar Del Plata on pitches that cut up horribly and of having Argentina play their last game after their own had finished.

Nor did it stop there, for before the Final had begun Holland's players came out onto the field five minutes before the home team, who instantly added to that piece of gamesmanship by objecting to the cast that was being worn by Rene Van der Kerkhof on his right wrist. He had suffered the injury in the first game of the tournament but none of the succeeding five opponents of the Dutch had objected! Eventually he was allowed to keep it on with a covering of bandage, but the psychological damage had been done. It was small wonder Holland began to play in a distressed and ugly mood. In addition, they had two further causes for worry: some most feeble refereeing by Sergio Gonella and the fact that Mario Kempès was in the most splendid form. For a long period the Argentina defence made mistake after mistake with Fillol making two superb saves from Rep and Rensenbrink and then suddenly, in the thirty-seventh minute, Argentina took the lead: Ardiles to Luque to Kempès who slid the ball into the goal, underneath the advancing Jongbloed.

In the first period of the second half each side made two substitutions: Nanninga for Rep, Larrosa for Ardiles, Suurbier for Jansen and Houseman for Ortiz. And it was the first-named of these who headed in a centre from the right in the eighty-first minute. Holland pressed forward even more aggressively and in the eighty-ninth minute Rensenbrink hit a post. Extra time, therefore; the first occasion in a Final since 1966 when another host country, England, had beaten the redoubtable West Germans. And it was during this period when Mario Kempès really came into his own, playing with all the skill, all the speed and all the composure that he knew. Bertoni put him through to score the goal that made him the highest scorer in the competition (although he hadn't scored at all in the first round): in the hundred-and-fourth minute when he struck in a rebound from his original shot; and ten minutes later he was able to play a one-two with Bertoni after which the winger scored. The host team had won for the second time in succession and Holland had had the chagrin of twice being defeated finalists.

102 goals had been scored, much good and entertaining football had been played; there had been thunderous goals from Haan, Rep, Cubillas and Luque, and clever ones from Dirceu, Gemmill, Schachner; there had been much intelligent running with the ball; a fair proportion of the refereeing had been wayward or weak and there had been some incredibly poor decisions – decisions which could have caused changes in some results. But overall the tournament was immensely better than one had dared to hope for and if the number of outstanding individuals was diminished then the mannner in which teamwork had improved since the last tournament was most marked.

The final word, however, must be cautionary. Pressures on teams and their managers were far too intense and, with the idea of playing the first section of games in groups, we have the situation in which both the last two winners of the tournament had been beaten before they ever reached the Final (West Germany by East Germany in 1974 and Argentina by Italy in 1978). With the next tournament being expanded to include 24 teams, the number of unimportant matches, the amount of bad and boring football, and mistakes by referees was bound to rise, and all the prestige of the World Cup sharply fall.

# 1978 Final Stages

## Group A

| | | | | | | | |
|---|---|---|---|---|---|---|---|
| HOLLAND | 3 | 2 | 1 | 0 | 9 | 4 | 5 |
| ITALY | 3 | 1 | 1 | 1 | 2 | 2 | 3 |
| WEST GERMANY | 3 | 0 | 2 | 1 | 4 | 5 | 2 |
| AUSTRIA | 3 | 1 | 0 | 2 | 4 | 8 | 2 |

## Group B

| | | | | | | | |
|---|---|---|---|---|---|---|---|
| ARGENTINA | 3 | 2 | 1 | 0 | 8 | 0 | 5 |
| BRAZIL | 3 | 2 | 1 | 0 | 6 | 1 | 5 |
| POLAND | 3 | 1 | 0 | 2 | 2 | 5 | 2 |
| PERU | 3 | 0 | 0 | 3 | 0 | 10 | 0 |

## Third Place Match played in Buenos Aires

BRAZIL 2, ITALY 1 (0–1) Nelinho, Dirceu for Brazil, Causio for Italy

BRAZIL: Leao; Nelinho, Oscar, Amaral, Neto; Cerezo (Rivelino), Batista, Dirceu; Gil (Reinaldo), Mendonca, Roberto
ITALY: Zoff; Cuccureddu, Gentile, Scirea, Cabrini; Maldera, Antognoni (Sala C.), Sala P.; Causio, Rossi, Bettega

# Final played in Buenos Aires

ARGENTINA 3, HOLLAND 1 (1–0) (1–1) Kempès (2), Bertoni for Argentina, Nanninga for Holland

ARGENTINA: Fillol; Olguin, Galvan, Passarella, Tarantini; Ardiles (Darrosa), Gallego, Kempès; Bertoni, Luque, Ortiz (Houseman)
HOLLAND: Jongbloed; Poortvliet, Brandts, Krol, Jansen (Suurbier); Haan, Neeskens, Van der Kerkhof W.; Rep (Nanninga), Rensenbrink, Van der Kerkhof R.

# 4 ITALY TRIUMPH FOR THE THIRD TIME

The 1982 edition of the World Cup, as forecast by many, proved to be far too cumbersome for its own good. Compared with the original edition, held in Uruguay in 1930 (which had seen 18 matches played in 17 days), it was positively elephantine, providing a total of 52 matches in a period of 28 days. The fact that the number of countries permitted to take part in the Finals had risen to 24 – for the first time – of course ensured that many of the games played were comparatively meaningless since the knock-out principle applied to only the last four matches. Equally negative was the fact that the number of rest days was too few, causing the Semi-final between France and West Germany to be decided by a penalty shoot-out: the first occasion on which this controversial practice had been used to decide a match in the World Cup. Much more fair, surely, to have the match replayed. But no – providing yet another example of the manner in which the game of football had been hijacked by the television and the promotions people so that the rights of the players often seemed to be of secondary importance.

Time and again this could be the only conclusion. Several matches were played in the most appalling heat (the Northern Ireland match against Austria took place in temperature which rose to 45 degrees in Centigrade); the players of France were forced to sit exhausted on their suitcases and watch while plane after plane took off from Seville airport after their Semi-final match against West Germany (small wonder that when it came to the play-off for the Third place the French team was much depleted) and throughout the competition came ceaseless complaints concerning the manner in which the common dignities of the players were being abused by the authorities.

There was no outstanding favourite for the tournament. Brazil were tipped by many and, indeed, possessed a wealth of talent in midfield. Cerezo, Socrates and Zico had provided Brazilian supporters with many moments of magic during the previous two years and to these had been added Falcao, known as 'Il Divino', who had been triumphing in Italy during the same period. He was especially eager to make a point since in 1978 he had been astonishingly omitted from the Brazilian party. The 1982 side, however, possessed another in that long line of forgettable goalkeepers in Waldir Peres and caused its supporters no end of torment by having a defence that was prone to lose concentration.

Argentina's hopes had been high at the start of the year. Many members of the successful side of four years previously were still available including the chief scorer, Mario Kempès, who had experienced success in Spain ever since 1976. If Cesar-Luis Menotti was still the manager, the authoritative Daniel Passarella was still in charge of the team on the pitch, and on this occasion it had another arrow in its quiver – Diego Maradona, a thick-thighed 21-year-old who was being hailed as the most outstanding player in the world. On March 31, however, General Galtieri decided to reclaim the Falkland Islands (or Las Malvinas as they are known in Argentina) by force – and there is no telling the emotive effect that living through reports of the war meant on the Argentine players, more than one of whom lost relatives or friends in the fighting.

Of the previous winners of the tournament that came from Europe, England were mightily fortunate to be competing in the Final stages at all – and this only after Rumania had amazingly lost 1–2 at home to Switzerland in a match from the Qualifying tournament. However, after Don Howe (who represented England as right-back in the 1958 tournament) was called in to organise the defence, England started to look more the part and in Bryan Robson possessed undoubtedly one of the most gifted midfield players in the world. West Germany, as so often, seemed to be a most solid side. The gigantic Horst Hrubesch, who had been outstanding during the 1980 European Nations Championship, was vying for a place; Karl-Heinz Rummenigge had been performing so splendidly for his club side of Bayern Munich that he had been elected European Footballer of the Year for the second successive time, and there was a thrilling newcomer in Pierre Littbarski who was as slippery as an eel and possessed a venomous shot. If there was disappointment that Bernd Schuster had been ruled out by injury while playing for his club side, FC Barcelona, this was mitigated by the fact that two other members of the team possessed vast experience of Spanish footballing conditions: Paul Breitner having performed recently in midfield for Real Madrid, the club which currently had on its books his compatriot, Uli Stielike, the West German sweeper.

The third of these former champions, Italy, entered the tournament in a most pessimistic state. Paolo Rossi had just 'emerged' from a two-year ban for having been involved in a bribery scandal, and drastically lacked match fitness. One of the heroes of four years previously, Roberto Bettega, had failed to recover from a cruel injury received in a European Cup game during October while another of their stars, the highly-talented midfielder, Giancarlo Antognoni, had just resumed playing after having received a near-fatal head wound in a club game at the end of November. Not surprisingly, Italy had lost recently against both France and East Germany and had been thankful to gain a draw with Switzerland. The portents seemed ominous. There is no job in football which equals the pressures placed upon the shoulders of the Italian manager, and the likeable Enzo Bearzot found himself on the receiving end of advice that arrived daily in the Italian sporting press and which eventually became so sour that the players ceased to give interviews.

Last of those teams that might have anticipated victory in this edition of the tournament came the host country, Spain. However, it had presented a most modest showing at the 1980 European Nations Championship and the results since had been very mixed. On that occasion the team had been managed by the brilliant ex-Hungarian inside-forward, Ladislao Kubala, and had been inspired from midfield by the Real Sociedad driving-force, Jesus Zamora. Now the former had been replaced by the former Uruguayan centre-back, Jose Santamaria, and the latter was disastrously out-of-form. A third consecutive victory by a side playing at home seemed, therefore, to be a remote possibility.

These six seeded countries had the immense advantage of being able to play all their matches in a specific city and were not

# World Cup 1982

required to travel, which could be a most gruelling task. Italy were allotted to Vigo on the western coast of Spain while on the northern and cooler coast West Germany were bound to Gijon and England to Bilbao. All games from these groups in the First Round took place, however, in the late afternoon while evening games were played by teams in the other three groups – Argentina being based in Barcelona, Spain in Valencia and the favourites, Brazil, in Seville.

Possible victors among sides outside this privileged sextet were not many. The Soviet Union had among its forwards the legendary Oleg Blokhin, an authoritative sweeper in Alexandr Chivadze and a highly-acclaimed young goalkeeper in Renat Dassaev but since injury had robbed them of the authority and flair of David Kipiani in the midfield the team lacked a play-maker of quality. Poland had one of the outstanding individuals from four years previously, Zbigniew Boniek, and Wladyslaw Zmuda was still an imposing figure in the centre of the defence, but the team seemed to be short of players of real quality. Belgium had never found a successor for Wilfred Van Moer who by now was in his thirty-seventh year and France, while it had a gloriously-gifted midfield marshalled by Michel Platini and the diminutive Alain Giresse, had a suspect defence, despite the authoritative play of Marius Tresor. Scotland were thought to have a good chance by their supporters (thousands of whom congregated in the bars of Malaga and Seville) and had an outstanding captain in Graeme Souness but sadly for them one of its few world-class players, Kenny Dalglish, was wretchedly out of form and the defence was sometimes prone to lapses in concentration.

The opening match of the tournament made a refreshing change from the norm. It was the first occasion for 20 years that the result was not a draw and the first occasion since 1950 (when Italy lost in Sao Paulo against Sweden – the Olympic champions two years earlier) that a defending champion had been beaten. The victors were Belgium, who smothered Maradona, used their advantages in height and weight to good purpose, and might easily have scored more than once – the crucial goal coming in the sixty-second minute from Frankie Vercauteren. The pundits who

had 'arranged' the Draw six months earlier had been proved
mistaken at the first hurdle since it became very unlikely that
Argentina would head Group One. (To make matters worse for
the players this was soon succeeded by reports that the Falkland
Islands had been retaken by the British.) Two days later came a
game which witnessed the highest score in the competition when
Hungary pulverised El Salvador 10–1, but then followed a match
that brought the Hungarians swiftly back to earth when Argentina
(with Maradona on outstanding form) beat them 4–1. In turn,
Belgium could only put one goal past El Salvador so, given the
massive goal-difference that Hungary had built up, victory against
the Belgians would have been sufficient to see them through to the
Second Round. It was not to be, however, the Hungarians allowing Alex Czerniatynski to grab a reply to an early goal by Joszef
Varga. Thus, with Argentina beating El Salvador 2–0 (despite
having recaptured their former indifferent form) it was they who
accompanied Belgium into the Second Round.

Considerably more dramatic were events in Groups One and
Two. The opening match in Group One was a disappointing
goalless draw between Italy and Poland which saw a masterly
display in the Italian midfield by Giancarlo Antognoni. Poland's
star – Boniek – was well marshalled by his future club comrade,
Marco Tardelli (who hit the bar during the second half), and there
were several half-chances for the Italians. Also goalless was the
game between Peru and Cameroon, one of the 'surprise' sides on
view. Roger Milla was one of a handful who had gained fame
outside his native country due to playing in France but Thomas
N'kono turned in a display that showed him to be one of the most
gifted goalkeepers in the tournament and in truth Cameroon were
unfortunate not to win the game. For Peru the star everyone
expected great things from, Julio Cesar Uribe, was a huge disappointment; the much-travelled Teofilo Cubillas was clearly
ageing fast and it was only some acrobatic goalkeeping by Ramon
Quiroga (known affectionately as 'El Loco') that kept Peru in the
game. The side performed with more adventure in its next match
against Italy, a 1–1 draw with Toribio Diaz answering an early goal
by the effervescent Italian winger, Bruno Conti. Indeed Peru were

unlucky not to be awarded a penalty when Juan-Carlos Oblitas was tripped inside the area by Claudio Gentile (of whom more anon!).

The players of Cameroon again displayed their worth by putting on a superb performance against a stilted Poland. Agreed, they had to survive two narrow attempts on their goal from Boniek and the man who had been the top scorer in 1974, Gregorz Lato, but saw several attempts saved by the Poland goalkeeper, Josef Mylnarczk, and it came as little surprise to find Roger Milla (who had played an outstanding game) having his name taken towards the end for throwing the ball in the face of an opponent in sheer frustration.

Only two goals had come in four matches so far and Group One appeared destined to set all sorts of records. The statistics were turned upside down three days later, however, when Poland thrashed Peru 5–1, all the goals coming in the second half of the game. Credit where credit is due – in spite of receiving this pasting, the Peruvian players never allowed themselves to become despondent and, in fact, scored the final goal. It was sad, however, to see an unfit Cubillas – a great star in 1970 when the competition was last held in Mexico – being substituted in the second half. So – to the last game between Italy and Cameroon which would see who would accompany Poland into the Second Round.

Cameroon gained a draw for the third time. Conti blazed over the bar when put through. Collovati and Tardelli saw shots saved by N'kono – and it was only when he slipped that Italy finally managed to score. Within 60 seconds, however, Cameroon had equalised that goal of Graziani's – a rush producing a goal for Gregoire M'bida. Alas for them, however; they were unable to score another – leaving Italy to go through to the Second Round: the two countries had the same number of points but Italy had scored that crucial extra goal. The Cameroon players would have the consolation of being the first team to depart from the competition unbeaten in addition to having given abundant proof of how quickly the game had developed throughout Africa.

Group Two provided still further evidence of this theme with its opening match in which Algeria beat the seeded West Germany by the odd goal in three – a result 'against the form book' that bears comparison with the North Korean victory against Italy in 1966 and the game in the 1950 tournament when England lost to the USA. As with Cameroon, Algeria had several players who belonged to club sides in France in addition to having the current African Footballer of the Year in Lakhdar Belloumi, a 24-year-old midfield player with boundless talent. Their players were also much more used to playing in the humidity experienced in Gijon during the late afternoon. With the skilful Nourredine Kourichi and Mahmoud Gendouz sealing up the middle of the defence the Germans found it almost impossible to carve a way through, so it came as little surprise when a pass from Salah Assad to Belloumi was driven through the German defence, for Rabah Madjer to score after Belloumi's shot had been blocked. It was Belloumi himself who scored the second Algerian goal, sliding a right-foot ball past Harald Schumacher a minute after Karl-Heinz Rummenigge had equalised in the sixty-seventh minute. No more goals, however, and the Germans were left to console themselves with the thought that whenever the country had been victorious it had suffered defeats in the first round: in 1954 by Hungary, in 1974 by East Germany.

Chile showed themselves to be the weakest country in this group, losing 0–1 to Austria and then 1–4 to West Germany, Rummenigge scoring a hat trick. The side also lost to Algeria by the odd goal in five after the Algerians had been beaten 2–0 by Austria. So West Germany positively *had* to win the last game in the Group to be sure of going through to the Second Round. However, if they did so by four goals or more that would permit Algeria to go through on goal difference. Shameful as it was, once the Germans had gone ahead in the tenth minute through Horst Hrubesch, the game came to resemble a match between sleepwalkers, neither side making any effort whatsoever. A disgrace. No wonder the Algerians were incensed – and it raised again the question as to why games should not be played simultaneously (bringing back memories of Argentina's 6–0 victory against Peru in 1978).

In Group Four England made a perfect start when Bryan Robson scored after just 27 seconds against France – the fastest goal in the history of the competition. Although the French replied through Gerard Soler who latched onto a pass from Giresse, Platini had a disappointing match and England were able to finish 3–1, winners thanks to another goal by Robson and one by Paul Mariner. With the plucky Kuwaitis gallantly holding Czechoslovakia to a draw the Group seemed to be smiling on the chances of England qualifying for the Second Round, which hope was confirmed when England beat a demoralised Czechoslovakia 2–0, both goals coming in the second-half. On the debit side, Bryan Robson injured a groin, but as the England manager, Ron Greenwood, pleasantly remarked afterwards the memory of England having qualified 'through the back door' was a thing of the past.

The following day France beat Kuwait 4–1 in the worst-refereed match of the tournament. The Russian official made mistake after mistake, culminating in his disallowing a perfectly good goal by Maxime Bossis, France's left-back, in the sixty-ninth minute when France were already 3–0 in the lead. The Kuwaitis hit back five minutes later but several minutes afterwards came an explosion as the Kuwaitis stopped playing, claiming to have heard a whistle from the crowd signalling that Giresse was off-side when he scored. Bedlam ensued as the referee at first indicated that a goal had been scored – only to change his mind nine minutes later after a protest by the President of the Kuwaiti FA. Three days later France drew 1–1 with the Czechs who had five minutes of frantic hope because Antonin Panenka equalised with a penalty in the eighty-fifth minute. Victory was not forthcoming, however, so it was France who would go through to the Second Stage. The intensity of play during that period was demonstrated by the fact that two minutes afterwards Ladislav Vizek had the ignominy of being the first man to be sent off in the tournament. England finished their spell in the First Round by defeating Kuwait 1–0 so could proudly go forward as one of only two sides to emerge from the First Round with maximum points.

The other side to achieve this feat was Brazil whose first match proved to be one of the best in the tournament. It was against the solid side representing the Soviet Union, which, controlling much of the early play, took the lead in the thirty-third minute through

Andrei Baal. 1–0 the score remained at half-time and long into the second half until Socrates equalised in the seventy-fifth minute with a spectacular shot. 12 minutes later came the final goal from Eder, who collected a pass after Falcao had bewitched his way through the Soviet defence. 2–1 was the final score but this had been a most entertaining match and hopes of neutrals were high that the Soviet Union would progress farther. Certainly, many thought that the refereeing was pitifully inadequate, the Soviet Union being denied two firm claims for a penalty and Brazil one.

24 hours later Scotland beat New Zealand 5–2, a fair result but those two lapses in the defence were to prove costly. When the team met Brazil three days later all returned to milk and honey during the first half-hour as David Narey scored after 18 minutes with a thunderbolt of a shot. That caused Scotland's supporters to feel that their team could go a long way in the tournament; soon after, however, the Brazilians moved up a gear – Zico equalising during the first half – and the second period was almost entirely devoted to the magic of Brazilian football as the South Americans ran in three further goals through Oscar, Eder and Falcao. Since the Soviet Union defeated New Zealand 3–0, Scotland knew that they would have to gain a victory over the USSR to proceed further with their challenge in the tournament. Some wit in the crowd (presumably a Scot!) had made an enormous banner which declaimed the match to be one of ALCOHOLISM versus COMMUNISM and Jock Stein brought back Joe Jordan to remind the Soviets that he meant business. In fact it was Jordan who scored after 15 minutes and, with Graeme Souness organising the side in masterly fashion, a win seemed most possible. But then came one of those failings that so often plague Scotland's goalkeepers when Chivadze, who was not closed down, was given room to strike a shot through a ruck of players; and in the eighty-fourth minute Scotland's central defenders became hopelessly mixed up and allowed Ramon Shengalia enough room to score. Souness made it 2–2 two minutes later but Scotland were eliminated. New Zealand's players found that gallantry was not enough against the Brazilians and went down 0–4 to goals which were among the best in the tournament from Zico and Falcao.

# World Cup 1982

Group Five proved to be most dramatic. According to the form-book both Spain and Yugoslavia would progress easily to the Second Round – convincingly beating Northern Ireland and Honduras. But it was not to be. Honduras announced to everybody that they would not lie down quietly by holding the hosts to a draw, 1–1. Only 24 hours before Hungary had trounced El Salvador, suggesting that both Central American sides might be easy meat! Not so in fact – Honduras scoring after only seven minutes. To equalise, Spain required a penalty and throughout the match displayed apathetic form, while for Honduras Julio Cesar Arzu (in goal) and Allan Costly (in the centre of the defence) showed themselves to be players of the highest class. The following day Northern Ireland drew 0–0 with Yugoslavia, with Norman Whiteside – the youngest player ever to appear in the competition – having a typically robust game in attack and Sammy McIlroy playing his heart out in midfield. Three days later Spain gained that much-desired victory, not against the supposedly-weaker Northern Ireland but instead against Yugoslavia. They required a twice-taken penalty in the fourteenth minute to reply to the Yugoslav goal, which had been scored four minutes earlier by Ivan Gudelj, and it was only a piece of carelessness by Ivica Surjak from a corner in the sixty-sixth minute which permitted the substitute Enrique Saura to race in to score. So Spain won a dull match in which they had played the worse football; in contrast, the following evening came an entertaining 1–1 draw between two of the supposedly weaker sides in the tournament – Honduras and Northern Ireland. Three evenings later the former went on to lose by a single goal to Yugoslavia in a scrappy confrontation, having their midfield player, Gilberto Yearwood, sent off.

The same fate befell Mal Donaghy the day after when Northern Ireland defeated Spain 1–0, Gerry Armstrong scoring just after half-time with the hundredth goal of the tournament. Most referees would have simply booked Donaghy but when you are officiating in the Luis Casanova stadium in Valencia with 50,000 locals wanting blood it can be very easy to be swayed by the crowd – so off Donaghy went. Spain, frankly, were pathetic and only went through to the Second Round as a result of having scored a greater number of goals than Yugoslavia, who also disappointed.

Into the Second Round of the competition went POLAND and ITALY; AUSTRIA and WEST GERMANY; BELGIUM and ARGENTINA; ENGLAND and FRANCE; NORTHERN IRELAND and SPAIN; and BRAZIL and the USSR. Four seeded countries had failed to head their Groups (ITALY, WEST GERMANY, ARGENTINA and SPAIN) but the organisers of the event, must have been most distressed when one of the Second Round groups saw paired together Brazil, Argentina and Italy while Spain, far from being in the supposedly easy group along with Austria and France, saw itself in a group with West Germany and England, both of which were sides Spain feared. Long faces all round.

In Group A a dazzling performance by Boniek helped Poland thrash Belgium 3–0. Moved to play in the attack between Smolarek on the left and the effervescent Lato on the right, Boniek laid on a devastating display of skills and scored a hat-trick of thrilling goals – which almost guaranteed that Poland would go through to the Semi-final stage. That became a certainty after the Soviet Union only managed to beat Belgium 1–0 so that all Poland were required to do in their next game was to hold the winners to a draw. It turned out to be a 'Goalless Grimmie'; one of the few highlights off the pitch being the appearance of several banners supporting Solidarity, which were removed, presumably on the orders of the Soviet authorities.

Group B started with a goalless draw between West Germany and England – a result that suited Spain, whose players turned up half-an-hour before the kick-off and received the loudest cheer of the night. The match proved to be a disappointing contest, England's best football coming during the first half when Harald Schumacher was forced to make crucial saves from Ray Wilkins and Bryan Robson, but as the game went on the English players began to tire quickly in the strength-sapping heat. Three days later West Germany beat Spain 2–1 in a game that saw much more action than the first contest. Zamora returned after injury but the other Spanish player of flair, Juanito, was injured just before half-time and substituted, leaving the host country without ideas of how to get goals. West Germany, on the other hand, really sparked for the first time in this competition – Pierre Littbarski, on viperish form in the forward line, opening the scoring just after half-time. A welcome goal, particularly given that Rummenigge had been unable to come out after the interval. With Klaus Fischer adding a second in the seventy-fifth minute, Zamora's goal for Spain appeared to be almost an irrelevancy.

So England had to play Spain, seeking to win by two clear goals or by 3–2 or 4–3: a difference that would permit them to overtake the Germans. Sadly for them they could manage nothing better than a goalless draw – with misses taking place at each end. In the sixty-third minute Ron Greenwood brought on Trevor Brooking and Kevin Keegan but while Brooking looked sharp and creative, Kevin Keegan just failed to glance into the Spanish goal a cross from Bryan Robson and clearly lacked match-fitness. 0–0 therefore, and England were out (as were Spain) but with the satisfaction of being unbeaten. If only Brooking and Keegan had been fit throughout. In the end, however, England could only blame their inability to take the chances offered.

Group C saw the meeting of three of the Titans in the history of the tournament – and every match proved to be full of interest. Italy met Argentina in a bruiser of a contest which saw five players being booked – two Italian, three Argentinian – one where so often footballing skills became submerged by the importance of the occasion. The entire first-half, in fact, was taken up with the two sides testing each other out but Italy took the lead in the fifty-sixth minute in dramatic fashion – Antognoni slipping through a perfect pass for his midfield colleague, Tardelli, to race through and score. As the Argentinian players strove to equalise, sadly for them, they left gaps in their defence and after Ubaldo Fillol had fouled Paolo Rossi, Bruno Conti retrieved the ball and gave it to the oncoming Antonio Cabrini to score. Although the Argentine captain, Daniel Passarella, pulled back a goal, 2–1 was the final score. Thus it would be Argentina who would perform next against their arch-rivals Brazil, but would be prevented from calling on their midfield player, Amerigo Gallego, who had been dismissed from the field five minutes from the end.

Matches between the two South-American countries are always

tense – and this particular match was no exception to that dictum. It was almost killed stone-dead, however, in the eleventh minute when Eder bent a free-kick from 30 metres out against the bar, only for Zico to scramble the ball home. Two further scores came from the Brazilians in the second-half but there came only a solitary reply by Ramon Diaz in the last minute to make the score 3-1. Maradona in the previous match had been forced to endure some savage tackling on the part of Claudio Gentile but in this match he committed a foul on Batista of which Gentile would have been proud, and was sent off for his pains. He turned out to have experienced a most disappointing World Cup, his only match of note having been the game against Hungary.

Three days later followed a match which will enter the Pantheon of outstanding games in the history of the tournament when Italy beat Brazil 3-2 in a totally absorbing contest. Paolo Rossi suddenly came into electrifying form in the attack, scoring all three Italian goals – his first in the competition – and Giancarlo Antognoni can have had few better games in the Italian midfield. Rossi scored after five and 25 minutes (following a crass mistake by the Brazilian defence) but Brazil replied dramatically after 12 minutes through Socrates and 68 minutes when Falcao scored one of the goals of the championship, shimmering his way through the Italian defence. With Gentile giving Zico a dose of the treatment he had meted out a week earlier to Maradona, one of the principal threats to Italy was shackled as firmly as had been the Argentinian. When Falcao's goal was scored the hearts of many Italian supporters must have sunk but such had been the spirit of determination induced in his players by Enzo Bearzot, the Italian manager, that anything seemed possible and it was 'The Prodigal Son' who scored the third goal six minutes later which took Italy into the Semi-final stage, where they would play Poland, with whom they had played a goalless draw in the First Round. On this occasion, however, it would be essential to win.

Group D saw Northern Ireland initially waiting on the sidelines while France played Austria. Now the knock-out principle was partly in use (the losers of a Group match automatically going on to play in the following match), the French team started to display

## World Cup 1982

what it was capable of. With Alain Giresse in corruscating form in midfield and Dominique Rocheteau becoming sharper in attack, with Marius Tresor displaying all his experience at centre-back and with many of the Austrians playing as if in a comatose state, France was able to dominate an entertaining game, although only scoring once when Bernard Genghini curled in a direct free kick that stunned the Austrian defence. Three days later, another lively match between Northern Ireland and Austria finished as a 2-2 draw, the Ulster men deservedly taking the lead through Billy Hamilton who put in a second after Austria had scored twice in the second half. Neither team, however, was able to add a decisive third goal so that when they met France three days later Northern Ireland knew they required a victory to be sure of reaching the Semi-final stage.

Unfortunately for them, Northern Ireland had to play in broiling conditions which they found most taxing. France, at last enjoying a streak of glorious form, took the lead in the thirty-third minute thanks to Giresse who tapped home a cross from Michel Platini, having his best match to date in the competition. Rocheteau added two further goals before Armstrong was able to score for the Irish but with a win being necessary, the hope of scoring three further goals in the last 16 minutes was beyond the realms of possibility and at the finish France went through 4-1 Giresse heading home in the eightieth minute. The Irish were eliminated from the tournament but could hold their heads high, while for the first time since 1958 France had reached the last four in the World Cup and would advance to the Semi-final stage, in which they would meet West Germany. (Even the valiant goalkeeper, Pat Jennings, could do nothing.)

This was the first occasion since 1966 that all four Semi-finalists came from Europe. The less intricate of the games saw a revitalised Italy beating Poland 2-0 in the Nou Camp stadium at Barcelona, both goals being scored by Paolo Rossi, who seemed to have completely rediscovered his instincts as a predator. The Polish players appeared to enter the game with an attitude that was totally pessimistic. Agreed, the heat was more taxing to them than it was to the Italians; agreed the suspension of their most gifted player – Boniek – had been a crucial blow. However, on the other hand, Antognoni was forced to leave the field injured in the twenty-ninth minute, seven minutes after Rossi had scored his first goal, causing a certain amount of reorganisation in the Italian side. But Poland were unable to take advantage of that piece of fortune, the only threat to the Italian goal coming from long-range shooting by the Polish midfield player Janusz Kupcewicz. In the seventy-third minute a classic header by Rossi from a centre by Conti sewed up the match for Italy who thus became the first team to appear in four Finals in the year history of the World Cup.

Soon after, Italy would have to share that record with West Germany but the other Semi-final deserves a chapter on its own for containing superb drama in addition to heart-bursting emotion. Just examine the scoreline: 1–1 at half-time, 1–1 at full time, 3–3 after extra-time – so the contest had to be resolved by a penalty shoot-out. An engrossing contest, this between German organisation and French skill, with Michel Platini at last playing at the peak of his form. It was Platini, in fact, who scored France's equaliser ten minutes after Littbarski had given West Germany the lead in the seventeenth minute, hitting home a penalty. Although the match continued to thrill, the crucial moment came in the fifty-sixth minute when Platini hit a superb pass through the German defence for Patrick Battiston – who had come on only six minutes earlier as a substitute – to run on unmarked towards the German goal. That was when Schumacher chose to come out at speed and – with no attempt to play the ball – to clummock Battiston to the ground, unconscious and minus two teeth. It took over three minutes for a stretcher to be brought onto the field (so security-conscious were the authorities that the Red Cross officials had been banned from the pitch), which delay served to make the incident seem even more dramatic.

Instead of being dismissed from the field by the Dutch referee, Corver, the German goalkeeper was simply shown a yellow card – which fact appeared even more shameful as the game went into extra-time. During that period France took a 3–1 lead, thanks to goals by Tresor and Giresse, only for West Germany to equalise through Rummenigge (who had just come on as a substitute) and

# World Cup 1982

Fischer. 3-3 then, and the first penalty shoot-out in the history of the tournament saw each side strike home four of its first five attempts to score – Stielike and then Six going through the agony of seeing their shots saved by the opposing goalkeeper. It became an affair of sudden-death at that stage with poor Maxime Bossis next in line: his shot smacked against the bar and rebounded into play. Hrubesch made no mistake with his shot – and West Germany proceeded to its second Final in three World Cups fully aware that Dame Fortune had been smiling on them, instead of on the unfortunate French.

Little wonder that when the Third Place match took place two days later France took the field against Poland with only four of the men who had started the match against West Germany – the tireless Marius Tresor, Amoros, Janvion (in defence) and Jean Tigana (in midfield). It turned out to be an entertaining contest which they would lose but only by the odd goal in five. France, in fact, took the lead in the twelfth minute through Girard but another old favourite from the side that had come third in 1974, Andrzej Szarmach, replied in the fortieth minute when he scored after accepting a telling pass by Boniek. Seconds before half-time Majewski headed in a second which was followed two minutes after the interval by a curling free-kick by Kupcewicz. 3-1 to Poland, then, with three goals having come in the space of seven minutes. France, however, then sprang to the challenge, mounting attack after attack and Alain Couriol made it 3-2 in the seventy-third minute. Which made for a dramatic final seventeen minutes as France attempted to score an equaliser. It was not to be but neutrals would point out that France had been forced to play only forty-eight hours after that traumatic meeting with West Germany in addition to having been exhausted by playing that particular encounter in the heat of Madrid instead of the comparative cool of Barcelona.

The same argument might also be applied to West Germany in the Final the following day. But few felt much sympathy for the Germans, having seen them beaten in their opening match by Algeria, and two games later coming that insult of a match between West Germany and Austria. The Germans even had fortune on their side in the Final when Giancarlo Antognoni was declared unfit at the last minute and received a further slice of luck since Graziani had to be helped off the field in the seventh minute when he injured a shoulder. Their largest slice of good fortune came in the twenty-fourth minute when Cabrini sliced wide a penalty-kick after Briegel had pulled down Conti inside the area, the first-ever penalty miss in the history of the competition. Conti, in fact, was Italy's most dangerous attacker and came close to scoring on several occasions but the first half finished goalless.

What a pleasing change in the second-half! Italy took the lead in the fifty-sixth minute when Rossi hit home at the near-post after a cross from Gentile, and that goal was added to 12 minutes later as Tardelli shot home after Gentile had finished a glorious move by the Italian midfield. 12 minutes after *that*, as the Germans allowed their discipline to wander after Briegel had been refused a penalty, Bruno Conti sprinted more than half the length of the field to put across a perfect pass for Altobelli to shoot past Schumacher. Although West Germany scored in the eighty-second minute through Brietner, Bearzot had the last word by putting on as substitute one of his favourites in the squad, Franco Causio, with only two minutes to play.

When Dino Zoff lifted the World Cup trophy soon after, he became only the second goalkeeper to captain a victorious side (the first being his fellow-countryman Giampiero Combi in 1934). Few could argue that Italy had not deserved to take the trophy for the third time, the first European country to achieve this feat. The form displayed by the side during the First Round had distressed its many followers throughout the world, and Enzo Bearzot must have given a vast sigh of relief when the match against Cameroon was finished and Italy were sure of progressing in the tournament. To be drawn at the Second Stage, however alongside those giants from South America, Brazil and Argentina, must have provided a fresh torment. Both teams possessed individuals of great talent who were capable of creating a goal out of nothing. Enter Claudio Gentile who by means fair or foul (very often the latter) entirely shackled up first Diego Maradona of Argentina and then Zico of Brazil. He was extremely fortunate not

# World Cup 1982

to be dismissed from the field but the psychological impact of his rigid marking was enormous.

In addition, Bearzot knew that he had another ace up his sleeve, an ace called Paolo Rossi who, with every game he played, was getting rid of the cobwebs of having been out of action for the past two years. Giancarlo Antognoni had slotted back into the side in a masterly fashion after having been out of the game for several months with a head injury and the faith that Bearzot also held for Rossi was justly rewarded by the thrilling goals which he scored in those last three games. Above all, Bearzot, not a spiteful man, must have received a fair amount of glee from reading the copy in the sports papers and pages from correspondents having to swallow their words. Not a few of those – even as late as May – had called for him to be replaced as manager.

Italy had the highest number of players booked in the competition (11) but theirs was a triumph for spirit over adversity; they splendidly beat Brazil, the team favoured by many as well as that which had scored most goals in the tournament (15) and although the Final tended to disappoint, few could doubt Italy were worthy champions.

# 1982 Final Stages

## Second Stage

## Group A

|         | P | W | D | L | F | A | Pts |
|---------|---|---|---|---|---|---|-----|
| POLAND  | 2 | 1 | 1 | 0 | 3 | 0 | 3   |
| USSR    | 2 | 0 | 1 | 0 | 1 | 0 | 3   |
| BELGIUM | 2 | 0 | 0 | 2 | 0 | 4 | 0   |

## Group B

| | | | | | | | |
|---|---|---|---|---|---|---|---|
| WEST GERMANY | 2 | 1 | 1 | 0 | 2 | 1 | 3 |
| ENGLAND | 2 | 0 | 2 | 0 | 0 | 0 | 2 |
| SPAIN | 2 | 0 | 1 | 1 | 1 | 2 | 1 |

## Group C

| | | | | | | | |
|---|---|---|---|---|---|---|---|
| ITALY | 2 | 2 | 0 | 0 | 5 | 3 | 4 |
| BRAZIL | 2 | 1 | 0 | 1 | 5 | 4 | 2 |
| ARGENTINA | 2 | 0 | 0 | 2 | 2 | 5 | 0 |

## Group D

| | | | | | | | |
|---|---|---|---|---|---|---|---|
| FRANCE | 2 | 2 | 0 | 0 | 5 | 1 | 4 |
| AUSTRIA | 2 | 0 | 1 | 1 | 2 | 3 | 1 |
| NORTHERN IRELAND | 2 | 0 | 1 | 1 | 2 | 6 | 1 |

## Semi-Final Stage

POLAND 0, ITALY 2 (0–1) Rossi (2) for Italy

POLAND: Mylnarczyk, Dziuba, Zmuda, Janas, Majewski, Kupcewicz, Buncol, Matysik, Lato, Ciolek (Palasz), Smolarek (Kusto).
ITALY: Zoff, Bergomi, Collovati, Scirea, Cabrini, Oriali, Antognoni (Marini), Tardelli, Conti, Rossi, Graziani (Altobelli).

# World Cup 1982

WEST GERMANY 3, FRANCE 3 (1-1) aet, Littbarski, Rummenigge, Fischer for West Germany; Platini (pen.), Tresor, Giresse for France

WEST GERMANY: Schumacher, Kaltz, Förster K. H., Stielike, Förster B., Briegel (Rummenigge), Dremmler, Brietner, Littbarski, Fischer, Magath (Hrubesch).
FRANCE: Ettori, Amoros, Janvion, Tresor, Bossis, Genghini (Battiston then Lopez), Platini, Giresse, Rocheteau, Six, Tigana.

West Germany won 5-4 on penalties: Kaltz, Brietner, Littbarski, Rummenigge and Hrubesch scored as did Giresse, Amoros, Rocheteau and Platini. Stielike's shot was saved as were those of Six and Bossis for France.

## Third Place Match played in Alicante

POLAND 3, FRANCE 2 (2-1) Szarmach, Majewski, Buncol for Poland; Girard, Couriol for France

POLAND: Mylnarczyk, Dziuba, Janas, Zmuda, Majewski, Kupcewicz, Matysik (Wojicki), Lato, Buncol, Boniek, Szarmach.
FRANCE: Castaneda, Amoros, Mahut, Tresor, Janvion (Lopez), Tigana (Six), Larios, Girard, Couriol, Soler, Bellone.

## Final played in Madrid

ITALY 3, WEST GERMANY 1 (0-0) Rossi, Tardelli, Altobelli for Italy, Breitner for West Germany

ITALY: Zoff, Gentile, Collovati, Scirea, Cabrini, Oriali, Bergomi, Tardelli, Conti, Rossi, Graziani (Altobelli then Causio).
WEST GERMANY: Schumacher, Kaltz, Förster K. H., Stielike, Briegel, Dremmler (Hrubesch), Breitner, Förster, B., Rummenigge (Müller), Fischer, Littbarski.

# 5 THE HAND OF DIEGO

If the abiding memory of the 1970 final tournament is of the stature and skills of the incomparable Pele, playing in his fourth finals, then that of 1986, again played in Mexico, would come from another South American genius in Diego Armando Maradona. As a captain whose form was inspirational, Maradona led Argentina to victory for its second triumph in three tournaments; at the quarter-final stage against England he became notorious when a goal allowed was scored with his left hand, but later in that match and in the semi-final against Belgium he produced goals (using his left foot on these occasions) that will remain long in the memory.

The final stages came to Mexico for the second time in sixteen years due to the unwillingness of Colombia, the original choice, to act as the Host country. Now extended to an unwieldy clutch of 24 teams in six groups, the final stages have become so cumbersome and elephantine that Colombia was unwilling to produce the extra finance required – as was its giant neighbour, Brazil. Eventually the choice fell upon Mexico, which had been eager to become the first country to host the World Cup finals twice.

Problems presented themselves, however. Although most of the stadiums which had been built or renovated for the 1970 tournament were deemed to be in a sufficiently smart state, and only one, at Queretaro, required building from scratch, the elements were a different proposition. If there had been no calamity to compare with the earthquake which had devastated Peru in 1970 and had killed thousands of people, two earth-tremors had occurred in Mexico during September 1985, reminding the authorities about the ever-present risk of a disaster from natural causes. The hostile altitudes and the intense heat were further negative aspects. Certain teams from Europe such as Belgium, England, France and West Germany provided immensely improved performances in the expanded knock-out stage after they had acclimatised to these natural enemies, so that several of their later matches became worthy to set alongside the best of previous tournaments.

# The hand of Diego

Despite the competition grossing more than the equivalent of £60 million, with each finalist receiving over £200,000 (up 25 per cent on the championship in 1982), ticket sales were dealt with in a 'very unsatisfactory' way according to Joseph Blatter, the General Secretary of FIFA. Grounds in many first-round matches were half-empty, and pitifully lacked atmosphere since no attempt had been made to fill them. Most of the finance accrued in the World Cup finals comes from the sale of television rights or from advertising rights for film, television, newspapers, magazines and hoardings, with the finance coming from advance ticket sales producing only a very slender percentage of the overall total. Surely, therefore, many of the population who could not afford the full price of a ticket might have been admitted at the last minute at more moderate prices? But no.

The standard of refereeing varied greatly. If there were authoritative performances from officials such as Luigi Agnolin of Italy and George Courtney of England, there were many erroneous decisions which tended to encourage cheating (Maradona's goal by the 'hand of God' being the most monstrous example), and the feebleness of some officials in allowing free-kicks to be taken when opposing players were clearly less than ten metres away effectively sabotaged the point. The few referees who remained firm in their intent ordered the freekick to be taken from ten metres further up the field, and it was pleasing to see the punishment fit the crime. Another problem looked on in a desultory fashion, as it had been in 1982, was the lack of good accommodation and hotel facilities for the players, since priority inevitably had been given to sponsors, officials and the media.

The desperate requirements of an impoverished country like Mexico necessitated the exposure of the tournament on the international stage through the bear-like grip of satellite television, so that inevitably the kick-off times for some matches were prostituted to the needs of television stations in Europe. The opening match between the Holders, Italy, and Bulgaria, was one of over thirty games which kicked off under a fierce midday sun, and at the high altitude of Mexico City. Italy had failed to qualify for the 1984 European Championships, and many of the subsequent 21 friendlies had been against teams not of the highest class, making some of the new players raw in their approach. Enzo Bearzot had to cope with injuries to important stars such as Giancarlo Antognoni, but Bruno Conti, whose play on the right wing had been so critical in 1982, had lost some of his zest, and Paolo Rossi had been too slow to acclimatize. If Giuseppe Bergomi and Gaetano Scirea remained authoritative defenders, and Antonio Cabrini a splendid attacking fullback, Giovanni Galli had several moments of uncertainty in goal and rarely gave confidence to his defence.

Italy's goal in the 1-1 draw with Bulgaria was scored, just before half-time, by Sandro Altobelli, who had scored the last of its goals in the 3-1 victory over West Germany in Madrid; but sadly the team could not take the few other chances in a lively game and in the six minutes from time, paid the penalty when Nasko Sirakov headed the equaliser. Italy's goal in their following game against Argentina, who had beaten South Korea 3-1, also came from Altobelli, a penalty awarded in the sixth minute after Jorge Burruchaga had clearly handled the ball. This early token of comfort was answered in the thirty-fourth minute by Maradona who placed a precise shot past a hesitant Galli. Although in the second half Conti struck a post and Salvatore Bagni blazed a shot over the bar, the game developed into a brawl and all were glad when it finished as a 1-1 draw.

Italian anxieties mounted over the next few days in anticipation of the meeting with South Korea, who had also drawn 1-1 with Bulgaria. They were eased after the dependable Altobelli scored in the eighteenth minute, but South Korea equalised in the sixty-second minute with a fierce shot from the gifted Choi Soon Ho. There followed eleven minutes of anxiety until Altobelli tapped in a free-kick from Bruno Conti, and nine minutes later Altobelli helped to make the score 3-1 when he forced Cho Kwang Rae to give away an own-goal after a forceful header by midfielder Fernando De Napoli. Although a minute from the end Huh Jung Moo made the final score 3-2, Italy proceeded to the next round, but with Argentina defeating Bulgaria 2-0 thanks to goals in the third minute by Valdano and in the seventy-fourth from

## The hand of Diego

Burruchaga, it was they who entered the knockout stage as the leading team in Group A.

Under the careful eye of its Yugoslavian coach, Bora Milutinovic, Mexico had withdrawn a clutch of its best players from the national championship and had drilled them during the previous two years, playing scores of friendlies against teams from Europe and South America. The star of the team would be Hugo Sanchez, who had been signed by Real Madrid.

Against an experienced but wayward Belgian side, Mexico scored twice in the first thirty-eight minutes through Fernando Quirarte and Hugo Sanchez, but the visitors were grateful for some haphazard goalkeeping by Pablo Larios which permitted them to pull back a goal just before half-time through Erwin Vandenbergh. No further goals were scored in a game that became too scrappy, but despite this initial set-back Belgium would proceed to the semi-final stage. After Paraguay had defeated Iraq 1-0 with a splendid goal from their Brazil-based South American Footballer of the Year, Julio Romero, the meeting between Mexico and Paraguay promised to tell which of the two would head the table. It turned out to be a disappointing match. Mexico took a lead in the second minute thanks to Luis Flores, although Paraguay gradually increased its hold on the game and it came as just reward when six minutes from time an equaliser was headed by Romero. Further drama was to come two minutes from the close when Hugo Sanchez was brought down inside the penalty area – but Sanchez himself failed in his attempt to score as Roberto Fernandez managed to deflect the ball against a post. The following day saw Belgium win 2-1 against an over-physical Iraq; and a goal by Quirarte for Mexico was enough to dispatch Iraq from the tournament three days later. The departing quote from their Brazilian coach that Iraq had not 'come here to win the disciplinary title. Soccer is strong. We play strong,' left an unpleasant taste in the mouth. Belgium and Paraguay drew the deciding and thrilling game 2-2, with goals from Frank Vercauteren and Daniel Veyt being answered by two from Roberto Cabanas, so that both teams would also proceed in the tournament, together with the Hosts.

France, fourth in the 1982 tournament and inspired by Michel Platini to triumph in the 1984 European Championships, had been seeded in Group C. In their opening match, however, the French made extremely heavy weather of defeating a plucky Canadian side (coached by the former England goalkeeper Tony Waiters) and did not score until the seventy-eighth minute thanks to a header by the normally incisive Jean-Pierre Papin. The following day the Soviet Union showed how it should be done by dismantling the fancied Hungary 6–0, scoring two goals inside the first four minutes with screaming shots by Pavel Yakovenko and Sergei Aleinikov.

The day after France and the Soviet Union had drawn 1–1, with goals from Luis Fernandez and Vasili Rats, a shell-shocked Hungary recovered enough to defeat Canada 2–0 in a game which Hungary's manager Gyorgy Mezey knew they 'had to win'. Although the Greek-based Marton Esterhazy scored after two minutes, Lajos Detari scored the second with only fifteen minutes of a bruising contest left; four minutes from the end Mike Sweeney had the dubious distinction of being the first person to be dismissed the field in the tournament. Given their disastrously negative goal-difference, the Hungarians also needed a victory in their third match, but when they came to meet France three days later, they were outplayed and beaten 3–0 by a side which was gradually showing people why it had become champions of Europe two years earlier, goals coming from Yannick Stopyra, Jean Tigana and Domenique Rocheteau. The Soviet Union defeated a courageous Canada 2–0 thanks to goals by Oleg Blokhin and the talented midfielder Alexandr Zavarov, although the losers might well have scored a consolation goal had the usually reliable Dale Mitchell been more accurate with his free-kick.

The other Group from which only two teams were to proceed would be Group D, which had the noisily supported Brazilians, and teams representing Algeria, Spain and Northern Ireland. Brazil had players of enormous talent, but it was a side in the middle of transition. The peerless Zico had not yet recovered from injury, while of the other experienced players Cerezo, Eder, Leandro and Dirceu had been dropped; and while Junior and

# The hand of Diego

Socrates had been selected, the new names included Josimar and Branco as full-backs, the prolific Careca and the promising Muller as the strike-force, and the midfield included Alemao, and Elzo, highly rated by Falcao whose place in the side he took. Brazil won 1-0 against a Spain deprived of Ramon Caldere and Rafael Gordillo, both stricken by Montezuma's Revenge. It was a nervous match which should have seen a goal allowed for Spain after Michel's shot struck the underside of the bar and rocketed down inside the goal. It might also have seen two penalties for Brazil, who received some justice in a poorly-refereed game when Socrates headed home the only goal from a rebound although he had been standing offside at the time that the original shot from Careca had hit the woodwork. Algeria drew 1-1 with Northern Ireland in a bruising encounter – both goals coming from free-kicks, by Norman Whiteside as early as the fifth minute and by Djamel Zidane in the fifty-eighth. Three days later Brazil gained another 1-0 victory, on this occasion against a spirited and skilful Algerian side which included Nassereddine Drid, their leading goalkeeper, as well as Lakhdir Belloumi, the midfield star, both of whom had been left out against Northern Ireland. Careca it was who turned in a centre from Muller, but Branco had earlier struck a post, and the Brazilians at last displayed their flair.

The following day Spain made an uplifting start against Northern Ireland, who had beaten them in the 1982 finals, by scoring in the very first minute, thanks to Emilio Butragueno who struck home a defence-splitting pass from Michel. Spain increased its lead in the eighteenth minute through Julio Salinas before the promising Alan McDonald and his fellow-defenders managed to prevent further goals. Although Northern Ireland pulled a goal back in the first minute of the second half when Colin Clarke headed past Andoni Zubizarreta, the Irish couldn't score the equaliser. In the final games in the group Spain won a bad-tempered and badly-refereed game against Algeria 3-0 with the goals being scored by Caldere (twice) and Eloy. It was a result precisely echoed in the other match when a superb display by Brazil overwhelmed Northern Ireland on the forty-first birthday of its celebrated goalkeeper, Pat Jennings, who played superbly and helped keep the score respectable. More important, however, might have been the first sight of Zico who came on to thunderous applause in the sixty-third minute and helped make the third Brazilian goal for Careca three minutes before the final whistle. Careca had opened the scoring in the fifteenth minute, and Brazil had gone into a 2–0 lead thanks to a pile-driving shot by their new right-back, Josimar, which screamed into the net to the right of Jennings's right shoulder. After the match the Irish goalkeeper, who could look back over a distinguished international career that had lasted over twenty years, announced his retirement.

When the Draw had been made in January, not unsurprisingly the Uruguayan manager, Omar Borras, had morosely referred to Group E as being 'El Grupo del Morte', 'The Group of Death'. Uruguay, with stars like Daniel Gutierrez, Enzo Francescoli and Wilmar Cabrera and a team fancied by many to triumph, had had the misfortune to be drawn against West Germany, the beaten finalists from 1982, Scotland, who had qualified for the fourth successive occasion and were reputed to be strong, and Denmark, the side that contained all the flair of Holland in the Seventies and was fancied by many. Borras was simply stating that Group E was by far the strongest, implying that each of the three matches would be savagely contested. They would be, with many Uruguayan players unfortunately choosing to hide their undoubted skills. Victorious in the 1980 European Championship and finalists in the 1982 World Cup, West Germany had performed disappointingly in the 1984 European Championships under Jupp Derwall, but when he was replaced by the legendary Franz Beckenbauer, optimism had returned, and although there was rumoured to be dissatisfaction among the players, West Germany are always a difficult side to beat, and usually rise to the occasion.

Alex Ferguson, who had taken over as manager of Scotland after the tragic death in November 1985 of the celebrated Jock Stein, astonishingly omitted Alan Hansen, one of the most cultured central defenders in Europe. His side was further weakened by the withdrawal through injury of Kenny Dalglish who wrenched a knee in April and decided not to risk it. In his first season as player-manager, he had just led Liverpool to a 'double'

## The hand of Diego

by winning both the League and the Cup. He would have been appearing in his fourth Finals, and his immense stature as a player would inevitably be sorely missed – but nevertheless Scotland still had some players of class. Denmark, coached by Sepp Piontek and appearing in the Finals for the first time, was very much the team in form. As long ago as June 1981, Enzo Bearzot had tipped Denmark as being 'the team of the future' after it had won a qualifying game against Italy in the previous World Cup. Indeed Denmark had gone on to qualify for the 1984 European Championship, and its talented players were gaining experience with successful club sides in England, Italy, West Germany, Belgium, France and Spain. On the afternoon of 4 June it got off to the right type of start by beating Scotland 1–0, thanks to a rather fortunate goal by Elkjaer. It turned out to be a game played with a good deal of skill at a pace that at times was ferocious, with splendid attacks being made for Denmark by their Italian-based forwards, Preben Elkjaer and Michael Laudrup, and for Scotland by Frank McAvennie and Charlie Nicholas until he was injured thanks to a distasteful foul by Klaus Berggreen. The other match witnessed an uneasy West German side come back after conceding a goal after only four minutes, scored for a sadly cynical Uruguay by Antonio Alzamendi, whose shot bounced down from the crossbar – but they didn't equalise until six minutes from the final whistle, the scorer being Klaus Allofs. Four days later West Germany performed much better to defeat Scotland 2–1, coming from behind after Gordon Strachan, who had a superb game, had given the Scots the lead in the seventeenth minute with a fine shot to the left of Toni Schumacher. However an unmarked Rudi Voller equalised five minutes later, hitting home a cross from Allofs, and it was Allofs himself who scored the crucial goal four minutes after half-time, sliding the ball past the advancing Jim Leighton after a goalmouth tangle.

Later that day Denmark performed in an authoritative manner when it demolished Uruguay 6–1, four of the goals coming after the interval, including a memorable score early in the second half when Michael Laudrup displayed all his skills in taking the ball past two defenders on the edge of the Uruguayan box before sliding it home from an acute angle. Enzo Francescoli had reduced the two-goal lead when he struck home a penalty on the stroke of half-time, and although Uruguay had been forced to play with only ten men after Bossio had been ordered off in the nineteenth minute after having collected two bookings, few teams could have beaten the Danes in this exuberant mood. The powerful Elkjaer scored a hat-trick, with the other Danish goals coming from Soren Lerby and Jesper Olsen.

When Scotland played Uruguay five days later requiring a victory, the game finished 0–0, but another Uruguayan was ordered off – this time after only 55 seconds when Batista was ordered off the field of play for having scythed down Gordon Strachan. Forseeably, after the match, an irate Omar Barros said that 'there was a murderer out there on the pitch today – the referee'. However it was Uruguay who would go through to the knock-out stage, despite having conceded those six goals to Denmark. Although Graeme Souness, who had been out of form, had been replaced by Paul McStay, the Scots were simply unable to score and thereby gain the point they required to move on to the next stage, while as the match progressed the superior skills of the South Americans became more influential. Truthfully, from Scotland's team, only Leighton in goal, Richard Gough at right back, along with Roy Aitken and Strachan in midfield, could feel as though they had done themselves justice, and it was therefore a dispirited collection of players who flew back to Glasgow having been unable to add to its previous tally of victories against Zaire in 1974, Holland in 1978 and New Zealand in 1982.

At the same time as Uruguay was collecting that vital point, Denmark defeated West Germany 2–0 thanks to goals by Jesper Olsen, who struck a penalty just before half-time into the left side of the goal as Toni Schumacher leapt the other way, and John Eriksen in the second half who slid home a cross from Frank Arnesen. Both teams were assured of qualification, however, and West Germany took the field without Klaus Augenthaler, Hans-Pieter Briegel, Pierre Littbarski and Karl-Heinz Rummenigge, clearly not unhappy to lose the match and thus meet Morocco instead of Spain in the next round. Denmark, however, had to

## The hand of Diego

cope with the suspension of their best player, Frank Arnesen, which would mean that he would be banned from playing against Spain; and it should still be noticed that West Germany went on to become Finalists despite being beaten in a match at the Group stage (by Algeria in 1982, by Denmark in 1986).

Of the teams playing in friendly Monterrey, Poland had quite justly been seeded thanks to having gained third place in the 1982 tournament. England, however, were also expected to perform creditably, and certainly to defeat the other two countries in the Group – Portugal, appearing for the first time since 1966, and Morocco, who hadn't appeared in the final stages since the previous tournament in Mexico in 1970. Although Bobby Robson's England had received a blow just before the tournament when their tall ball-playing centre-half, Mark Wright, broke a leg, it had been on a splendid run during the previous 20 months, losing merely three games out of 22, two of which had been at high altitude when they had played in a tournament in Mexico City in 1985. Especially heartening had been a 1–0 victory against the Soviet Union at Tbilisi and a 2–1 victory against a Souness-inspired Scotland at Wembley in a game in which no quarter was given or granted. On 2 June Poland were unable to score against a skilful Morocco side in a match which finished as a goalless draw, but imagine the intense shock when in their opening match England lost 1–0 to Portugal after Carlos Manuel struck home a cross from Diamantino who had beaten the normally dependable Kenny Sansom on the right. Indeed, after a goalless first period, England had come to dominate the second half, causing Portugal to bring on its gifted 17-year-old substitute, Paulo Futre in the seventy-first minute, four minutes before Carlos Manuel scored. Worse was to follow for England. In the following match, in which the team played poorly against Morocco, the experienced Ray Wilkins was sent off after having received two bookings (the second for uncharacteristically throwing the ball at the referee), but more importantly the inspiring captain Bryan Robson had to leave the field because his suspect shoulder had again been damaged, and was replaced by Steve Hodge. (This occurred only a few days after it had been dislocated for the fourth time in a friendly against Mexico. Thus Bryan Robson would take no farther part in the tournament.) With only ten men and on a scorchingly hot day, England held on to gain a goalless draw, but as a result of these calamities Bobby Robson clearly had to change the balance of the side for the next crucial game against Poland, who had defeated Portugal thanks to a goal from Wlodzimierz Smolarek, playing in his third World Cup.

England replaced Mark Hateley in the forward line with an effervescent Peter Beardsley, and into the centre of midfield brought the combative Peter Reid to play alongside the inspiring Glenn Hoddle, moved in from the right side where his talents could not be fully appreciated, with Steve Hodge and Trevor Steven playing wide. In a match it simply had to win, England triumphed 3-0, all its goals being scored in the first half by Gary Lineker. It was indeed the first occasion that England had won a game in the World Cup Finals by three clear goals, and psychologically the victory helped raise heads which had been drooping. In the other match Morocco beat Portugal 3-1 to lead Group F, with Abderrazak Khairi rifling in two shots within the first half-hour and Merry Krimau adding a third before Diamantino scored a consolation goal. Thus Portugal, who had caused the first major surprise of the competition, returned home empty-handed.

The sixteen sides who qualified to play in the eighth-finals, therefore, were: Argentina, Italy and Bulgaria from Group A, Mexico, Paraguay and Belgium from Group B, the Soviet Union and France from Group C, Brazil and Spain from Group D, Denmark, West Germany and Uruguay from Group E, and Morocco, England and Poland from Group F.

Belgium defeated the Soviet Union 4-3 in a sparkling game at Leon which flowed from end to end and showed the Belgians, after having given mediocre displays in the opening part of the tournament, at their glorious best. The first goal in the hat-trick scored by Igor Belanov came after twenty-seven minutes when he made to the right of the pitch and from 25 metres out unleashed a shot which screamed into Belgium's net. Enzo Scifo equalised in the fifty-fourth minute, but fifteen minutes later the irresistible Belanov slid the ball under the body of Pfaff to turn the match once

# The hand of Diego

again in the favour of the Soviet Union. Not for long, however, because in the seventy-fifth minute Ceulemans turned brilliantly and struck the ball past Dassayev in the opposing goal. Extra time came, but by now the Belgians had got their tails up and Belanov's third goal from a penalty in the one hundred and eleventh minute came after Belgium had taken a 4–2 lead. This succeeded a match in which Mexico defeated a thoroughly inept Bulgaria 2–0, the opening goal being a delight since it came from an acrobatic bicycle kick by Manuel Negrete that placed the ball to the right of goalkeeper Borislav Mikhailov. With the midfielder Raul Servin adding a second in the sixty-first minute, the game was truly finished, with the feeble Bulgaria having shown little stomach for the fight.

The following day the Brazilians showed that in their previous match against Northern Ireland they'd been only warming up, by defeating Poland 4–0. They scored only one goal in the first half from a penalty from Socrates, and nearly gave two goals away to the experienced Zbigniew Boniek and the sharp-shooting newcomer Dariusz Dziekanowski, but in the second half they began to play with real flair. Another goal was rifled in from the left by Josimar, the centre back Edinho scored in the seventy-eighth minute, and Careca, who had made a glorious run before that goal, added a penalty a minute after, the ball just squeezing over the line following a good save by Mlynarczyk. There were two interesting substitutions. As in the match against Northern Ireland, the barely fit but nevertheless inspirational Zico was brought on with twenty minutes remaining, and with only seven minutes to go the Polish centre-back Wladyslaw Zmuda was brought on in his fourth World Cup Finals, and equalled the record of appearances in World Cup matches of twenty-one held by Uwe Seeler of West Germany.

Argentina met Uruguay in a match whose anticipated passions were kept under control by the excellent refereeing of Luigi Agnolin. These two countries have met on countless occasions previously in South America, but in the World Cup this was their first meeting since the original Final in Uruguay in 1930, a game which Uruguay had won. On this occasion they were outplayed in midfield and Maradona, as though particularly charged by meeting another South American team, played with masterly control, crossing perfectly in the eleventh minute for Jorge Valdano, who alas failed to connect properly, and only minutes later struck the bar with a free-kick. A minute later Maradona started the move which led to the only goal of the game being scored by Pedro Pasculli in the forty-first minute when he latched on to a cross by Burruchaga – but two minutes later saw a shot go over the bar from Francescoli. The second half continued to be as exciting as the first, with chances at both ends and with the Uruguyans on their best behaviour after having received a warning and fine from FIFA, but in the sixty-sixth minute an electrical storm put an end to tidy football and left Argentina to go through.

Italy's hesitant World Cup challenge came to an end when it was beaten 2–0 by France. Just as the two sides were weighing each other up, Michel Platini found himself unmarked inside the area, ran on to a fine pass from Dominique Rocheteau, and chipped the ball over the advancing Giovanni Galli. That score came in the thirteenth minute and made a nervous Italy even more uncertain. The few attacking runs by Bruno Conti were tragically wasted and when the French got their second goal in the fifty-sixth minute it stood as a fine example of their growing confidence. Rocheteau was again involved, this time unselfishly passing to Yannick Stopyra who rocketed in a right-foot drive; by so doing he scored the hundredth goal of this World Cup. Although Italy brought on a promising new attacker in Gianluca Vialli with an hour to go, there was nothing to be done and the players could hardly complain at having been beaten by a better team. The ever-truthful Enzo Bearzot absolved his players of any sin. 'The mistakes were mine,' he admitted, and the *Corriere della Sport* was not being unfair when it claimed that 'The Bluff Has Finished'.

On the same day, however, West Germany, recalling Rummenigge for the first time in its starting line-up, won 1–0 against the talented Moroccans, but it didn't score until there were only 85 seconds to go, when Lothar Mattheaus scored with a free-kick curled round the wall to the left of Zaki – this while Jose Faria, Morocco's Brazilian coach, was warming up his substitutes ready

## The hand of Diego

for extra time! Although the Germans seemed slow in the first half of the game, they looked sharper after the introduction of Littbarski in the second period, but found the gifted Zaki in the Morocco goal on exceptional form.

The renovated England beat a paranoid Paraguay 3-0 thanks to two goals by Lineker and one by his new partner Beardsley. Terry Fenwick had been suspended, his place alongside the dependable Butcher in the centre of the defence being taken by Alvin Martin, but otherwise the team was that which had arisen from the dead against Poland. It was Paraguay's first appearance in the competition since 1958, and although it had players of skill and flair in Romero and Roberto Cabanas, the team lacked the resolution to come back after Lineker scored in the thirty-first minute, striking home a cross from Glenn Hoddle which had been touched on by Steve Hodge. Beardsley scored in the fifty-fifth minute when he ran on to another cross from Hoddle, and Hoddle was involved in helping Lineker score his third from a corner. A far cry this from the miseries against Portugal and Morocco, and only petulance on the part of the Paraguayans spoilt the delight of the performance.

The gifted Danes proved just how inexperienced they were when Denmark came to confront Spain, the team which had brought a halt to its progress in the 1984 European Championship, winning 6-5 after a penalty shoot-out. After Jesper Olsen had provided the lead in the thirty-second minute with a penalty, the Danes continued to play the most glorious football, even without the suspended Frank Arnesen in midfield. Alas for Denmark, a suicidal back to back by Jesper Olsen allowed Butragueno to collect the ball and to equalise just before half-time – psychologically the worst possible moment. Then followed a rush of four goals for Spain in the second half, two of them from penalties, one scored by Goicoechea and the other three scored by the man known as 'El Buitre', or 'The Vulture', his fourth from a penalty in the last minute when he equalled a record of scoring four goals in a single match last set by the legendary Eusebio for Portugal against North Korea in the tournament of 1966. So out of the competition went its most colourful debutant, a team which bore comparison with the Holland of the Seventies. In their match against Spain the Danes had shown themselves to be most skilful, but also showed that they were relaxed to a point of being casual, and naturally the fact that their wives and girlfriends had joined them on this trip was seen as the cause of that laid-back feeling.

From the Americas Argentina turned out to be the only side to enter the Semi-finals. As in 1982, when it was defeated by Italy, who went on to become Winners, Brazil let itself down in its Quarter-final against France, almost conceding a goal in the third minute, and in the fortieth minute allowing Platini to strike home a cross from Rocheteau which had caused chaos in Brazil's defence. This equalised a delightful goal in the sixteenth minute which had been scored by Careca following fine passing from Junior and Muller. In the seventy-first minute, after further chances had gone begging at each end, the latter was substituted by Zico. A minute later Zico, before he could have possibly become acclimatised to the nature of the game, was given the responsibility of taking a penalty, after Branco had been brought down inside the area by Joel Bats, and missed. He attempted to compensate several minutes later, only to see his fierce header saved by Bats at point-blank range, and must have been relieved moments later when Rocheteau failed to take a golden opportunity to win the match. Extra time came and went with further chances at both ends, and none taken, but the first penalty, struck by Socrates, was saved by Bats flying to his right. The following six penalties were all struck effectively, and then up stepped Michel Platini, perhaps the most effective kicker of a dead-ball of recent times – who promptly hit the ball to the left of the goal. Brazil's delight in the natural order being restored, however, was short-lived.

Julio Cesar drove the next penalty against the right-hand post of Bats, and in so doing restored an advantage which Luis Fernandez sealed by placing his penalty slightly to the left of Carlos inside the Brazilian goal. This was probably the most thrilling game of the Finals, a match to savour between Brazil and the team many referred to as being 'the Brazilians of Europe', both of them worthy of a place in the Final; and one greatly mourns the fact that Zico was fit to play in only 89 minutes of Brazil's five matches.

## The hand of Diego

What a contrast to this feast of football was the deplorable contest that succeeded it on the afternoon of 21 June between West Germany and Mexico. Any hopes that West Germany might have been eager not to repeat the last minute victory from their previous match against Morocco would be dashed, but in a bruising contest the physical strength of its players proved decisive. Thomas Berthold, the promising new German defender, was dismissed after a brutal foul on Quirarte, Javier Aguirre followed him in extra time and the yellow card was shown to a further seven players. West Germany made few attempts to attack, and as the match went goalless into extra time it became obvious that the Germans were confident of being able to win the penalty shoot-out – which they did, thanks to some inspired goalkeeping by Schumacher who saved the strikes by Quirarte (with his left leg) and Raul Servin, and thus helped to give West Germany a winning 4–1 advantage. So Mexico went out, along with Brazil a country with an unbeaten record if you ignore the penalty shoot-out, who at times had played some very skilful football.

On the afternoon of 22 June Belgium continued to show good form by defeating Spain on penalties, after another thrilling contest had finished in a 1–1 draw – its defence firm and Jean-Marie Pfaff proving on several occasions that he was among the best goalkeepers in the competition. After Julio Salinas had failed to beat him in the twenty-eighth minute, Belgium went into the lead six minutes later, Jan Ceulemans diving into the Spanish defence to fiercely head a cross from Frank Vercauteren past Zubizarreta's left arm. In the fifty-second minute the Belgians should have scored again when Nico Claesen laid the ball off to the unmarked Ceulemans, who instead of shooting decided to pass to Daniel Veyt to his right. Veyt's shot skidded past Zubizarreta – but thenceforth, with Spanish players almost continually in the Belgian half, an equaliser seemed inevitable. It came six minutes from time, Juan Senior rifling home a long strike from a pass by Victor. Extra time came and went, Georges Grun failing to tie up the match for Belgium when he had only the goalkeeper to beat; but in this particular penalty contest everyone made his strike count except for Eloy, who had been brought on as a substitute for

Salinas. So with the score of penalties at 5–5, up stepped Leo Van Der Elst to strike the winner into the right of Spain's goal as Zubizarreta dived to his left – and by so doing taking Belgium further in this competition than it had ever been.

If three of the four Quarter-finals turned out to be close games which had to be decided after extra time and penalties, the fourth, in which Argentina defeated England 2–1, provided the moment that people will talk about for years. There were no goals in the first half of the game which opened at midday on the same day, but with Glenn Hoddle being marked man to man, England's inspiration in midfield was lacking. Maradona's first goal when it came in the fiftieth minute was sensational – but for the wrong reason. When Steve Hodge sliced the ball back to Peter Shilton, the Argentinian leapt for and reached it just before the England goalkeeper, but the Tunisian referee, Ben Nasser was one of those who failed to notice that Maradona had struck the ball with his hand and not his head – and Maradona himself failed to be truthful. England's players were understandably distressed by the goal having been allowed, and some of them chased the referee back to the centre circle to argue their case. (According to Pelé, if Argentina had been playing a side from Brazil or Uruguay, Maradona would have been lynched!) Four minutes later, however, came a second goal from Maradona which showed what a magical player he can be. He collected the ball just inside his own half and set off a long slalom of a run in which his sleight of foot confused all England's defenders and left him to beat the advancing Shilton with a low left foot strike. He thereby painfully confirmed the prophecy of Bobby Robson that 'Maradona can win a game on his own in five minutes.'

It was over an hour before England made their first attack, but with Chris Waddle being brought on in the sixty-third minute and John Barnes eleven minutes later, the last twenty minutes of the match were very even and well-balanced. Ten minutes from time Lineker scored from a cross by Barnes, who made several further telling runs, and the game ended with Argentina very relieved to hear the sound of the final whistle. Whether England could have scored another goal given a few more minutes will always remain

# The hand of Diego

debatable. At least the players (19 of whom were used) could return home with their heads held high and Gary Lineker with the satisfaction of being the highest scorer in the tournament with a tally of six goals – the first occasion this has been achieved by anyone from the British Isles.

By proceeding thus far West Germany had scored only four goals in its first 5 matches, but against France at noon on 25 June – the second time in four years that the sides had met at the semi-final stage – it went ahead in the ninth minute. Following a free-kick by Magath, awarded when Rummenigge was fouled on the end of the area, Joel Bats (who otherwise played faultlessly) allowed a shot by Andreas Brehme to slide under his body. Even without the injured Rocheteau France had three golden opportunities to equalise during the following five minutes through Alain Giresse, Platini and Maxime Bossis, and the remaining period in the first half saw scoring opportunities missed at both ends. Platini and Stopyra failed to convert good chances in the second half, but for West Germany, while Magath was a tremendous orchestrator in midfield, Mattheaus was inspiring on the right, and the longer the game went on, the more tired the French appeared to become. In the last minute Rudi Voller, who had replaced Rummenigge in the fifty-sixth minute, scored the decisive second goal. He latched on to a cross from Allofs, calmly lobbed the approaching Bats, and then ran round France's goalkeeper before sliding the ball home with his right foot.

In the afternoon Argentina eased its way into the Final thanks to two more incomparable strikes by Diego Maradona. During the first half, the Belgian defence played in a resolute manner, and a greasy pitch helped to militate against the close passing of the confident Argentinians. What a different story in the second half! In the fifty-first minute the incomparable Maradona darted between two defenders in the penalty area to lob the ball over the head of the approaching Pfaff, and twelve minutes later, he doubled the score, making a run that bettered the one he had made against England, weaving his way through the right-hand side of Belgium's defence, and beating Pfaff with a shot into the corner of the Argentinian net. Belgium bravely replaced Michel Renquin with Philippe Desmet, but without Rene Vandereycken in the midfield and Erwin Vandenburgh in the forward line, who had both been injured, Belgium simply could not summon up enough fire-power.

Three days later Belgium lost its third match in these Finals when it was beaten 4–2 by an equally weakened France, who thus finished one place higher than it had done in 1982. It had been unable to choose Bats, Bossis, Giresse, Platini and Rocheteau, so when Ceulemans raced down the right flank and fired a shot past Albert Rust in the tenth minute, matters looked serious for the French. Against the run of play, however, Jean-Marc Ferreri equalised in the twenty-sixth minute with a fierce right-foot shot from just beyond the penalty box, and three minutes before half-time Papin hit a cross from Tigana past the advancing Pfaff. Nico Claesan made sure that Belgium remained in the game when he struck home a pass from Danny Veyt in the seventy-second minute, and it required goals during extra time from Bernard Genghini and Manuel Amoros from a penalty to provide France with the victory. It thereby equalled the best position it had achieved in the World Cup of 1958; but the players of Belgium could congratulate themselves on reaching their highest position ever.

The Final saw its first twenty minutes taken up with the two teams, Argentina and West Germany measuring each other up, and, as had England and Belgium, West Germany was having a difficult time penetrating the five-man Argentinian midfield. In the twenty-first minute Argentina took the lead, thanks not to a player from that midfield, but to Jose Luis Brown, the sweeper who had kept out of the side Daniel Passarella, captain of the victorious side in the 1978 tournament. He moved into the opposing half and headed a free-kick from the outstanding Jorge Burruchaga past the right shoulder of the advancing Schumacher into the left corner of his goal. If Diego Maradona failed to score in this game, his influence was all-pervasive, and Lothar Mattheaus, his personal watchman, couldn't prevent him having a part in all three goals. It was his foul on Maradona that provided the free-kick from which Brown scored; ten minutes after half-time

# The hand of Diego

Maradona collected the ball in his own half from Enrique, moved forward a fair degree, and then passed it to his left to the dangerous Valdano, who had been involved in the first place and sprinted across the field to strike it fiercely past Schumacher's outreaching left hand into the corner of the net; and then with the score 2-2, with only six minutes left, he fed a pass to Jorge Burruchaga, who had been consistently good throughout the championship but in this particular game had played in a slightly more advanced position, that allowed him to race past Briegel and shoot through the arms of Schumacher to score the final goal.

It proved to be handsome timing, since just before this Argentina had been reminded that one can never, never, never discount West Germany. With Rummenigge, Voller and Littbarski far from fully fit, during its first five matches the side from Europe had taken four hundred and eighty minutes to score four goals; but in the space of eight minutes midway through the second half the Germans scored twice. In the seventy-third minute Rummenigge ran forward to knock home a header from Voller, who had come on as substitute for Allofs at half-time, and with only nine to go it was Voller himself who dived in to apply the finishing touch after the gifted attacking right back, Thomas Berthold, gained possession in the penalty area and headed the ball to him.

That winning goal from Burruchaga, therefore, was vitally significant. It ensured that the trophy passed into the hands of a team which had known when to bring the forceful Enrique and the combative Olarticoechea into its midfield, and who 'were worthy world champions' according to the West German manager, Franz Beckenbauer, and a team that profited from the genius of the most talented player of his time – Diego Armando Maradona.

## Semi-Final Stage

ARGENTINA 2, BELGIUM 0 (0–0) Maradona (2) for Argentina.
ARGENTINA: Pumpido; Ruggeri, Brown, Cuciuffo; Giusti, Enrique, Batista, Burruchaga (Bochini 84), Olarticoechea; Valdano, Maradona.
BELGIUM: Pfaff; Gerets, Renquin (Desmet 66), De Mol, Vervoot; Scifo, Veyt, Broos, Ceulemans, Vercauteren; Claesen.

WEST GERMANY 2, FRANCE 0 (1–0) Brehme, Voller for West Germany
WEST GERMANY: Schumacher; Berthold, Jakobs, K. Forster, Brehme; Mattheaus, Magath, Eder, Rolff; Rummenigge (Voller 56), Allofs.
FRANCE: Bats; Ayache, Bossis, Battiston, Amoros; Fernandez, Giresse (Vercruysse 72), Tigana, Platini; Bellone (Xuereb 66), Stopyra.

## Third Place Match played at Puebla

FRANCE 4, BELGIUM 2 (2–1) a.e.t. Ferreri, Papin, Genghini and Amoros for France; Ceulemans, Claesen for Belgium.

FRANCE: Rust; Ayache, Battiston, Le Roux (Bossis 53), Amoros; Bibard, Ferreri, Tigana, Vercruysse; Papin, Bellone.
BELGIUM: Pfaff; Gerets, Renquin (F. Van der Elst 46), De Mol, Veroort; Scifo (L. Van der Elst 64), Grun, Mommens, Ceulemans; Veyt, Claesen.

## Final played in Mexico City

ARGENTINA 3, WEST GERMANY 2 (1–0) Brown, Valdano and Burruchaga for Argentina; Rummenigge and Voller for West Germany.

## The hand of Diego

ARGENTINA: Pumpido; Ruggeri, Brown, Cuciuffo; Giusti, Enrique, Batista, Burruchaga (Trobbiani 90), Olarticoechea; Valdano, Maradona.

WEST GERMANY: Schumacher; Berthold, Jakobs, K. Forster, Brehme; Mattheaus, Magath (Hoeness 61), Eder, Briegel; K-H Rummenigge, Allofs (Voller 46).

# Final Classification 1986

|     |                  | P | W | D | L | F  | A  |
|-----|------------------|---|---|---|---|----|----|
| 1.  | ARGENTINA        | 7 | 6 | 1 | 0 | 14 | 5  |
| 2.  | WEST GERMANY     | 7 | 3 | 2 | 2 | 8  | 7  |
| 3.  | FRANCE           | 7 | 5 | 1 | 1 | 12 | 6  |
| 4.  | BELGIUM          | 7 | 2 | 2 | 3 | 12 | 15 |
| 5.  | BRAZIL           | 5 | 4 | 1 | 0 | 10 | 1  |
| 6.  | MEXICO           | 5 | 3 | 2 | 0 | 6  | 2  |
| 7.  | SPAIN            | 5 | 3 | 1 | 1 | 11 | 4  |
| 8.  | ENGLAND          | 5 | 2 | 1 | 2 | 7  | 3  |
| 9.  | DENMARK          | 4 | 3 | 0 | 1 | 10 | 6  |
| 10. | SOVIET UNION     | 4 | 2 | 1 | 1 | 12 | 5  |
| 11. | MOROCCO          | 4 | 1 | 2 | 1 | 3  | 2  |
| 12. | ITALY            | 4 | 1 | 2 | 1 | 5  | 6  |
| 13. | PARAGUAY         | 4 | 1 | 2 | 1 | 4  | 6  |
| 14. | POLAND           | 4 | 1 | 1 | 2 | 1  | 7  |
| 15. | BULGARIA         | 4 | 0 | 2 | 2 | 2  | 6  |
| 16. | URUGUAY          | 4 | 0 | 2 | 2 | 2  | 8  |
| 17. | PORTUGAL         | 3 | 1 | 0 | 2 | 2  | 4  |
| 18. | HUNGARY          | 3 | 1 | 0 | 2 | 2  | 9  |
| 19. | SCOTLAND         | 3 | 0 | 1 | 2 | 1  | 3  |
| 20. | SOUTH KOREA      | 3 | 0 | 1 | 2 | 4  | 7  |
| 21. | NORTHERN IRELAND | 3 | 0 | 1 | 2 | 2  | 6  |
| 22. | ALGERIA          | 3 | 0 | 1 | 2 | 1  | 5  |
| 23. | IRAQ             | 3 | 0 | 0 | 3 | 0  | 5  |
| 24. | CANADA           | 3 | 0 | 0 | 3 | 0  | 5  |

# 6 SOME STATISTICS

## Number of Entries

1930 in Uruguay – 13
1934 in Italy – 32
1938 in France – 36
1950 in Brazil – 32
1954 in Switzerland – 38
1958 in Sweden – 53
1962 in Chile – 56
1966 in England – 71
1970 in Mexico – 70
1974 in West Germany – 99
1978 in Argentina – 106
1982 in Spain – 109
1986 in Mexico – 121
1990 in Italy – 114

## Attendances at Final Matches

1930 at Montevideo–90,000   URUGUAY 4 ARGENTINA 2
1934 at Rome–50,000   ITALY 2 CZECHOSLOVAKIA 1
(after extra time)
1938 at Paris–45,000   ITALY 4 HUNGARY 2
1950 at Rio de Janeiro–199,850   URUGUAY 2 BRAZIL 1
1954 at Berne–60,000   WEST GERMANY 3 HUNGARY 2
1958 at Stockholm–49,737   BRAZIL 5 SWEDEN 2
1962 at Santiago–68,679   BRAZIL 3 CZECHOSLOVAKIA 1
1966 at London–93,802   ENGLAND 4 WEST GERMANY 2
(after extra time)
1970 at Mexico City–107,412   BRAZIL 4 ITALY 1
1974 at Munich–77,833   WEST GERMANY 2 HOLLAND 1
1978 at Buenos Aires–77,000   ARGENTINA 3 HOLLAND 1
(after extra time)
1982 at Madrid–90,089   ITALY 3 WEST GERMANY 1
1986 at Mexico City–115,026   ARGENTINA 3 WEST GERMANY 2

## Analysis of the winning teams in the World Cup

|      |         | P | W | D | L | F  | A |
|------|---------|---|---|---|---|----|---|
| 1930 | URUGUAY | 4 | 4 | 0 | 0 | 15 | 3 |

*15 players used.* Ballesteros, Nasazzi, Cea, Andrade (J), Fernandez, Gestido, Iriarte 4 apps. each; Dorado, Mascheroni, Scarone 3 each; Castro, Anselmo 2 each; Tejera, Petrone, Urdinaran 1 each.

## Some statistics

**1934 ITALY**      5   4   1   0   12   3
*17 players used.* Combi, Allemandi, Monti, Meazza, Orsi 5 each; Monzeglio, Bertolini, Schiavio, Ferrari, Guiata 4 each; Ferraris IV 3; Pizziolo 2; Rosetta, Guarisi, Castellazzi, Borel, Demaris 1 each.

**1938 ITALY**      4   4   0   0   11   5
*14 players used.* Olivieri, Rava, Serantoni, Andreolo, Locatelli, Meazza, Piolo, Ferrari 4 each; Foni, Biavati, Colaussi 3 each; Monzeglio, Pasinati, Ferraris 1 each.

**1950 URUGUAY**      4   3   1   0   15   5
*14 players used.* Gonzales M., Tejera, Valera, Andrade R., Ghiggia, Perez, Miguez, Schiaffino 4 each; Maspoli, Vidal 3 each; Gonzales W., Gambetta 2 each; Paz, Moran 1 each.

**1954 WEST GERMANY**      6   5   0   1   25   14
*18 players used.* Eckel, Walter F. 6 each; Turek, Kohlmeyer, Posipal, Mai, Morlock, Walter O., Schafer 5 each; Liebrich, Rahn 4 each; Laband 3; Klodt, Bauer 2 each; Mebus, Hermann, Kwaitowski, Pfaff 1 each.

**1958 BRAZIL**      6   5   1   0   16   4
*16 players used.* Gilmar, Nilton Santos, Bellini, Orlando, Didi, Zagalo 6 each; De Sordi 5; Vavà, Zito, Garrincha, Pelé 4 each; Mazzola 3; Dino, Joel 2 each; Djalma Santos, Didì 1 each.

**1962 BRAZIL**      6   5   1   0   14   5
*12 players used (the lowest number by any Winner).* Gilmar, Santos D., Santos N., Zozimo, Mauro, Zito, Didì, Vava, Garrincha, Zagalo 6 each; Amarildo 4; Pelé 2.

**1966 ENGLAND**      6   5   1   0   14   3
*15 players used.* Banks, Cohen, Wilson, Stiles, Charlton J., Moore, Hunt, Charlton R. 6 each; Peters 5; Ball 4; Greaves, Hurst 3 each; Paine, Callaghan, Connelly 1 each.

**1970 BRAZIL**      6   6   0   0   19   7
*16 players used.* Felix, Carlos, Alberto, Piazza, Brito, Clodoaldo, Jairzinho, Pelé, Tostao 6 each; Everaldo, Rivelino 5 each; Gerson 4; Paulo Cesar 2 + 2 subs; Marco Antonio 1 + 1 sub; Roberto 2 subs; Fontana 1; Edu 1 sub.

**1974 WEST GERMANY**      7   6   0   1   13   4
*18 players used.* Maier, Vogts, Breitner, Schwarzenbeck, Beckenbauer, Muller, Overath 7 each; Hoeness 6 + 1 sub; Grabowski 5 + 1 sub; Bonhof 4; Holzenbein 4 + 2 subs; Cullman 3; Heynckes, Herzog 2 each; Flohe 1 + 2 subs; Wimmer 1 + 1 sub; Netzer, Hottges 1 sub each.

1978 ARGENTINA 7 5 1 1 15 4
*17 players used.* Fillol, Galvan L., Olguin, Passarella, Tarantini, Gallego, Kempès 7 each; Ardiles 6; Bertoni 5 + 1 sub; Ortiz 4 + 2 subs; Luque 5; Houseman 3 + 3 subs; Valencia 4; Larrosa 1 + 1 sub; Alonso 3 subs; Villa 2 subs.

1982 ITALY 7 4 3 0 12 6
*15 players used.* Zoff, Cabrini, Collovati, Scirea, Conti B., Tardelli, Rossi, Graziani 7 each; Antognoni, Gentile 6 each; Oriali 5; Marini 2 + 3 subs; Bergomi 2 + 1 sub; Altobelli 3 subs; Causio 2 subs.

1986 ARGENTINA 7 6 1 0 14 5
*18 players used.* Pumpido, Brown, Ruggeri, Giusti, Batista, Burruchaga, Maradona, Valdano 7 each; Cuciuffo 6; Garre 4; Olarticoechea 3 + 4 subs; Enrique 3 + 2 subs; Borghi, Pasculli 2; Clausen 1; Tapin 2 subs; Bochini, Trobbiani 1 sub.

Uruguay (1930), Italy (1938) and Brazil (1970) have been the only winners with 100% records.

# Leading Scorers

| 1930 | 8 | STABILE (Argentina) |
| | 5 | CEA (Uruguay) |
| 1934 | 4 | SCHIAVIO (Italy), CONEN (Germany) and NEJEDLY (Czechoslovakia) |
| 1938 | 8 | LEONIDAS (Brazil) |
| | 7 | SZENGELLER (Hungary) |
| | 5 | PIOLA (Italy) |
| 1950 | 7 | ADEMIR (Brazil) |
| | 5 | SCHIAFFINO (Uruguay), BASORA (Spain) |
| 1954 | 11 | KOCSIS (Hungary) |
| | 6 | MORLOCK (West Germany), PROBST (Austria) |
| | 5 | HUGI (Switzerland) |
| 1958 | 13 | FONTAINE (France) |
| | 6 | PELÉ (Brazil), RAHN (West Germany) |
| | 5 | VAVA (Brazil), McPARLAND (Northern Ireland) |
| 1962 | 5 | JERKOVIC (Yugoslavia) |
| | 4 | ALBERT (Hungary), GARRINCHA (Brazil), IVANOV (USSR), SANCHEZ (Chile), VAVA (Brazil) |
| 1966 | 9 | EUSEBIO (Portugal) |
| | 5 | HALLER (West Germany) |
| | 4 | HURST (England), BENE (Hungary), PORKUIAN (USSR), BECKENBAUER (West Germany) |

## Some statistics

1970   10  MULLER (West Germany)
       7  JAIRZINHO (Brazil) who scored in each game played by the Winners
       5  CUBILLAS (Peru)

1974    7  LATO (Poland)
       5  SZARMACH (Poland), NEESKENS (Holland)
       4  MULLER (West Germany), REP (Holland), EDSTROEM (Sweden)

1978    6  KEMPÈS (Argentina)
       5  RENSENBRINK (Holland), CUBILLAS (Peru)
       4  LUQUE (Argentina), KRANKL (Austria)

1982    6  ROSSI (Italy)
       5  RUMMENIGGE (West Germany)
       4  BONIEK (Poland), ZICO (Brazil)

1986    6  LINEKER (England)
       5  BUTRAGUENO (Spain), CARECA (Brazil), MARADONA (Argentina)
       4  ALTOBELLI (Italy), BELANOV (USSR), ELKAER-LARSEN (Denmark), VALDANO (Argentina)

*Placed together the best individual goal-scoring performances in the World Cup Final tournaments go like this:*

| | |
|---|---|
| 13 Fontaine 1958 | 6 Probst 1954 |
| 11 Kocsis 1954 |    Morlock 1954 |
| 10 Muller 1970 |    Pelé 1958 |
|  9 Eusebio 1966 |    Rahn 1958 |
|  8 Stabile 1930 |    Kempes 1978 |
|    Leonidas 1938 |    Rossi 1982 |
|  7 Szengeller 1938 |    Lineker 1986 |
|    Ademir 1950 | |
|    Jairzinho 1970 | |
|    Lato 1974 | |

*The catalogue of best all-time goal-scorers is as follows:*

14 Muller (West Germany) in 1970 and 1974
13 Fontaine (France) in 1958
12 Pelé (Brazil) in 1958, 1962, 1966 and 1970
11 Kocsis (Hungary) in 1954
10 Cubillas (Peru) in 1970 and 1978
   Lato (Poland) in 1974, 1978 and 1982
   Rahn (West Germany) in 1954 and 1958

9   Eusebio (Portugal) in 1966
    Jairzinho (Brazil) in 1970 and 1974
    Rossi (Italy) in 1978 and 1982
    Seeler (West Germany) in 1958, 1962, 1966 and 1970
    Vava (Brazil) in 1958 and 1962
8   Leonidas (Brazil) in 1938
    Stabile (Argentina) in 1930
    Rummenigge (West Germany) in 1978, 1982 and 1986

# Some Interesting Records

ANTONIO CARBAJAL (Mexico) is the player to have appeared in most World Cup tournaments. He kept goal in 1950, 1954, 1958, 1962 and 1966.

UWE SEELER (West Germany) is one of the two players to have appeared in most matches, playing on 21 occasions in the Finals of 1958, 1962, 1966 and 1970. The other is WLADISLAV ZMUDA (Poland) who played in the Finals of 1974, 1978, 1982 and 1986.

MARIO ZAGALO (Brazil) is the only man so far to have played in (1958 and 1962) and managed (1970) winning teams.

BRYAN ROBSON (England) became the scorer of the *fastest goal* in the history of the World Cup when he scored after only 27 seconds in the match against France on 16 June 1982.

NORMAN WHITESIDE (Northern Ireland) became the *youngest* player ever to compete in a World Cup Final tournament when he played against Yugoslavia on 17 June 1982.

When PORTUGAL defeated WEST GERMANY by 1-0 on 16 October 1985, it was the first occasion that the country had been beaten in the Qualifying Rounds of a World Cup tournament (it failed to enter in 1930, was banned from entry 20 years later and was victorious in the 1954 and the 1974 editions of the tournament, the last of which it hosted). Before this historic defeat it had won 32 and drawn four of its 36 matches. A truly astonishing record.

GEOFF HURST (England) is the only player to date to have scored a hat-trick in a World Cup Final but the record for scoring goals in any World Cup match is four, a feat which has been achieved on nine occasions:

**Some statistics** 135

| | |
|---|---|
| GUSTAV WETTERSTROEM | Sweden v Cuba 1938 |
| LEONIDAS DA SILVA | Brazil v Poland 1938 |
| ERNEST WILLIMOWSKI | Poland v Brazil 1938 |
| ADEMIR | Brazil v Sweden 1950 |
| JUAN SCHIAFFINO | Uruguay v Bolivia 1950 |
| SANDOR KOCSIS | Hungary v West Germany 1954 |
| JUST FONTAINE | France v West Germany 1958 |
| EUSEBIO | Portugal v North Korea 1966 |
| BUTRAGUENO | Spain v Denmark 1986 |

# Goal milestones in the World Cup

1st goal: LAURENT (France) 13 July 1930 against Mexico (4–1)
100th goal: JONASSON (Sweden) 1934 against Argentina (3–2)
200th goal: WETTERSTROEM (Sweden) 1938 against Cuba (8–0)
300th goal: CHICO (Brazil) 1950 against Spain (6–1)
400th goal: LEFTER (Turkey) 1954 against West Germany (2–7)
500th goal: RAHN (West Germany) 1958 against Czechoslovakia (2–2)
600th goal: JERKOVIC (Yugoslavia) 1962 against Hungary (3–1)
700th goal: BOBBY CHARLTON (England) 1966 against Mexico (2–0)
800th goal: JAIRZINHO (Brazil) 1970 against England (1–0)
900th goal: YAZALDE (Argentina) 1974 against Haiti (4–1)
1000th goal: RENSENBRINK (Holland) 1978 against Scotland (2–3)
1100th goal: BLOKHIN (USSR) 1982 against New Zealand (3–0)
1200th goal: PAPIN (France) 1986 against Canada (1–0)
1300th goal: LINEKER (England) 1986 against Paraguay (3–0)
1400th goal: ................................................................
1500th goal: ................................................................

# Attendances and Goals World Cup 1930–1986

| YEAR | VENUE | ATTENDANCES | AVERAGE | MATCHES | GOALS | AVERAGE |
|------|-------|-------------|---------|---------|-------|---------|
| 1930 | URUGUAY | 434,500 | 24,139 | 18 | 70 | 3.88 |
| 1934 | ITALY | 395,000 | 23,235 | 17 | 70 | 4.11 |
| 1938 | FRANCE | 483,000 | 26,833 | 18 | 84 | 4.66 |
| 1950 | BRAZIL | 1,337,000 | 60,772 | 22 | 88 | 4.00 |
| 1954 | SWITZERLAND | 943,000 | 36,270 | 26 | 140 | 5.38 |
| 1958 | SWEDEN | 868,000 | 24,800 | 35 | 126 | 3.60 |
| 1962 | CHILE | 776,000 | 24,250 | 32 | 89 | 2.78 |
| 1966 | ENGLAND | 1,614,677 | 50,458 | 32 | 89 | 2.78 |
| 1970 | MEXICO | 1,673,975 | 52,312 | 32 | 95 | 2.96 |
| 1974 | WEST GERMANY | 1,774,022 | 46,685 | 38 | 97 | 2.55 |
| 1978 | ARGENTINA | 1,610,215 | 42,374 | 38 | 102 | 2.68 |
| 1982 | SPAIN | 1,766,277 | 33,967 | 52 | 146 | 2.8 |
| 1986 | MEXICO | 2,406,511 | 47,432 | 52 | 132 | 2.54 |

## Some statistics
# The Trophy

The Jules Rimet Trophy – won outright by the Brazilians in 1970 on account of their third victory – was designed by the French sculptor, Abel Lafleur, stood a foot high and weighed in the region of nine pounds of gold. The present trophy – competed for in 1974 for the first time and known as the FIFA World Cup – was designed by an Italian, Silvio Gazzaniga, cost £8,000, was made in eighteen-carat gold and weighs about ten pounds.

*Only six countries have won the World Cup:*

Brazil (1958, 1962 and 1970), Italy (1934, 1938 and 1982), Uruguay (1930 and 1950), West Germany (1954 and 1974), Argentina (1978 and 1986), and England (1966).

Of these, Brazil is the only country to have gained all her victories away from home (she unexpectedly lost the 1950 Final match to Uruguay in Rio de Janeiro) in addition to being the only country to succeed in different continents (Sweden in 1958 and Mexico in 1970).

*'Host' countries for the final stages have been:*

Uruguay (1930)
Italy (1934)
England (1966)
West Germany (1974)
and Argentina (1978)

*The only players to have the distinction of gaining winners' medals in TWO World Cups are:*

GIOVANNI FERRARI (Italy 1934 and 1938)
GIUSEPPE MEAZZA (Italy 1934 and 1938)
and
PELÉ (Brazil 1958 and 1970) – the only man to have scored in two Finals.

# Expulsions During Previous Tournaments

| | |
|---|---|
| URUGUAY 1930 | Cierro (Argentina) |
| FRANCE 1938 | Machados and Zeze (Brazil) Riha (Czechoslovakia) |
| SWITZERLAND 1954 | Nilton Santos and Tozzi (Brazil) Bozsik (Hungary) |
| SWEDEN 1958 | Bubernik (Czechoslovakia) Sipos (Hungary) Juskowiak (West Germany) |
| CHILE 1962 | David and Ferrini (Italy) |
| ENGLAND 1966 | Rattin (Argentina) Silva and Troche (Uruguay) |
| WEST GERMANY 1974 | Caszely (Chile) Richards (Australia) Ndaye (Zaire) Montero Castillo (Uruguay) Luis Pereira (Brazil) |
| ARGENTINA 1978 | Nyilasi and Toroscik (Hungary) Naninga (Holland) |
| SPAIN 1982 | Vizek (Czechoslovakia), Gilberto Yearwood (Honduras), Donaghy (Northern Ireland), Gallego and Maradona (Argentina) |
| MEXICO 1986 | Sweeney (Canada), Wilkins (England), Gourgies (Iraq), Bossio and Batista (Uruguay), Arnesen (Denmark), Berthold (West Germany), Aguirre (Mexico) |

# 7 SUMMARY OF MATCHES IN WORLD CUP FINALS 1930–1986

|  | Q | P | W | D | L | F | A | Pts. |
|---|---|---|---|---|---|---|---|---|
| *BRAZIL | 13 | 62 | 41 | 10 | 11 | 144 | 63 | 92 |
| *WEST GERMANY | 11 | 61 | 35 | 12 | 24 | 130 | 85 | 83 |
| *ITALY | 11 | 47 | 25 | 11 | 11 | 79 | 52 | 61 |
| *ARGENTINA | 9 | 41 | 22 | 6 | 13 | 77 | 55 | 50 |
| FRANCE | 9 | 34 | 16 | 4 | 14 | 71 | 56 | 36 |
| HUNGARY | 9 | 32 | 15 | 3 | 14 | 87 | 57 | 33 |
| MEXICO | 9 | 29 | 6 | 5 | 18 | 27 | 64 | 17 |
| *ENGLAND | 8 | 34 | 15 | 9 | 10 | 47 | 32 | 39 |
| *URUGUAY | 8 | 33 | 14 | 7 | 12 | 59 | 47 | 35 |
| *SWEDEN | 7 | 28 | 11 | 6 | 11 | 48 | 46 | 28 |
| *YUGOSLAVIA | 7 | 28 | 11 | 6 | 11 | 47 | 36 | 28 |
| *SPAIN | 7 | 28 | 11 | 5 | 12 | 37 | 34 | 27 |
| *CZECHOSLOVAKIA | 7 | 25 | 8 | 5 | 12 | 34 | 40 | 21 |
| *BELGIUM | 7 | 21 | 6 | 3 | 12 | 27 | 45 | 15 |
| *USSR | 6 | 28 | 14 | 6 | 8 | 49 | 30 | 34 |
| CHILE | 6 | 21 | 7 | 3 | 11 | 26 | 32 | 17 |
| SWITZERLAND | 6 | 18 | 5 | 2 | 11 | 28 | 44 | 12 |
| *SCOTLAND | 6 | 17 | 3 | 6 | 8 | 21 | 32 | 12 |
| POLAND | 5 | 25 | 13 | 5 | 8 | 39 | 29 | 31 |
| *AUSTRIA | 5 | 23 | 11 | 2 | 10 | 38 | 40 | 24 |
| BULGARIA | 5 | 16 | 0 | 6 | 10 | 11 | 35 | 6 |
| *HOLLAND | 4 | 16 | 8 | 3 | 5 | 32 | 19 | 19 |
| PERU | 4 | 15 | 4 | 3 | 8 | 19 | 31 | 11 |
| PARAGUAY | 4 | 11 | 3 | 4 | 4 | 16 | 25 | 10 |
| *RUMANIA | 4 | 8 | 2 | 1 | 5 | 12 | 17 | 5 |
| NORTHERN IRELAND | 3 | 13 | 3 | 5 | 5 | 14 | 23 | 11 |
| *UNITED STATES | 3 | 7 | 3 | 0 | 9 | 12 | 21 | 6 |
| PORTUGAL | 2 | 9 | 6 | 0 | 3 | 19 | 12 | 12 |
| MOROCCO | 2 | 7 | 1 | 3 | 3 | 5 | 8 | 5 |
| ALGERIA | 2 | 6 | 2 | 1 | 3 | 6 | 10 | 5 |
| *SOUTH KOREA | 2 | 5 | 0 | 1 | 4 | 4 | 23 | 1 |
| EL SALVADOR | 2 | 6 | 0 | 0 | 6 | 1 | 22 | 0 |
| BOLIVIA | 2 | 3 | 0 | 0 | 3 | 0 | 16 | 0 |
| DENMARK | 1 | 4 | 3 | 0 | 1 | 10 | 6 | 6 |
| EAST GERMANY | 1 | 6 | 2 | 2 | 2 | 5 | 5 | 6 |
| WALES | 1 | 5 | 1 | 3 | 1 | 4 | 4 | 5 |
| NORTH KOREA | 1 | 4 | 1 | 1 | 2 | 5 | 9 | 3 |
| TUNISIA | 1 | 3 | 1 | 1 | 1 | 3 | 2 | 3 |

| | | | | | | | | |
|---|---|---|---|---|---|---|---|---|
| *CAMEROON | 1 | 3 | 0 | 3 | 0 | 1 | 1 | 3 |
| CUBA | 1 | 3 | 1 | 1 | 1 | 5 | 12 | 3 |
| HONDURAS | 1 | 3 | 0 | 2 | 1 | 2 | 3 | 2 |
| ISRAEL | 1 | 3 | 0 | 2 | 1 | 1 | 3 | 2 |
| TURKEY | 1 | 3 | 1 | 0 | 2 | 10 | 11 | 2 |
| *COLOMBIA | 1 | 3 | 0 | 1 | 2 | 5 | 11 | 1 |
| KUWAIT | 1 | 3 | 0 | 1 | 2 | 2 | 6 | 1 |
| IRAN | 1 | 3 | 0 | 1 | 2 | 2 | 8 | 1 |
| AUSTRALIA | 1 | 3 | 0 | 1 | 2 | 0 | 5 | 1 |
| NEW ZEALAND | 1 | 3 | 0 | 0 | 3 | 2 | 12 | 0 |
| HAITI | 1 | 3 | 0 | 0 | 3 | 2 | 14 | 0 |
| IRAQ | 1 | 3 | 0 | 0 | 3 | 1 | 4 | 0 |
| CANADA | 1 | 3 | 0 | 0 | 3 | 0 | 5 | 0 |
| ZAIRE | 1 | 3 | 0 | 0 | 1 | 0 | 14 | 0 |
| NORWAY | 1 | 1 | 0 | 0 | 1 | 1 | 2 | 0 |
| *EGYPT | 1 | 1 | 0 | 0 | 1 | 2 | 4 | 0 |
| DUTCH EAST INDIES | 1 | 1 | 0 | 0 | 1 | 0 | 6 | 0 |

*Countries that have qualified

The REPUBLIC OF IRELAND, the UNITED ARAB EMIRATES and COSTA RICA are appearing for the first time.

As can be noted BRAZIL is the only country to have participated in all of the final tournaments; WEST GERMANY, who did not enter the original tournament, was barred from entering in 1950; while ITALY, who also chose to avoid the first World Cup, was prevented from competing in 1958 after being knocked out of the qualifying group by NORTHERN IRELAND.

It is interesting to compare the records of HOLLAND (19 points from 16 matches), POLAND (31 points from 25 matches) and PORTUGAL (12 points from 9 matches) with those of MEXICO (17 points from 29 matches); as it is to note that from merely 4 matches DENMARK has acquired the same number of points (6) as has BULGARIA, although requiring only a quarter of the number of games; and that from its one appearance in 1958 WALES has scored as many points as RUMANIA, who has appeared on 4 occasions.

# 8 THE TEAMS WHO WILL BE COMPETING

Of the total of 152 countries which have taken part in all stages of the World Cup since the competition started in 1930, 114 entered for the finals of 1990 (including Italy, the Hosts, and Argentina, the current champions). Twenty-four teams will partake in the events in June and early July after seeing a total of 692 goals from 313 matches played over a period of 19 months.

On this occasion certain teams qualified who had been Finalists or Semi-finalists in previous competitions, but who had been absent in 1986: AUSTRIA, CZECHOSLOVAKIA, HOLLAND, SWEDEN and YUGOSLAVIA from Europe together with the UNITED STATES (Semi-finalists in the 1930 World Cup) from the CONCACAF Group. Their participation promises a considerably stronger World Cup than that of 1986. Those not taking part, however include HUNGARY (Finalists in 1938 and 1954), FRANCE (Semi-finalists in 1958, 1982 and 1986), CHILE (Semi-finalists in 1962), PORTUGAL (Semi-finalists in 1966) and POLAND (Semi-finalists in 1974 and 1982). Only nine countries have taken part in the last three editions of the tournament: BELGIUM, ENGLAND, ITALY, SCOTLAND, SOVIET UNION, SPAIN and WEST GERMANY from Europe and ARGENTINA and BRAZIL from South America.

Drama certainly existed during the first weekend in September 1989. First came the deaths in motoring accidents of past heroes of the World Cup in Kazimierz Deyna (Poland 1974, 1978) and Gaetano Scirea (Italy 1978, 1982 and 1986), which were succeeded on 3 September by a monstrous display of cheating which made that used by Maradona to score with 'The Hand of God' appear trivial. It occurred during the final match in the South American Group 3 between Brazil and Chile. Trouble had been expected. During the first match between these sides, a 1–1 draw at Santiago on 22 August, two players had been sent off the field within the first twelve minutes, a further seven booked and the match had been punctuated by bouts of fisticuffs and general mayhem. Despite attempts to cool matters down between the sides, it came as little surprise when the Brazil-Chile match at Maracana Stadium was stopped in the sixty-ninth minute (with Brazil leading 1–0 through a goal by Careca), when a flare appeared to strike the Chilean goalkeeper, Roberto Rojas. Chile's players promptly marched off the pitch – and in doing so forfeited the match, which was granted to Brazil by FIFA a week later 2–0 (making it the only country to have played in all final tournaments, although Brazil would have much preferred to gain the ultimate victory on the field of play rather than at a table of judgement). The incident appeared serious – and it was, but for the wrong reason. An inquiry discovered that the flare had not struck Rojas, and that the 'blood' on his head turned out to be red dye secreted inside a bracelet. Rojas was later banned from international competition for life, along with the association's doctor and president, and the team manager and vice-captain were banned for five years. Chile was debarred from participating in the 1994 World Cup.

The other moment of true drama affected the United States, who knew they were to be Hosts in 1994, but intended to qualify on this occasion to show the world that they planned to take the event seriously. In the absence of Mexico, banned from playing international football for two years due to playing overage players in an Under-20 tournament, Costa Rica took a commanding position at the top of the Central and North American Qualifying Group, gaining 11 points from its 8 games, all played between March and July 1989. Although at one stage Trinidad and Tobago seemed likely to join them, at the last the team representing the United States foiled them. On 17 September the United States beat El Salvador 1–0 in Tecigulpa in Honduras, thanks to a goal scored in the second half by Hugo Perez (who was born in El Salvador), but they were unable to score in the return match, which finished as a goalless draw, as had the match away to Guatemala. The United States, therefore, had to register a victory

# The teams who will be competing

in its final match against Trinidad and Tobago, who only required a draw to be sure of qualifying.

This confrontation took place on 19 November, in Port of Spain and in front of 30,000 impassioned fans who had taken up their places fully five hours before the start of the match, who wore red favours and were determined to see the team from Trinidad become the first side from the West Indies ever to qualify for the World Cup Finals. They went away disappointed, with the only goal being scored for the United States after 30 minutes by Paul Caligiuri, and Trinidad not able to penetrate an outstanding defence, in particular the young goalkeeper, Tony Meola. It was a disappointing finish for Trinidad, who had won the opening match of the entire competition by defeating Guyana in Georgetown on 17 April 1988, and brought back memories of 1973 when they again failed to win a final, deciding contest (on that occasion against Haiti). For the United States, however, who were the last to qualify, 19 November 1989 became a date equal in importance to that of 29 June 1950 when they unexpectedly defeated England 1–0 at Belo Horizonte in Brazil during the 1950 World Cup – as well as a most handsome portent for the World Cup of 1994.

## Group A: Italy

*Federazione Italiana Giuoco Calcio founded 1898. Joined FIFA 1905.*

*Previous appearances:* 1934 (Winners), 1938 (Winners), 1950, 1954, 1962, 1966, 1970 (Finalists), 1974, 1978 (Fourth), 1982 (Winners) and 1986.

*Present tournament:* Qualified automatically as Hosts.

*The manager and players:* the charming AZEGLIO VICINI (54), assistant to ENZO BEARZOT, took over when he resigned in 1986 and has seen an almost complete replenishment of players. WALTER ZENGA (30 on 28 April) is another in a fine line of Italian goalkeepers with STEFANO TACCONI (33 on 13 May) and GIANLUCA PAGLIUCA (23) as his deputies. The defence will be drawn from GIUSEPPE BERGOMI (26), who played in the 1982 and 1986 World Cups, while as stopper will be his clubmate with Internazionale RICCARDO FERRI (26), and the other two members of the defence come from A.C.Milan – the authoritative libero FRANCO BARESI (30 on 8 May), the promising PAULO MALDINI (22 on 26 June), whose father, Cesare, played in the 1962 World Cup, while the reserves will be CIRO FERRARI (23) who played in the 1988 Olympic team, PIETRO VIERCHOWOD (31), LUCA DE AGOSTINI (29 on 7 April) and GIOVANNI FRANCINI (26). In midfield will be ROBERTO DONADONI (26), FERNANDO DE NAPOLI (26), NICOLA BERTI (24), CARLO ANCELOTTI (31 on 10 June), that brilliant attacking goal-scorer ROBERTO BAGGIO (23), GIANCARLO MAROCCHI (25 on 4 July), LUCA FUSI (27 on 7 June) and the playmaker for Roma GIUSEPPE GIAN-NINI (25). In attack will be ALDO SERENA (29), ROBERTO MANCINI (25), ANDREA CARNEVALE (29) who played in the 1988 Olympic team, GIANLUCA VIALLI (26 on 9 July), another player to have played in the 1986 World Cup, and maybe SALVATORE SCHILLACI (25) will be brought in at the last moment. Playing at grounds familiar to them will undoubtedly be an advantage to the Italian players, although their supporters can be very fickle, and are not slow to turn against their team when matters go less than smoothly.

## United States

*United States Soccer Federation founded 1913. Joined FIFA 1913.*

*Previous tournaments:* 1930 (Semi-finalists), 1934 and 1950.

*Present competition:* Finished Second in CONCACAF Group with 11 points from 8 games behind COSTA RICA (0–1 away and 1–0 at home) but ahead of TRINIDAD AND TOBAGO (1–0 at home and 1–0 away), GUATEMALA (2–1 at home and 0–0 away) and EL SALVADOR (1–0 away and 0–0 at home).

*The manager and team:* Born in Hungary 1 July 1941, BOB GANSLER came to the United States when he was eleven, and went on to play in the Olympic Games of 1964 and 1968. He was put in charge of the United States team at the start of 1989, and straightaway took the USA squad to Saudi Arabia for the 1989

Pelé and Bobby Moore exchange shirts after Brazil had beaten England 1 – 0 in the 1970 World Cup.

Francis Lee busy in action during the Quarter-final game in the 1970 World Cup which England lost 2 – 3 in extra time after having led 2 – 0. Those watching are Brian Labone, Klaus Fichtel, Franz Beckenbauer, Sepp Maier, Uwe Seeler and Berti Vogts.

World Cup Final 1970. Jairzinho moments after he had scored Brazil's third goal. Pelé is the other Brazilian player while the Italians are Mazzola, Facchetti, Burgnich and De Sisti.

The face of Billy Bremner tells the story as he watches his shot skimming just past on the wrong side of the Brazilian goal. Leao is the beaten goalkeeper, Hay and Piazza the other players.

Daniel Bertoni races away after scoring Argentina's last goal in the 3 – 1 victory over Holland in the 1978 Final. The other players are Mario Kempès, Leopoldo Luque and the beaten goalkeeper is Jan Jongbloed, who is appealing for offside.

Bryan Robson scoring the fastest goal in the hstory of the tournament after only 27 seconds against France. Jean-Luc Ettori is the hapless goalkeeper.

Antonio Cabrini and Gaetano Scirea (No. 7) watching as Claudio Gentile of Italy decidedly does *not* live up to his name. The victim is Diego Maradona of Argentina. In the following match the Italian turned his attentions to the Brazilian Zico.

Paolo Rossi slides the ball past the Brazilian goalkeeper, Waldir Peres, to score his third goal in the 3 – 2 victory over the Brazilians. In the background are Socrates of Brazil (who replied to Rossi's first goal) and Giancarlo Antognoni of Italy who also had an outstanding match.

Gordon Strachan about to score Scotland's only goal of the tournament in the game against West Germany, which they lost 2 – 1. The German defender is Klaus Augenthaler.

The first of three goals scored by Gary Lineker in an uplifting English victory against Poland. The Polish players are Stefan Majewski and goalkeeper Joszef Mlynarczyk, the other English player, Peter Reid.

Michel Platini about to score France's first goal in the 2 – 0 victory against Italy. The Italian player is Antonio Cabrini.

Jan Ceulemans of Belgium dives into the Spanish defence to head the ball past the left arm of Andoni Zubizarreta during the Quarter-final. The other Spanish defender is Ricardo Gallego, currently with Udinese.

Diego Maradona using what he later called 'The Hand of God' to score the first goal of Argentina's 2 – 1 Quarter-final victory against England.

Maradona attempts to absolve his act of fraud by scoring a magical second goal. The goalkeeper is Peter Shilton, the long-legged defender, Terry Butcher.

Rudi Voller heads a goal that confuses the Argentina goalkeeper Nery Pumpido and defender Jorge Olarticoechea and levels the score of the Final at 2 – 2 in the eighty-first minute.

In the eighty-fourth minute Jorge Burruchaga strikes home the final goal in Argentina's 3 – 2 victory against West Germany. The despairing defender is Hans-Peter Briegel, the beaten goalkeeper Harald Schumacher.

# The teams who will be competing

World Youth Cup – where it finished fourth. His goalkeepers are TONY MEOLA (21), DAVID VANOLE (27) and KASEY KELLER (20); while his defence comes from PAUL KRUMPE (27), DESMOND ARMSTRONG (25), STEVE TRITTSCHUH (25 on 24 April), JIMMY BANKS (26), JOHN DOYLE (24), the determined MIKE WINDISCHMANN (24) and MARCELO BALBOA (22). The Uruguayan-born TABARE RAMOS (23) is a creative midfielder and is joined the fearless JOHN HARKES (23) whose grandparents are Scottish, BRIAN BLISS (24), the experienced PAUL CALIGIURI (26) who scored the vital goal against Trinidad and Tobago, JOHN STOLLMEYER (27) and HUGO PEREZ (26) who plays for Red Star, Paris. Among the forwards are BRUCE MURRAY (24), ERIC EICHMANN (25 on 7 May), the goal-scoring BRENT GOULET (26 on 19 May) who has played in England, PHILIP GYAU (25), PETER VERMES (23), a determined central striker who plays in Holland, and FRANK KLOPAS (23) who plays in Greece, although an inspired addition at the final moment could be the London-based ROY WEGERLE (26). The leading scorers were FRANK KLOPAS and HUGO PEREZ with 2 goals each.

## Austria

*Oesterreichischer Fussball-Bund founded in 1904. Joined FIFA 1905.*

*Previous appearances:* 1934 (Fourth), 1954 (Third), 1958, 1978 and 1982 (Second Round).

*Present tournament:* Finished Second in European Group 3 with 9 points from 8 matches behind the SOVIET UNION (0–2 away and 0–0 at home) but ahead of TURKEY (3–2 at home and 0–3 away), EAST GERMANY (1–1 away and 3–0 at home) and ICELAND (0–0 away and 2–1 at home).

*The manager and players:* JOSEF HICKERSBERGER (42 on 27 April), a former international (who played in the 1978 World Cup in Argentina), took over in February 1988 and has steered Austria to its first major competition since 1982. The first-choice goalkeeper will be KLAUS LINDENBERGER (33 on May 28),

MICHAEL KONSEL (28) and OTTO KONRAD (28) being in reserve. The defence will be drawn from ROBERT PECL (24) as stopper, KURT ROSS (25) on his right, the hard tackling ANTON PFEFFER (24) on his left, with as libero the youthful ERNST AIGNER (23) or the experienced HERIBERT WEBER (35 on June 28). Among the midfielders are the fierce-shooting MANFRED ZSAK (25), GERALD WILFURTH (27), MANFRED LINZMAIER (27), with tight-marking PETER ARTNER (24 on 20 May) ANDREAS HERZOG (21) who is a fine attacking midfielder and CHRISTIAN KEGLEVITS (29), the new playmaker in the team following the retirement of that experienced tactician HERBERT PROHASKA (34). Among the forwards are ANDREAS OGRIS (25), the inexperienced HEIMO PFEIFENBERGER (23), GERHARD RODAX (24) who is a star in the making, and ANTON POLSTER (26), who was the leading scorer with 5 out of the total 9 goals.

## Czechoslovakia

*Ceskoslovensky Fotbalovy Svaz founded in 1881. Joined FIFA 1906.*

*Previous appearances:* 1934 (Second), 1938 (Quarter-finalists), 1954, 1958, 1962 (Second), 1970 and 1982.

*Present tournament:* Finished Second in European Group 7 with 12 points from 8 matches behind BELGIUM (0-0 at home and 1-2 away) on goal difference but ahead of PORTUGAL (3-1 at home and 0-0 away), SWITZERLAND (1-0 away and 3-0 at home) and LUXEMBURG (4-0 at home and 2-0 away).

*The manager and players:* JOZEF VENGLOS (53) has been in charge since January 1988 (when he succeeded JOSEF MASOPUST), and has experience of Italian conditions since under his aegis Czechoslovakia defeated Italy on penalties to seize third place in the 1980 European Nations Championship. First-choice goalkeeper is JAN STEJSKAL (27) of Sparta Prague with the experienced LUDEK MIKLOSKO (29) as his deputy; JAN KOCIAN (31) has recently played as sweeper with, in front of him, FRANTISEK STRAKA (31), another experienced central defender, while on the left will be either MIROSLAV

KADIEC (25) or LUDOMIR VIK (25) and on the right JULIUS BIELEK (28). The former libero JOSZEF CHOVANEC (30 on May 7) will play just in front of the defence, while also in midfield will be the skilful LUBOS KUBIK (26), the quick-thinking and fleet-footed LUDOMIR MORAVCIK (25 on June 22), the fierce-shooting MICHAL BILEK (25 on April 13) together with his partner at Sparta Prague IVAN HASEK (26), the hard-running VLADIMIR WEISS (25), and the talented VACLAV NEMECEK (23). Among the forwards will be the highly impressive TOMAS SKUHRAVY (25), the central striker STANISLAV GRIGA (28), and MILAN LUHOVY (26). The leading scorers with 4 each out of the final 13 were TOMAS SKUHRAVY and MICHAL BILEK.

## Group B: Argentina

*Asociacion de Futbol Argentino founded in 1893. Joined FIFA in 1912.*

*Previous appearances:* 1930 (Runners-up), 1934, 1958, 1962, 1966 (Quarter-finalists), 1974 (Second Round), 1978 (Winners), 1982 (Second Round) and 1986 (Winners).

*Present tournament:* Qualified as Victors of the previous tournament.

*The manager and players:* CARLOS SALVADOR BILARDO, 59 and a doctor of medicine, succeeded CESAR LUIS MENOTTI as manager in May 1983 but his plans keep being rudely interrupted by the exodus of the most talented players to Europe. Two such are the first-choice goalkeeper NERY PUMPIDO (32) of Betis and LUIS ISLAS (24) of Logrones who both were in the party for 1986, the third choice being SERGIO GOYOECHEA (25). In contention for the defence are JORGE OLARTICOECHEA (29) and ROBERTO SENSINI (23) with Udinese. OSCAR RUGGERI (28) of Real Madrid is an experienced stopper, JOSE LUIS BROWN (34) is the established libero, and the gifted JUAN SIMON (30), PEDRO MONZON (28) and NESTOR FABBRI (25) have also played. The midfield can call upon the experienced JORGE BURRUCHAGA (27) of Nantes, SERGIO DANIEL BATISTA (27), RICARDO GIUSTI (33),

NESTOR GOROSITO (24), PEDRO TROGLIO (24) who is in Rome playing for Lazio, CARLOS ENRIQUE (27), JOSE BASUALDO (26), GABRIEL CALDERON (30) with Paris Saint Germain and DIEGO MARADONA (29) with Napoli. They will link up with the attack which will be drawn from the long-haired and immensely talented CLAUDIO CANIGGIA (23) who has spent two seasons in Italy, PEDRO PASCULLI (30 on 17 May) who plays for Lecce, CARLOS ALEJANDRO ALFARO MORENO (26), ABEL BALBO (24 on 1 June) who moved in 1989 from River Plate to Udinese, the ball-playing GUSTAVO ABEL DEZOTTI (25) bought by Cremonese from Lazio who likes to make long runs down the left, and Bilardo will hope to use JORGE VALDANO (34) recovered after being struck down by hepatitis in March 1987. As was shown in 1986 when you are blessed with a genius like MARADONA, anything is possible, but . . .

## Soviet Union
*Federation founded 1912. Joined FIFA 1946.*

*Previous appearances:* 1958 (Quarter-finalists), 1962 (Quarter-finalists), 1966 (Fourth), 1970 (Quarter-finalists), 1982 (Second Round) and 1986.

*Present tournament*: Headed European Group 3 with 11 points from 8 matches ahead of AUSTRIA (2–0 at home and 0–0 away), TURKEY (1–0 away and 2–0 at home), EAST GERMANY (3–0 at home and 1–2 away) and ICELAND (1–1 away and 1–1 at home).

*The manager and players:* VALERY LOBANOVSKY (51), who has been in charge of the Soviet team since May 1986, guided it in the European Championship of 1988, in which it lost a thrilling Final to Holland. The outstanding RENAT DASSAEV (33 on 13 April) has lost form since his move to play for Seville in Spain and could well be replaced by VICTOR CHANOV (30) or by the promising DMITRI KHARIN (21). At right-back could be either the experienced VLADIMIR BESSONOV (32) or the young

OLEG LUZNHYI (21). The Toulouse-based VAGIZ KHIDIA-TULLIN (31) is a resourceful libero, OLEG KUZNETSOV (27 on 22 March) a redoubtable stopper, SERGEI GORLUKOVICH (28) will be at left-back, while the experienced ANATOLY DEMI-ANENKO (31) and the promising VALERI KULKOV (24 on 11 June) will also be available. The master of the midfield will be the long-striding ALEXEI MIKHAILICHENKO (27 on 30 March), his companions being FIODOR CHERENKOV (30), ANDREI ZYCMANTOVICH (27), GENNADI LIVTOCHENKO (26), fierce-shooting VASSILY RATS (29 on 25 April), IVAN JAREM-CHUK (28), and the pair playing for Juventus in Torino, SERGEI ALEINIKOV (28) and the graceful ALEXANDR ZAVAROV (29 on 26 April). In the attack will be the resourceful and high-scoring OLEG PROTASOV (26), SERGEI RODIONOV (23), IGOR BELANOV (30 on 20 April), the promising YURI SAVICHEV (25), and another star of the victorious team in the 1988 Olympic games IGOR DOBROVOLSKI (22). GENNADI LIVOCH-ENKO and OLEG PROTASOV were the chief scorers with 3 goals each out of the total 11.

## Rumania

*Federatia Romana de Fotbal founded in 1908. Joined FIFA 1929.*

*Previous appearances:* 1930, 1934, 1938 and 1970.

*Present tournament:* Finished top of European Group 1 with 9 points from 6 games, ahead of DENMARK (0-3 away and 3-1 at home), GREECE (3-0 at home and 0-0 away) and BULGARIA (3-1 away and 1-0 at home).

*The manager and players:* The chess-playing enthusiast EMER-ICH JENEI (52 on 28 March) took over from his predecessor, MIRCEA LUCESCU, in September 1986 a few months after having steered the club side of Steaua Bucharest to victory in the 1986 European Cup, the first side from Eastern Europe to win the trophy. The experienced SILVIU LUNG (33) will be in goal, with BOGDAN STELEA (22) as his deputy. STEFAN IOVAN (29) is an authoritative right-back, IOAN ANDONE (30), NICO-LAE UNGUREANU (33), ADRIAN BUMBESCU (30) form an experienced defence, and MIRCEA REDNIC (28 on 9 April) is a proven full-back with JOSIF ROTARIU (27) as his deputy. Although recently returned after an eleven-month sojourn in Yugoslavia MIODRAG BELODEDECI (26 on 20 May) is an attacking libero of great poise. The key player in midfield is the mercurial GHEORGHE HAGI (25) who has alongside him the goal-scoring GAVRIL BALINT (27), GHEORGHE POPESCU (22), the experienced MICHAEL KLEIN (30) and an immensely promising youngster in IOAN SABAU (22), together with DORIN MATEUT (25), the chief goal-scorer in Europe last season, and DANUT LUPU (23). The star of the attack will be MARIUS LACATUS (26 on 5 April) with alongside him either the experienced RODION CAMATARU (32 on 22 June) or CLAUDIU VAISCOVICI (27). The chief scorers with two goals each were BALINT, CAMATARU, MATEUT and SABAU.

## Cameroon

*Federation Camerounaise de Football founded in 1960. Joined FIFA in 1962.*

*Previous appearance:* 1982.

*Present tournament:* Headed Group table with 9 points from 6 games against NIGERIA (0–2 away and 1–0 at home), ANGOLA (1–1 at home and 2–1 away) and GABON (3–1 away and 2–1 at home). At the semi-final stage Cameroon beat TUNISIA (2–0 at home and 1–0 away).

*The manager and players:* The Soviet coach VALERI NEPOM-NIACIJ (46) will be hoping to emulate Cameroon's last appearance in 1982 when they left the competition unbeaten. He will recall, however, how just weeks before those finals were due to start, the Yugoslavian coach Branko Zutic was replaced by the former French international Jean Vincent. Its outstanding goalkeeper from that tournament, THOMAS N'KONO (34), has been in Spain for the last eight years, but his successor is the inspiring JOSEPH-ANTOINE BELL (35), who plays for Bordeaux and was recently voted the best goalkeeper in France.

## The teams who will be competing

The exceptional captain and right-sided defender is the speedy STEPHEN TATAW (27 on 31 March) who likes to set up attacks, while alongside him could be BENJAMIN MASSING (29 on 20 June), the French-based JEAN-CLAUDE PAGAL (25), JULES DENIS ONANA (31 on 12 June), JACOB EBWELLE (27), the promising HANS AGBO (20) and VICTOR AHEN N'DIP (22), while the libero will be EMMANUEL KUNDE (34 on 15 July), who took part in the 1982 World Cup finals, has experience of playing in France, and scored in the last minute of the home match against a five-man Tunisian defence. In midfield will be ANDRE KANA BIYIK (24), MBELLA NGOM (24), the left-sided BONAVENTURE DJONKEP (28), EMILE M'BOUH M'BOUH (24 on 30 May), CYRILLE MAKANAKI (25 on 26 May) who plays for Toulon, EUGENE EKEKE (30 on 15 May) who plays for Valenciennes and LOUIS-PAUL M'FEDE (28), who scored first in the home match against Tunisia. In the attack will be YVES BELLE (25 on 8 June), ERNEST EBONGUE (28 on 15 May), ALPHONSE TCHANI (22), JEAN-PIERRE M'BOUM (24), GREGOIRE M'BIDA (31) and lastly the heir of Roger Milla, FRANCOIS OMAM BIYIK (26 on 21 May), known as 'the Black Van Basten', who plays for Stade Lavallois in France, scored the single goal in Tunis, and finished as leading scorer with 5 goals. In addition to its appearance in the 1982 World Cup finals, Cameroon were champions of Africa in 1984 and 1988.

## Group C: Brazil

*Confederaciao Brasileira do Futebol founded 1914. Joined FIFA in 1923.*

*Previous appearances:* 1930, 1934, 1938 (Third), 1950 (Finalists), 1954 (Quarter-finalists), 1958 (Winners), 1962 (Winners), 1966, 1970 (Winners), 1974 (Fourth), 1978 (Third), 1982 (Second Round) and 1986 (Quarter-finalists).

*Present tournament:* Headed South American Group 3 with 7 points from 4 matches against CHILE (1-1 away and 2-0 awarded at home) and VENEZUALA (4-0 away and 6-0 at home).

*The manager and players:* After the 1986 World Cup CARLOS ALBERTO SILVA was appointed as manager, but the CDB is notorious for being inconsistent, and not until 6 January 1989 was SEBASTAIO LAZARONI (39) confirmed as the man to regain honours for Brazil in the footballing world. He steered his team to victory in the 1989 South American Championship, the first trophy of any type that Brazil had won since the 1970 World Cup, and this proved a nice prelude to the Qualifying matches. However, with many leading players choosing to follow the more lucrative footballing life in Europe (many of them in Italy), the lack of stability has not helped the formation of a settled side; but although the flair which we have all come to expect from the Brazilians will be present, the highly-respected Lazaroni has stiffened the side defensively by using a libero behind two central defenders and two laterals, so that memories of the defeat against Italy in 1982 can be exorcised. The men in contention could be CLAUDIO TAFFAREL (24 on 8 May), ACACIO (31) or ZE CARLOS (28) in goal. In defence will be MAURO GALVAO (28), an authoritative libero, or the Marseilles-based JOSE-CARLOS MOZER (29), and in front of him on the right JOSIMAR (28), JORGINHO (25) who is with Bayer Leverkusen and can also play in midfield, the central defenders being the highly gifted ALDAIR (24), RICARDO ROCHA (28) and the left-footed ANDRE CRUZ (22), while on the left will be MAZINHO (23) or BRANCO (26 on 4 April), a skilful back who has experience of playing in Italy. In midfield are VALDO (26) now with Benfica, the combative DUNGA (26) who plays for Fiorentina, the foraging ALEMAO (28) who plays for Napoli, GEOVANI (26 on 6 April) who plays for Bologna, TITA (32 on 1 April) who plays for Pescara, the stylish and influential SILAS (24) and BISMARCK (20), one of the stars of the 1989 World Youth Cup. Among the forwards are the Dutch-based ROMARIO (24), the skilful CARECA (29) who plays for Napoli and scored 4 of Brazil's goals in the Qualifying tournament, the enormously talented if slightly-built BEBETO (26), the gifted MULLER (24) who has spent two seasons with Torino and the speedy JOAO PAULO (26), who plays for Bari.

# The teams who will be competing

## Scotland

*Scottish Football Association founded in 1873. Joined FIFA 1910–20, 1924–28, 1946.*

*Previous appearances:* 1954, 1958, 1974, 1978, 1982 and 1986.

*Present tournament:* Finished second in European Group 5 with 10 points from 8 games behind YUGOSLAVIA (1–1 at home and 1–3 away) but ahead of FRANCE (2–0 at home and 0–3 away), NORWAY (2–1 away and 1–1 at home) and CYPRUS (3–2 away and 2–1 at home).

*The manager and players:* ANDY ROXBURGH (46) took over after Scotland had experienced a disappointing time in the 1986 World Cup and steered them to a fifth consecutive qualification – a remarkable record for such a small footballing country. JIM LEIGHTON (31) plays in goal with ANDY GORAM (26 on 13 April) as his deputy, while the men in front of him could include the outstanding RICHARD GOUGH (28 on 5 April), the elegant CRAIG LEVEIN (25), GARY GILLESPIE (30 on 7 May), WILLIE MILLER (35 on 2 May), his colleague at Aberdeen ALEX McLEISH (31) and MAURICE MALPAS (27). The midfield can call upon the play-making PAUL McSTAY (25), STEVE NICOL (28), ROY AITKEN (31), MURDO McLEOD (22) who plays for Borussia Dortmund, JIM BETT (30), the gifted GARY McALLISTER (25), together with the Everton pair of the courageous STUART McCALL (24) and the exciting PAT NEVIN (27) who loves to run with the ball, as does the experienced GORDON STRACHAN (33). In the attack will be the prolific MAURICE JOHNSTON (27 on 13 April), his club mate at Rangers ALLY McCOIST (27), or four players from clubs outside Scotland, GORDON DURIE (24) of Chelsea, BRIAN McCLAIR of Manchester United, the speedy ROBERT FLECK (24) of Norwich and ALAN McINALLY (27) of Bayern Munich. The chief scorer with 6 goals was JOHNSTON.

## Sweden

*Svenska Fotbollforbundet founded 1904. Joined FIFA 1912.*

*Previous appearances:* 1934, 1938 (Fourth), 1950 (Third), 1958 (Second), 1970, 1974 and 1978.

*Present tournament:* Headed Group 2 with 10 points from 6 games ahead of ENGLAND (0-0 away and 0-0 at home), POLAND (2-1 at home and 2-0 away) and ALBANIA (2-1 away and 3-1 at home).

*The manager and players:* OLLE NORDIN (40), who played for Sweden when the country last qualified for the World Cup finals in 1978, has had to live with the problems caused by having many of his team playing abroad. The goalkeeper has been the dependable THOMAS RAVELLI (30) with as his deputies the promising SVEN ANDERSSON (26) and BENGT NILSSON (32). ROLAND NILSSON (26) has often been at right-back, while in the centre of the defence have been the inspiring libero GLENN HYSEN (30), PETER LARSSON (29) as stopper with at left-back the promising ROGER LJUNG (23), while among the reserves are ANDREAS RAVELLI (30), DENNIS SCHILLER (25) and STEFAN REHN (23). The midfield has stars currently playing in Italy such as the majestic GLENN STROMBERG (30) who is with Atalanta of Bergamo, ROBERT PRYTZ (30) now with Verona, the elegant ANDERS LIMPAR (24) with Cremonese, while other talent includes the promising JONAS THERN (23), LEIF ENGKVIST (27), JAN NILSSON (25) and HANS HOLMQUIST (30 on 27 April) who also plays in Italy. Among the forwards are JOHNNY EKSTROEM (25) now playing in France, who also has played in Italy, MATS MAGNUSSON (27 on 10 July), who has been scoring freely since his transfer from Malmoe to Benfica in 1987, HANS ESKILSSON (24), the exciting MARTIN DAHLIN (23) and STEFAN PETERSSON (27). EKSTROEM was the chief scorer with 2 goals.

## Costa Rica

*Federacion Costaricenese de Futbol founded 1921. Joined FIFA 1927.*

*Previous appearances:* None.

*Present tournament:* First Round beat PANAMA (1-1 at home, 2-0 away), passed through Second Round thanks to the disqualification of MEXICO, and in the Third Round finished top with 11 points from 8 matches above the UNITED STATES (1-0 at home and 0-1 away), TRINIDAD and TOBAGO (1-1 away

## The teams who will be competing

and 1-0 home), GUATEMALA (0-1 away and 2-1 home) and EL SALVADOR (4-2 away and 1-0 home).

*The manager and players:* The Uruguayan coach GUSTAVO DE SIMONE was replaced after the first game, a 0-1 loss to Guatemala in March 1989, by the Spaniard ANTONIO MOYANO REIAN, who in turn was soon succeeded by MARVIN RODRIGUEZ RAMIREZ (42). A small country in Central America which lies between Panama to the south and Nicaragua to the north, Costa Rica's opportunities of appearing in the finals of this tournament have been frequently nullified by the footballing strength of Mexico to its north. The players, who are part-timers, started preparing for the World Cup in February. The leading goalkeeper has been GABELO CONEJO (30) whose models are Walter Zenga and Renat Dassaev, with JORGE HIDALGO (26) and HERMIDIO BARRANTES (25) as his deputies. The defence will be drawn from VLADIMIR QUESADA (24 on 12 May), the captain ROGER FLORES (33 on 26 May), MAURICIO MONTERO (26), RONALD MARIN (27), ENRIQUE DIAZ (31) and JOSE CHAN (29 on 12 June). In midfield he can choose from GERMAN CHAVARRIA (31), the goal-scoring JUAN CAYASSO (29), CARLOS MARIO HIDALGO (28), OSCAR RAMIREZ (25), ALVARO SOLANO (29 on 25 June), and the powerful HECTOR MARCHENA (26). In the attack of this fluid 4-4-2 system will be the skilful and experienced EVARISTO CORONADO (29), who plays for Saprissa, the wealthiest team in Costa Rica, and the swift and highly promising HERNAN MEDFORD (22 on 23 May), with their deputies being CLAUDIO JARA (31 on 6 May), GILBERTO RHODEN (27), or the recently-selected PASTOR FERNANDEZ (27) – and maybe Marvin Rodriguez will choose some of the stars from the Costa Rican side at the 1989 World Youth Cup such as RONALD GONZALEZ (19), who can curl a mean free-kick, or HAROLD LOPEZ (20 on 19 June). Of the 10 goals 3 each were scored by FLORES and JUAN CAYASSO.

## Group D: West Germany

*Deutscher Fussball-Bund founded in 1900. Joined FIFA in 1904–1945, 1950.*

*Previous appearances (including pre-war Germany):* 1934 (Third), 1938, 1954 (Winners), 1958 (Fourth), 1962 (Quarter-finalists), 1966 (Finalists), 1970 (Third), 1974 (Winners), 1978 (Second Round), 1982 (Finalists) and 1986 (Finalists).

*Present tournament:* Second in European Group 4 with 9 points from 6 games behind HOLLAND (0–0 at home and 0–0 away) but in front of FINLAND (4–0 away and 6–0 at home) and WALES (0–0 away and 2–1 at home).

*The manager and players:* FRANZ BECKENBAUER (44) took over in July 1984 and in 1986 steered West Germany to a second appearance as beaten Finalists, although his team had several players not wholly fit. Indeed ever since then Beckenbauer has been blessed with so many injuries that only twice has he been able to field the same side. The goalkeeper has normally been BODO ILLGNER (23 on 7 April) with RAIMOND AUMANN (26) as his deputy. In defence will be the outstanding THOMAS BERTHOLD (25) who now plays for Roma, the straight-backed stopper GUIDO BUCHWALD (28), the fierce-shooting KLAUS AUGENTHALER (32) as libero, HANS PFUGLER (30), JURGEN KOHLER (24), ALOIS REINHARDT (28) and the formidable ANDREAS BREHME (29) who moved to play for Internazionale-Milan in 1988. ANDREAS MOELLER (22), a new star of the highest talent, has come into midfield along with THOMAS HAESSLER (24 on 30 May), the highly experienced LOTHAR MATTHEAUS (29) also with Inter, STEFAN REUTER (23), and the compact OLAF THON (24 on 1 May) together with his colleague at Bayern Munich HANS DORFNER (25 on 3 July). Among the forwards will be PIERRE LITTBARSKI (30 on 16 April), RUDI VOLLER (30 on 13 April), who plays with Roma, the gifted JURGEN KLINSMANN (25) who joined his compatriots at Internazionale in 1989, and the talented KARLHEINZ REIDLE (24). The chief scorer was RUDI VOLLER with 4 of the 13 goals. In the last nine editions of the World Cup, West Germany have been victorious in 1954 and

# The teams who will be competing

1974, Finalists in 1966, 1982 and 1986, Semi-finalists in 1958 and 1970 and Quarter-finalists in 1962. With a spine of five outstanding players intimate with Italian conditions, it should again perform most creditably.

## Yugoslavia
*Fudbalski Savez Jugoslavije founded 1919. Joined FIFA 1919.*

*Previous appearances:* 1930 (Semi-finalists), 1950, 1954 (Quarter-finalists), 1958 (Quarter-finalists), 1962 (Fourth), 1974 (Second Round) and 1982.

*Present tournament:* Headed European Group 5 with 14 points from 8 games against SCOTLAND (1–1 away and 3–1 at home), FRANCE (3–2 at home and 0–0 away), NORWAY (2–1 away and 1–0 at home) and CYPRUS (4–0 at home and 2–1 away).

*The manager and players:* IVICA OSIM (49 on 6 May) was appointed in June 1986 and although nearly dismissed following the 1–4 home defeat by England in November 1987, remained in charge and has guided Yugoslavia in triumphant and unbeaten fashion. He has been faced with the problem well known to all managers of Yugoslavia of having to assemble his players for crucial matches from countries all over Europe. In goal will be TOMISLAV IVKOVIC (29), with FAHRADIN OMEROVIC (28) as his deputy, while in front of him will be PREDRAG SPASIC (24), VUJADIN STANOJKOVIC (26), the polished MIRSAD BALJIC (28), the dependable centre-back FARUK HADZIBEGIC (32), DAVOR JOZIC (29) who plays for Cesena in Italy, BUDIMIR VUJACIC (26), BOSKO DJUROVISKI (28) and GORAN JURIC (28). In the midfield will be the gifted play-maker DRAGAN STOJKOVIC (24), DRAZ SLISKOVIC (31 on May 30), the tall SRECKO KATANEC (27) who recently moved to play in Genoa, MILAN JANKOVIC (30), the experienced SAFET SUSIC (35 on 13 April), ZORAN VUJOVIC (31) and the immensely promising ROBERT PROSINECKI (22), voted best player at the 1987 World Youth Cup (held in Chile and won by Yugoslavia), but the frequently selected MEHMED BAZDAREVIC (29) spoilt his chances of making the trip after he spat at the referee in the Yugoslavia–Norway match and was disqualified for a year. In the attack could play RADOMIR MIHAJLOVIC (25), a central striker who moved from Dinamo Zagreb to Bayern Munich, DEJAN SAVICEVIC (23), BORISLAV CVETKOVIC (27) who plays in Italy for Ascoli, HARIS SKORO (27) who plays for Torino, DARKO PANCEV (24), DRAGAN JAKOVLJIEVIC (27) and ZLATKO VUJOIC (31), who has gained over 60 selections. DEJAN SAVICEVIC was chief scorer with 3 of the 16 goals.

## Colombia
*Federacion Colombiana de Futbol founded 1924. Joined FIFA 1936.*
*Previous appearance:* 1962
*Present tournament:* Headed South American Group 2 over PARAGUAY (1–2 away and 2–1 at home) and ECUADOR (2–0 at home and 0–0 away). In the play-off against ISRAEL, the Header of the Oceania Group, Colombia won 1–0 at home and drew 0–0 away.
*The manager and players:* FRANCISCO 'CICHO' MATURANA (41), an orthodontist and a former central defender who played in the Qualifying competitions for the 1978 and 1982 World Cups, took over as manager in 1987. A year later the Colombians were much admired when they took part in the Rous Cup, and such was his progress that by May 1989 Colombia was generally considered to be the strongest side on the continent, in addition to being the most entertaining. The penalty-taking, colourful goalkeeper who also acts as an unofficial full-back or libero is RENE HIGUITA (23) with his deputies ALBERTO CALLE (32) and EDUARDO GARCIA (22). In defence will be WILSON PEREZ (22), the cultured central defender ANDRES ESCOBAR (23), the strong LUIS CARLOS PEREA (26) and CARLOS HOYOS (28), with the reserves LEON VILLA (30) and ALEXIS MENDOZA (29 on 8 June). The jewel of the side is CARLOS VALDERRAMA (28) who recently has played in France with alongside him the fierce-shooting LEONEL ALVAREZ (24), LUIS FARJADO (26), GABRIEL JAIME GO-

# The teams who will be competing

MEZ (30), the powerful BERNARDO REDIN (27) and RICARDO PEREZ MORALES (26). In attack the most explosive striker will be the experienced and widely-travelled ARNOLDO IGUARAN (33). RUBEN DARIO HERNANDEZ (23) is a most promising goal-scorer, while the tall ALVEIRO UZURIAGA (23) is a productive right-winger; on the left plays the acrobatic JAIRO TRELLEZ (22 on 29 April) with JAIME ARANGO (28), WILMER CABRERA (22) and GUSTAVO RESTREPO (27) being the likely replacements. The top scorer with 4 of the 6 goals was IGUARAN.

## United Arab Emirates

*UAE Football Association founded 1971. Joined FIFA 1972.*

*Previous appearances:* None.

*Present tournament:* First Round ahead of KUWAIT (3–2 away and 1–0 at home) and PAKISTAN (5–0 at home and 4–1 away). In the Final Pool the United Arab Emirates finished second with 6 points from 5 matches behind SOUTH KOREA (1–1) but in front of QATAR (1–1), CHINA (2–1), SAUDI ARABIA (0–0) and NORTH KOREA (0–0).

*The manager and players:* The man who has looked after the fortunes of the UAE recently has been MARIO ZAGALO (59), who played for Brazil in 1958 and 1962, steered the team to its third triumph in 1970, and was also in charge when Brazil finished fourth in 1974. The first manager to be attracted by the enormous stipend was Don Revie, who was succeeded by coaches from Hungary and Yugoslavia. In 1988 Zagalo took over as manager from CARLOS ALBERTO PEREIRA (previously manager of Kuwait when that country qualified in 1982 but who for this particular competition chose to manage Saudi Arabia) and really knit the side together. In January 1990, however, he was dismissed and replaced by the Dutch BERNARD BLAUT (40). In goal will be the excellent MUHSIN MUSABAH (25), the best goalkeeper in the final tournament, who will have ABDEL QADIR HASSAN (28) and ADEL ANAS MUBARAK (23) as his deputies; the defence will be drawn from EISA MEER NOUR (23), FAHAD

RAHMAN ABDULLA (28), KHALIL GHANEM MUBARAK (26) the captain and a well-built and goal-scoring defender, MUBARAK GHANIM MUBARAK (27), OBAID HELAL (23), IBRAHIM MEER NAIR (23). The midfielders available will be ABDUL RAHMAN ABDULLA (26), HASSAN AL SHAIBANI (27), the team's playmaker NASSER KHAMIS MUBARAK (25), ALI AL EHAWI (22), and another promising youngster in ABDUL RAZAQ IBRAHIM (22); while the attack will be drawn from FAHAD KHAMIS MUBARAK (22), HUSSAIN GHULAM ALI (21), ABDUL AZIZ KHADOR (23) and the dangerous ADNAN KHAMIS TALYANI (25) who scored 2 goals in the final competition. With the total number of players 1,787 and the total number of clubs 23, the UAE must be the smallest footballing country to participate in the Finals.

## Group E: Belgium

*Union Royale Belge des Societés de Football Association founded 1895. Joined FIFA 1904.*

*Previous appearances:* 1930, 1934, 1938, 1954, 1970, 1982 (Second Round) and 1986 (Fourth).

*Present tournament:* Headed European Group 7 with 12 points from 8 games ahead of CZECHOSLOVAKIA (0–0 away and 2–1 at home), PORTUGAL (1–1 away and 3–0 at home), SWITZERLAND (1–0 at home and 2–2 away) and LUXEMBOURG (5–0 away and 1–1 at home).

*The manager and players:* The 67-year-old GUY THYS retired as the widely respected manager in June 1989. Having been appointed in early 1976, he saw his team play almost a hundred matches, including the European Championships of 1980 (it reached the Final) and 1984, as well as the Finals of the World Cup of 1982 and 1986. When he retired in June 1989 Belgium was well on the road to qualifying for the 1990 Finals, and he is succeeded as manager by a former player WALTER MEEUWS (39 on 11 July). MICHEL PREUD'HOMME (30), the Footballer of the Year, has been in outstanding form as the regular goalkeeper, has a very useful deputy in FILIP DE WILDE (28),

## The teams who will be competing

and in front of him is a sure trusty defence. The authoritative ERIC GERETS (36 on 18 May), who played for A.C.Milan between 1983-4, has re-established himself as right-back in preference to GEORGES GRUN (28) who may be chosen as stopper instead of GEERT BROECKAERT (25). As libero will be the tall STEPHANE DEMOL (24) who recently spent a season with Bologna, or the experienced LEO CLIJSTERS (33), while the fierce-shooting BRUNO VERSAVEL (23) will be left-back, with MICHEL DE WOLF (33) JEAN-FRANCOIS DE SART (25) and PATRICK VERVOORT (26) also in the party. The playmaker should be VICENZO SCIFO (24), who may have alongside him the defensive FRANKY VAN DER ELST (29 on 30 April), MARC EMMERS (24), the gifted attacking midfielder JAN CEULEMANS (33) and MARC BOFFIN (24). Among the forwards will be the much-travelled NICO CLAESAN (27), the promising LUC NILIS (23 on 25 May), and the men who have been at the forefront of the attack MARC DEGRYSE (24) together with his partner at Anderlecht, MARC VAN DER LINDEN (26), who scored 7 of the 15 Belgian goals.

## Spain

*Real Federacion Espanola de Futbol founded 1913. Joined FIFA 1904.*

*Previous appearances:* 1934 (Quarter-finalists), 1950 (Fourth), 1962, 1966, 1978, 1982 and 1986 (Quarter-finalists).

*Present tournament:* Headed European Group 6 with 13 points from 8 games ahead of REPUBLIC OF IRELAND (2-0 at home and 0-1 away), HUNGARY (2-2 away and 4-0 at home), NORTHERN IRELAND (4-0 at home and 2-0 away) and MALTA (2-0 away and 4-0 at home).

*The manager and players:* LUIS SUAREZ (50), who played with such distinction for Barcelona and Internazionale-Milan as a midfield creator, took charge after Spain's disappointing performance in the 1988 European Nations Championship. Although his first match saw a home defeat against Yugoslavia in a friendly, the passage through the Qualifying Group saw the first five games being won. Suarez has a team of some talent. In goal will be the experienced ANDONI ZUBIZARETTA (28), who first played in January 1985, his deputy being FERNANDO BUYO (32), while the defence should be drawn from the newly-selected MIGUEL CHENDO (28), QUIQUE FLORES (25), MANUEL SANCHIS (25 on 23 May) who sometimes plays in midfield for Real Madrid, the sweeper GENARO ANDRINUA (26 on 9 May), JIMENEZ (26) and the promising FERNANDO HIERRO (22). Available in midfield are Real Madrid's fierce-shooting MICHEL (27), from Barcelona the dynamic AMOR (22), ROBERTO (28 on 5 May), the left-sided MARTIN VASQUEZ (28) and EUSEBIO (26 on 13 April) who has just come into the side, and settled in comfortably with Udinese is RICARDO GALLEGO (31). In attack the star undoubtedly is the graceful EMILIO BUTRAGUENO (26), while aiding and abetting him could be the small, incisive MANOLO (25), who plays for Atletico Madrid, JULIO SALINAS (27), AITOR BEGUIRISTAIN (25), the swift PACO LLORENTE (24) and the fast-moving ELOY (26 on 10 July). The chief scorer with 5 of the 15 goals was MANOLO while MICHEL scored 4.

## Uruguay
*Football Associacion founded in 1900. Joined FIFA in 1923.*

*Previous appearances:* 1930 (Winners), 1950 (Winners), 1954 (Semi-finalists), 1958, 1966 (Quarter-finalists), 1970 (Semi-finalists), 1974 and 1986.

*Present tournament:* Headed South American Group 1 with 6 points from 4 games against BOLIVIA (1–2 away and 2–0 at home) and PERU (2–0 away and 2–0 at home).

*The manager and players:* OSCAR WASHINGTON TABAREZ (43) decided he could not live with the habit of many of his best players of seeking employment in Europe, so from 13 February to 24 September 1989 there was a ban on further players going abroad so that the team could prepare for the South American Championships (in which Uruguay finished in the Final) and the eliminators for the World Cup. The first-choice goalkeeper will be EDUARDO PEREIRA (26) with OSCAR FERRO (23) and JAVIER

# The teams who will be competing

ZEOLI (28 on 2 May) as his standbys. The defence will be drawn from two full-backs eager to link with the midfield in JOSE HERRERA (25 on 17 June) and ALFONSO DOMINGUEZ (24), some powerful central defenders in NELSON GUTTIEREZ (28 on 13 April), who has spent the last two seasons in Italy, the experienced HUGO DE LEON (32) who now plays for River Plate in Buenos Aires, the reserves coming from JOSE SALDANA (26), NELSON CABRERA (22), JORGE GONCALVES (23) and DANIEL REVELEZ (30). In midfield are the very experienced ANTONIO ALZAMENDI (34), in the centre the authoritative SANTIAGO OSTALAZA (28 on 10 July), JOSE PERDOMO (25) together with his team mate in Italy RUBEN PAZ (30), with GABRIEL CORREA (22), RUBEN PEREIRA (22) and PABLO BENGOECHEA (25 on 27 June). In the forward line are the Genoa-based CARLOS AGUILERA (25), RUBEN DA SILVA (22), the recently capped SERGIO MARTINEZ (21), and the two jewels of the side, the free-running ENZO FRANCESCOLI (28), and the lively opportunist RUBEN SOSA (26 on 25 April), who also plays in Italy and scored 5 of the 7 goals. The skilful Uruguay will be a difficult side to beat, so long as they do not suicidally waste their energies committing acts of Grievous Bodily Harm (as they did in 1986).

## South Korea

*Football Association founded 1928. Joined FIFA in 1948.*

*Previous appearances:* 1954, 1986.

*Present tournament*: In its First Group South Korea finished top with 12 points from 6 games against MALAYSIA (3–0 at home and 3–0 away), SINGAPORE (3–0 at home and 3–0 away) and NEPAL (9–0 at home and 4–0 away). In the Final Group, a round-robin tournament in Singapore, South Korea finished top with 8 points from 5 matches ahead of UNITED ARAB EMIRATES (1–1), QATAR (0–0), CHINA (1–0), SAUDI ARABIA (2–0) and NORTH KOREA (1–0). All told 30 goals for and only 1 against, that goal conceded after South Korea were already assured of qualifying.

*The manager and players:* LEE HOE-TAIK (43), one of the best central strikers in Asia during the Seventies, took over from KIM CHUNG-NAM who had been in charge for both the 1986 World Cup finals and the 1988 Olympic Games. KIM PONG-JOO (25) is an excellent goalkeeper with YOO DAI-SOON (25) as his deputy. CHOI KANG-HEE (31 on 12 April), CHUNG YONG-HWAN (30) and PARK KYUNG-HOON (29) are gifted central defenders, with GU SANG-BUM (26 on 15 June), KIM SANG-HO (31) and CHO YOUNG-JEUNG (35) also in contention. In the midfield will be KIM SANG-HO (25), with alongside LEE YOUNG-JIN (26), YOON DEUK-YEO (28) and HWANGBO-KWAN (28) who has a ferocious free-kick. Among the forwards will be CHOI SOON-HO (28), who in 1986 rifled home a spectacular volley against Italy, HWANG SEON-HONG (22), a stylish centre-forward and on his left KIM JOO-SUNG (24), known as the 'Signor Rossi of Korea', who was voted the best player of the final tournament. Of the 30 goals scored by South Korea in the Qualifying Round, 7 came from HWANG SEON-HONG and 5 from KIM JOO-SUNG.

## Group F: England

*Football Association founded 1863. Joined FIFA 1905–20, 1924–28, 1946.*

*Previous appearances:* 1950, 1954 (Quarter-finalists), 1958, 1962 (Quarter-finalists), 1966 (Winners), 1970 (Quarter-finalists), 1982 (Second Round) and 1986 (Quarter-finalists).

*Present tournament:* Second in European Group 2 with 9 points from 6 matches behind SWEDEN (0–0 at home and 0–0 away) but ahead of POLAND (3–0 at home and 0–0 away) and ALBANIA (2–0 away and 5–0 at home).

*The manager and players:* BOBBY ROBSON (56) has seen England through six years of qualifying games for the World Cup and the European Championship without being defeated, and the final match in this tournament saw England as the only country to qualify without conceding a goal. The goalkeeper largely responsible for this has been the ever-green PETER

# The teams who will be competing

SHILTON (40), with the much-improved DAVID SEAMAN (26) and CHRIS WOODS (30) as his deputies. GARY STEVENS (27) has been the regular right-back, but PAUL PARKER (26 on 4 April) has also played there, while at left-back the fierce-shooting STUART PEARCE (28 on 24 April) has been a regular choice, with TONY DORIGO (24) as his deputy. The positions at the centre have been taken by the quick-silver DES WALKER (24), the experienced TERRY BUTCHER (31), or TONY ADAMS (23). Alongside the inspiring BRYAN ROBSON (33) in midfield could be NEIL WEBB (26) recently recovered from injury, the experienced STEVE HODGE (27), the strong-running STEVE McMAHON (28), the gifted PAUL GASCOIGNE (23 on 27 May), two players from Arsenal in the combative DAVID ROCASTLE (23 on 2 May) and MICHAEL THOMAS (22), who can also play full-back, the versatile PAUL LAKE (21) and late choice could be the graceful GORDON COWANS (30) who spent three seasons with Bari before returning to Aston Villa. The knack of scoring comes easily to GARY LINEKER (29), the knack of creating goals comes easily to PETER BEARDSLEY (29), and other forwards who have played regularly are the fluent CHRIS WADDLE (29), now with Marseilles, and the strong-running JOHN BARNES (26), who also plays effectively as a central striker. The prolific STEVE BULL (25 on 28 March), ALAN SMITH (29), and Aston Villa's lively DAVID PLATT (24 on 10 June) might also be selected. Of the 10 goals ROBSON, BARNES, BEARDSLEY and LINEKER scored 2 each.

## Holland
*Dutch Football League founded in 1889. Joined FIFA 1924.*

*Previous tournaments:* 1934, 1938, 1974 (Finalists), 1978 (Finalists).

*Present competition:* Finished top of European Group 4 with 10 points from 6 games above WEST GERMANY (0–0 away and 1–1 at home), FINLAND (1–0 away and 3–0 at home) and WALES (1–0 at home and 2–1 away).

*The manager and players:* THIJS LIBREGTS (49) will be attempting to emulate the triumph of two years ago when his celebrated predecessor RINUS MICHELS steered Holland to victory in the 1988 European Championship. He still has the backbone of that team. In goal will be HANS VAN BREUKELEN (33) with JOOP HIELE (31) as his replacement, while the defence can call upon GRAEME RUTJES (29), SJAAK TROOST (30), SONNY SILOOY (26), JOOP LANKHAAR (23), AARON WINTER (23), as stopper BERRY VAN AERLE (27), that superbly gifted centre-back RONALD KOEMAN (27), RONALD SPELBOS (36 on 8 July), JOHN DE WOLF (28), ADDICK KOOT (25), the recently-selected HENK FRASER (24 on 7 July), and the experienced ADRI VAN TIGGELEN (33 on 17 June) who can also play as sweeper. In midfield could be skilful GERALD VANENBURG (26), the Milan-based duo of the gifted FRANK RIJKAARD (27) and the inspiring RUUD GULLIT (27), HENDRIE KRUZEN (25), ERWIN KOEMAN (28), the hard-working JAN WOUTERS (29), MARTIN LAMMERS (23) and WIM HOFKENS (31). The attack could be represented by the lethal MARCO VAN BASTEN (25), JOHNNY VAN'T SCHIP (26), JOHNNY BOSMAN (25), WIM KIEFT (27), who also has experience of playing in Italy, while among those providing service could be the highly talented BRIAN ROY (20), and PETER HUISTRA (23) another outside-left of great potential.

## Republic of Ireland
*Association founded 1921. Joined FIFA 1923.*

*Previous appearances:* None.

*Present tournament:* Finished Second in European Group 6 with 12 points from 8 games behind SPAIN (0–2 away and 1–0 at home) but ahead of HUNGARY (0–0 away and 2–0 at home), NORTHERN IRELAND (0–0 away and 3–0 at home) and MALTA (2–0 at home and 2–0 away).

*The manager and players:* JACK CHARLTON (54), centre-half for England in the 1966 World Cup Finals, took over as manager

## The teams who will be competing 167

in early February 1986. Appearing for the first time in the final stages of the 1988 European Nations Championships, Ireland performed with immense success, beating England 1-0, drawing 1-1 with the USSR (who reached the final), and losing 0-1 to the eventual victors Holland – the Dutch goal not coming until eight minutes before the final whistle. Charlton believes firmly that when his team has possession of the ball, it should make full use of it, never be vulnerable to counter-attacks and 'must always be giving the opposition something to think about.' The success of this attitude was shown by Ireland giving away only two goals in eight qualifying matches in an arduous group which contained three countries which had played in the 1986 finals. In goal will be PADDY BONNER (30) with GARY PEYTON (34) as his deputy, while in front of him Charlton can call on CHRIS MORRIS (26), CHRIS HUGHTON (31), accomplished centre-backs in KEVIN MORAN (34 on 29 April), MICK McCARTHY (31) who plays for Lyons in France, DAVID O'LEARY (33) and PAUL McGRATH (30) with STEVE STAUNTON (21) the recently-chosen left-back linking up with his experienced midfield colleagues from Liverpool, the stylish RONNIE WHELAN (28) and the hardy RAY HOUGHTON (28). Other possible midfield players include ANDY TOWN-SEND (26), the talented JOHN SHERIDAN (25) and many will be hoping that the experienced LIAM BRADY (34) will be selected. Among the forwards are the fearless TONY CASCA-RINO (27), who can be lethal inside the box, with alongside him the highly-experienced FRANK STAPLETON (34 on 10 July) or JOHN ALDRIDGE (31), and KEVIN SHEEDY (30), a tricky winger who often curls free-kicks on to his forehead. JOHN BYRNE (29), TONY GALVIN (33) and the lanky NIALL QUINN (23) have also played recently. CASCARINO, HOUGHTON and ALDRIDGE scored 2 goals each. Like Denmark in the 1986 World Cup, Ireland are expected to be the most successful of the debutants.

# Egypt

*Egyptian Football Association founded 1921. Joined FIFA in 1923.*

*Previous appearance:* 1934.

*Present competition:* Finished top of First Qualifying Round with 8 points from 6 games ahead of LIBERIA (2–0 at home and 0–1 away), KENYA (0–1 away and 2–0 at home) and MALAWI (0–0 away and 1–0 at home). In Second Qualifying Round beat ALGERIA (0–0 away and 1–0 at home).

*The manager and players:* MAHMOUD EL-GOHARY (50), famous as a celebrated goalkeeper, took over in 1988 from the former coach of Wales MIKE SMITH. It was especially gratifying to knock out Algeria, whose players possessed much international experience, had qualified for the final stages of every competition during the decade, and were known as 'the Brazilians of Africa'. The goalkeeper will be the talented AHMED SHOUBEIR (29) who has AIMAN TAHIR (23) as his deputy; while the defence will be drawn from IBRAHIM HASSAN (23), an accomplished young libero in HANI RAMZI (21), HISHAM YAKAN (26), ASHRAF KASSEM (24), SABEIR AID (21), MOHAMMED OMAR (30), ASHRAF FERCAYI (22), RABIEH YASIN (26) and ALAN MAYHOUB (22). In midfield the experienced captain GAMAL ABDELHAMID (32), a player of great ability, will be joined by MAGDI ABDELGHANI (31 on 27 July) who now plays in Portugal for Beira-Mar, the promising AHMED EL-KASS (24), BAD RAGAB (21), YASSER FAROUK (21), and AHMED RANZI (25). Among the attacking players are the experienced TAHAR ADOU ZEID (34), ALI MAHOUB (23), MOHAMMED SIDKI (25), KHALID AID (25), and Ibrahim's twin brother HOSSAM HASSAN (23), a gifted centre-forward who scored that crucial goal in Cairo to delight 100,000 people all chanting a chorus of 'Misr! Misr!' ('Egypt! Egypt!'). The chief scorer with 3 of the 6 goals was HISHAM ABDEL-RASOUL who tragically broke his left thigh in a motoring accident late in December, and is unlikely to be well enough by June to be able to play. Egypt has only once qualified for the finals, in 1934 when they were first held in Italy, and played only one game, losing 2–4 to Hungary. In January 1986 England travelled to Cairo for their only meeting and beat Egypt 4–0.

# 9 LEADING PLAYERS IN THE TOURNAMENT

Carlos AGUILERA (Uruguay). Born 21 September 1964, he is a goal-poaching forward who moved to Italy from Penarol last summer. He scored the Uruguayan goal in their 1–1 draw with Italy in Verona in April 1989, and has been on outstanding form for Genoa this season.

Roy AITKEN (Scotland). Born 24 November 1958, he is a driving midfield player who in January 1990 moved to Newcastle United from Glasgow Celtic, for whom he first played in February 1976 and with whom he was involved in much European club competition. First selected in 1980, he has been a regular choice for Scotland since 1984, and took part in the 1986 edition of the World Cup.

ALDAIR (Brazil). Born 30 November 1965 and a footballer of great versatility, Aldair can play in roles as diverse as a strong-tackling sweeper or as a defence-splitting wing. In the summer of 1989 he joined Benfica in Portugal, and has undoubtedly benefitted from becoming familiar with the more intricate defensive systems of Europe.

John ALDRIDGE (Republic of Ireland). Born in Liverpool 18 September 1958, Aldridge returned to play for Liverpool for over two seasons, before he was transferred to Real Sociedad in September 1989. Played in the 1988 European Championship. Since he has been a prolific scorer for his club sides, supporters of Ireland will be hoping that Aldridge scores handsomely in the World Cup.

Antonio ALZAMENDI (Uruguay). Born 7 June 1956, Alzamendi is an experienced right-sided attacker who took part in the 1986 World Cup and now plays in Spain. He was voted South American Footballer of the Year for 1986.

Klaus AUGENTHALER (West Germany). Born 26 September 1957, Augenthaler is an inspiring figure at the centre of the defence who took part in the 1986 World Cup. He has played club football for Bayern Munich and frequently rifles home goals from a long distance.

John BARNES (England). Born 7 November 1963, the immensely talented Barnes, who now plays for Liverpool, is a poetic but most incisive runner with the ball, first selected in May 1983 while he was with Watford. He scored an outstanding goal in June 1984 when England travelled to and beat Brazil 2–0.

Sergio BATISTA (Argentina). Born 11 November 1962, Batista's displays as a defensive midfielder were crucial in helping to gain Argentina the 1986 World Cup.

Peter BEARDSLEY (England). Born 18 January 1961, the intuitive Beardsley gained his first cap in January 1986 against Egypt, and his form alongside Gary Lineker proved crucial during the 1986 World Cup. He was transferred from Newcastle to Liverpool before the 1987–88 season, and with his tantalising runs from midfield will be seeking to instigate more goal-chances this summer.

Thomas BERTHOLD (West Germany). Born 12 November 1964, Berthold was one of West Germany's stars throughout the 1986 World Cup as a full-back of immense authority. In 1987 he moved from Eintracht Frankfurt to Verona, but now plays as stopper for Roma.

Michel BILEK (Czechoslovakia). Born 13 April 1965, Bilek is a midfield player of great authority who frequently rifles goals from a distance. He has a formidable free-kick.

Paddy BONNER (Republic of Ireland)    Born 24 May 1960 and a sure goalkeeper for Glasgow Celtic, Bonner was first selected for Ireland in May 1981 and played outstandingly in the 1988 European Championships.

Liam BRADY (Republic of Ireland). Born 13 February 1956, Brady, one of the first to be transferred to Italy when foreign stars

## Leading players in the tournament 171

began to be re-imported in 1980, helped Juventus to win the title twice in his first two seasons, and returned to England in early 1987 and joined West Ham. First selected for Ireland in November 1974, he has played over 70 times, and his experience about Italian football will be invaluable to Jack Charlton, whether playing or advising.

Claudio BRANCO (Brazil). Born 4 April 1964, Branco spent two seasons with Brescia after his outstanding performances in the 1986 World Cup, and is now a most important figure on the left side of Brazil's defence.

Andreas BREHME (West Germany). Born 9 November 1960 and married to a Spanish wife, Brehme played for Kaiserslautern and Bayern Munich before being transferred in June 1988 to Internazionale Milan, whom he helped to win the Italian championship in the 1988/89 season. A strong attacking player on the left side of the defence, he was first selected for West Germany on 2 February 1984, played in the 1986 World Cup, and could well be one of the important figures in the final tournament.

Steve BULL (England). Born 28 March 1965, Bull was first selected in May 1989 and is a raw-boned striker of real aggression, who has been lethal at club level, and many will be wondering how many Bull's Eyes he will be scoring during the summer.

Jorge BURRUCHAGA (Argentina). Born 9 October 1962, Burruchaga's role on the right side of Argentina's five-man midfield proved crucial in the 1986 World Cup, a performance duly crowned when he scored the final goal of the tournament. He was transferred to Nantes in France during July 1985.

Terry BUTCHER (England). A tall and commanding central defender who was born 26 December 1958, Butcher started his England career in 1981 and played in the 1982 World Cup. A fixture in the England team ever since, he played in the 1986 finals, and his absence through injury was part of the reason why England performed so disappointingly in the 1988 European Championships. He plays for Glasgow Rangers, whom he joined from Ipswich Town after the 1986 World Cup.

Emilio BUTRAGUENO (Spain). Born 22 July 1963, the slim Butragueno is known as 'The Vulture' – and it's a nickname he frequently lives up to, not least during the 1986 World Cup when he scored four goals in Spain's 5–1 victory over Denmark. He plays his club football for Real Madrid alongside the flamboyant Mexican Hugo Sanchez.

Paul CALIGIURI (United States). Born 9 March 1964, he is an attacking midfield player who has experience of playing in West Germany. No goal he will ever score will be more important than that in the 1–0 victory in Port of Spain against Trinidad and Tobago – a game the US had to win against the odds to qualify for the 1990 finals.

Claudio Paul CANIGGIA (Argentina). Born 9 January 1967, the flaxen-haired and Italian-based Caniggia could prove one of the delights of the tournament. A talented right-sided striker who came to Italy in 1988, he was not permitted by his club, Verona, to play in the 1988 Olympic Games, but has been on outstanding form this season for Atalanta of Bergamo.

Antonio De Oliviera Filho CARECA (Brazil). Born 5 October 1960, he made his international debut in 1982, but injured himself just before the Finals. He compensated for this during the 1986 World Cup when he scored some superb goals, and a year later was transferred to Napoli. In January 1990 he broke a bone in his right foot during a training accident with his compatriot Alemao, but if all is healed he could dovetail well with the prolific Romario.

Tony CASCARINO (Republic of Ireland). Born 1 September 1962, Cascarino qualifies to play for Ireland because the name of his maternal grandfather was O'Malley. A tall striker who has greatly contributed to the recent success of Millwall, he was brought into the Irish side during 1986, and now leads the attack. His threatening aerial power will cause many headaches for defenders in Italy.

Jan CEULEMANS (Belgium). Born 28 February 1957, Ceulemans is an attacking midfield player of great distinction who has

## Leading players in the tournament

been a regular member of the Belgian side since the team reached the Final of the 1980 European Championships. He also took part with success in the 1982 and 1986 World Cup Finals, and in August 1989 broke the record of 81 appearances held by the legendary Paul Van Himst.

Jozef CHOVANEC (Czechoslovakia). Born 7 May 1960, Chovanec was transferred from Sparta Prague to PSV Eindhoven a year ago following the departure of that other outstanding libero, Ronald Koeman. Recently he has been playing in midfield, a perfect link between the defence and attack.

Hugo DE LEON (Uruguay). Born 27 February 1958, De Leon is a formidable centre-back who makes very few errors, and is an outstanding organizer of the team's play. A truly South American figure, De Leon was born on the borders with Brazil, started his career in Montevideo, was purchased in 1980 by Gremio of Brazil, and now plays in Argentina.

Igor DOBROVOLSKI (USSR). Born 27 August 1967, Dobrovolski made his first impact on the international scene when he shone as a midfield star in the Soviet team at the 1988 Olympic football tournament, helping the USSR to beat Brazil 2–1 in the Final itself, in which he scored. He now plays further forward and is a regular member of the full side.

Carlos DUNGA (Brazil). Born 31 October 1963, the tireless Dunga was transferred three seasons ago by Vasco da Gama to Fiorentina (for whom he now plays in midfield alongside Roberto Baggio) and became a regular member of the national side in 1987.

Andres ESCOBAR (Colombia). Born 13 March 1967 and a commanding, athletic central defender, Escobar has already gained over 40 selections, and is a player who will be much admired.

Enzo FRANCESCOLI (Uruguay). Born 12 November 1961 and South American Footballer of the Year 1984, Francescoli is a central striker of undoubted skill who came to Europe after playing in the 1986 World Cup. Last summer he was transferred from Racing Paris to Marseilles, where he has recovered his appetite for the game.

Richard GOUGH (Scotland). Born in Stockholm 5 April 1962 and a defender of the highest class, Gough was one of the few successes in the Scotland team in 1986, which led to his being transferred from Dundee United to Tottenham Hotspur. He is now with Glasgow Rangers.

Stanislav GRIGA (Czechoslovakia). Born 4 November 1961, Griga is an experienced central striker who moved from Sparta Prague to Feyenoord in Holland at the end of 1989. He scored both goals when Czechoslovakia visited and beat Austria 2–1 in April 1989.

Ruud GULLIT (Holland). Born 1 September 1962 and an outstanding attacking midfield player, Gullit was elected European Footballer of 1987. Played an instrumental part in helping to win the 1988 European Championship for Holland, the league title in that same year for A.C. Milan and in 1989 the European Cup. However, in April and July 1989 he underwent serious operations on his right knee, which may prevent him playing.

Nelson Daniel GUTIERREZ (Uruguay). Born 13 April 1962 and a much travelled man, Gutierrez opened his career with Penarol, spent a season playing for Nacional in Colombia and three for River Plate in Buenos Aires who sold him in the summer of 1988 to Lazio from where he was transferred a year later to Verona. A forceful defender, he came into the national side in 1983 and took part in all four of Uruguay's games in the last World Cup.

Gheorghe HAGI (Rumania). Born 5 February 1965, 'the Maradona of the Carpathians' didn't start to play football until he was 13, but within months he moved to Bucharest, progressed through the ranks of youth and junior football, and now is among the most inventive midfield players in Europe, the real motor of the Rumanian side.

## Leading players in the tournament

Thomas HAESSLER (West Germany). Born 30 May 1966, a player who might be compared to past midfield heroes such as Fritz Walter, Gunter Netzer and Wolfgang Overath, Hassler appeared on the international scene during 1988 and has provided much inspiration in an area of the field where West Germany has been noticeably weak in recent seasons.

Andreas HERZOG (Austria). Born 10 September 1968, he is an attacking midfield player of great gifts who has come into the side recently and could develop into a footballer of some stature.

Rene HIGUITA (Colombia). Born 28 August 1966 and one of the game's real eccentrics, the small but brave Higuita is a goalkeeper who takes penalties, likes to double as a substitute libero or fullback, and has been known to dribble the ball to the halfway line.

Ray HOUGHTON (Republic of Ireland). Born 9 January 1962, Houghton is an imaginative right-sided midfield player who is now with Liverpool. He gained his first selection in 1986, and played outstandingly in the 1988 European Championships.

Glenn HYSEN (Sweden). A central defender of great authority who was born 30 October 1959, Hysen played in Sweden for Gothenburg before spending three unhappy seasons with PSV Eindhoven, who played him out of position. He joined Fiorentina during the summer of 1987 where he spent two years until he was transferred to Liverpool in July 1989.

Stefan IOVAN (Rumania). Born 23 August 1960, although he plays as libero for his club side of Steaua Bucharest, Iovan has established his position on the right of Rumania's defence, frequently making surging runs which culminate in penetrating crosses.

Maurice JOHNSTON (Scotland). Born 13 April 1963, Johnston is a much-travelled player whose notoriety in becoming the first Catholic ever to be signed by Glasgow Rangers has tended to obscure his lethal talent as a striker. He was not taken to the 1986 World Cup but scored 6 goals in the Qualifying tournament.

**JORGINHO (Brazil).** Born as Jorge de Amorim Campos 17 August 1964, Jorginho is a lateral defender similar in style to the former international Junior, who moves at a lightning pace and loves to set up attacks. He plays his club football in West Germany for Leverkusen.

**Srecko KATANEC (Yugoslavia).** Born 16 July 1963, the tall Katanec made his international debut as a defensive midfielder in November 1983, and during 1984 played in all three of Yugoslavia's matches in the European Championship, succeeded by the Los Angeles Olympics (in which Yugoslavia finished third). In 1989 he moved from Stoccard in West Germany to play in Genoa for Sampdoria.

**Vagiz KHIDIATULIN (USSR).** Born 3 March 1959, he is an outstanding centre-back who was first selected in 1980, then appeared only irregularly before returning to represent the Soviet Union team in the 1988 European Championships. He now plays in France for Toulouse.

**Jurgen KLINSMANN (West Germany).** Born 30 July 1964 and a tall, lithe central striker, he joined Internazionale of Milan from Stoccard during 1989, and has settled in most effectively. He played in the 1988 European Championship, and must relish the prospect of taking part in this World Cup since West Germany have been seeded to play in Milan.

**Ronald KOEMAN (Holland).** Born 21 March 1963, he is a centre-back of immense distinction who was on outstanding form in June 1988 when Holland won the European Championships. A year later he was transferred from PSV Eindhoven to Barcelona whose manager is his compatriot Johan Cruyff. Strikes free-kicks with awesome ferocity.

**Lubos KUBIK (Czechoslovakia).** Born 20 January 1964, he is a compact and intelligent midfield player who was transferred to Fiorentina before the start of last season.

**Jim LEIGHTON (Scotland).** Born 24 July 1958, Leighton has been the first-choice goalkeeper for Scotland since 1985, and

## Leading players in the tournament

was outstanding in the 1986 World Cup. He used to be with Aberdeen (whom he helped to win the 1982-83 Cup Winners' Cup), but now he plays for Manchester United.

Gary LINEKER (England). Born 30 November 1960, Lineker started his career as a clever goalscorer with Leicester City, moved on to Everton before going on soon after the 1986 World Cup to play for Barcelona. An attack of hepatitis sadly affected his form during the 1988 European Championships, but he returned to play for Spurs in July 1989, and will be eager to equal his triumph of four years ago when he became the first Briton ever to become chief goalscorer.

Pierre LITTBARSKI (West Germany). Born 16 April 1960, Littbarski was first selected in October 1981 and scored two of the goals in the 3-1 victory against Austria in Vienna. A waspish player down both flanks, he has become a permanent fixture in West Germany's football in recent seasons.

Silviu LUNG (Rumania). Born 9 January 1957, Lung is a tall and commanding goalkeeper who has made himself a cornerstone in the Rumanian defence. First selected in 1980, he played in all of Rumania's matches in the 1984 European Championships.

Mick McCARTHY (Republic of Ireland). Born 7 February 1959, this tall and commanding centre-back who has a powerful throw, started his career with Barnsley before moving on to Manchester City and Glasgow Celtic, and was transferred in May 1989 to Lyons in France. First selected in 1985, he took part in all three of Eire's matches in the 1988 European Championships.

Paul McGRATH (Republic of Ireland). Born 4 December 1959, the versatile McGrath can either play as a stopper or take on defensive duties in midfield. He also scores important goals, one such being in Eire's 2-0 victory over Hungary in May 1988 when he unlocked the Hungarian defence with a powerful shot from 30 metres.

Paul McSTAY (Scotland). Born 22 October 1964 and first selected in 1984 McStay played in only one game during the

1986 World Cup. He has since become a permanent fixture in Scotland's midfield, and by playing for Glasgow Celtic has benefited from experiencing European club competition.

Mats MAGNUSSON (Sweden). Born 10 July 1963, Magnusson is a striker who moved from Malmoe to Servette in Switzerland. He is now with Benfica, for whom he scores very frequently, and has formed a close understanding with his clever midfield compatriot, Jonas Thern.

Diego MARADONA (Argentina). Born 30 October 1960 and the footballing phenomenon of this age, Diego Maradona has been selected more times than any other Argentinian player. First chosen by Argentinos Juniors when he was only 16 and elected South American Footballer of the Year for 1979 and 1980, he moved on to Boca Juniors before being transferred to Barcelona after the 1982 finals and to Napoli in 1984. Despite daily reports concerning his lack of fitness (from both Napoli and Buenos Aires), he captained Argentina in the World Cup of 1986, made some penetrative runs from midfield into the attack, and scored crucial goals with various parts of his body. For the second consecutive Finals, he could be the outstanding character; particularly since Argentina plays several of its games in Napoli, where Maradona is almost a deity.

Dorin MATEUT (Rumania). Born 5 February 1965, the fierce-shooting Mateut is a regular scorer, as was underlined last season when he scored the most goals in Europe.

Lothar MATTHEAUS (West Germany). Born 21 March 1961, Mattheaus is a midfield player of great talent, who also has a happy knack of scoring important goals. After spending five seasons with Borussia Moenchengladbach and four with Bayern Munich he moved to Internazionale of Milan after the 1988 European Nations Championship. He performed outstandingly for his country in the 1986 tournament.

MAURO GALVAO (Brazil). Born 19 December 1961, Mauro Galvao has been given the responsibility of strengthening Brazil's

## Leading players in the tournament

defence as a libero – a role that he fulfills superbly. A brilliant tackler, he is a very quick reader of the game.

Tony MEOLA (United States). Born 21 January 1969, the young Meola, whose grandparents are Italian, gained his first selection in June 1989 and progressed quickly last autumn to become his country's goalkeeper, ahead of the more experienced David Vanole. He had the uplifting experience of playing excellently in the vital match when USA beat Trinidad and Tobago 1–0 and should relish the amount of practice he will be given when the World Cup starts. In January he had trials with Sheffield Wednesday along with his midfield compatriot, John Harkes.

Alexei MICHAILICHENKO (USSR). Born 30 March 1963 and a long-striding and influential figure in midfield, he was outstanding in the European Championships and Olympic Games of 1988. Although recently he has been out of the game for a lengthy time he remains a Soviet player much coveted by wealthy clubs in Italy and Spain.

Andreas MOELLER (West Germany). Born 2 September 1967 and transferred for a record fee between German clubs in December 1987 when he moved from Eintracht Frankfurt to Borussia Dortmund, Moeller is a right-sided midfield player who was first selected in September 1988, and can be guaranteed to be one of the stars of the tournament.

Luis MULLER (Brazil). Born 31 January 1966, Muller is an athletic winger who came into the Brazil side during 1984 and played in the 1986 finals. He was transferred from Sao Paolo to Torino during 1988.

Steve NICOL (Scotland). Born 11 December 1961, Nicol is a commanding player on the right side of Liverpool and Scotland's midfield. First selected in 1965, the following year saw him providing displays of the highest class during the 1986 World Cup, and his all-round consistency means that Scotland will benefit again from his skills.

Ruben PAZ (Uruguay). Born 8 August 1959 and South American

Footballer of the Year 1988, Ruben Paz was transferred during July 1989 from Racing Avellaneda in Argentina to Genoa to join his compatriots Jose Perdomo and Carlos Aguilera, and now plays more as a provider than a poacher of goals.

Robert PECL (Austria). Born 15 November 1965, Pecl is a tight-marking central defender who plays for Rapid Vienna and will be watched closely by scouts for Italian clubs.

Hugo PEREZ (United States). Born 8 November 1963, the extrovert Perez was 14 when his parents decided to emigrate from El Salvador to San Diego where he soon found success as a midfield footballer who likes to join in with the attack. Indeed, few goals he will ever score will prove more vital than that he drove home in the 1-0 away victory against, ironically, San Salvador. At present he is playing in France.

Anton POLSTER (Austria). Born 10 March 1964, Polster was transferred by Austria Vienna to Torino in 1987, where he remained for only one season before moving on to Seville in Spain. He was first selected in 1984, since when he has been a regular choice, and has been lethal recently, as was amply demonstrated by his hat-trick against East Germany in November 1989 – a game that Austria had to win.

Oleg PROTASOV (USSR). Born 14 February 1964, Protasov has been a regular fixture as central striker in recent years and scores a goal in every other game, although he took part in only half a match during the 1986 World Cup.

Alberto PUMPIDO (Argentina). Born 30 July 1957, Nery Pumpido was called in to play for Argentina just prior to the 1986 World Cup, during which his outstanding displays gave much confidence to his defence.

Frank RIJKAARD (Holland). Born 30 September 1962 to a Dutch father and a mother from Surinam, he plays sweeper in front of rather than behind the defence. He was outstanding in the 1988 European Championships, and now playing for A.C. Milan, can be expected to repeat that success in the World Cup.

## Leading players in the tournament 181

Bryan ROBSON (England). Born 11 January 1957, first selected against Ireland in February 1980 and a crucial figure during the decade, the inspiring Robson has become essential to the well-being of English football. A driving midfield player who holds records for scoring speedy goals (World Cup in 27 seconds, at Wembley in 38). Although in early February he underwent an operation for a groin strain, he will relish playing in his third World Cup Finals, and put behind him the sad memories of that in 1986, and the tale of the dislocated shoulder.

ROMARIO de Souza (Brazil). Born 29 January 1966 and transferred in 1988 by Vasco da Gama to PSV Eindhoven, Romario is a most exciting central striker who finished as the leading scorer in the 1988 Olympic Games with 7 goals. He scored Brazil's goal in the Final when the South Americans lost 2–1 to USSR.

Oscar RUGGIERI (Argentina). Born 26 January 1962 and now gaining experience with Real Madrid, Ruggieri is a central defender of great determination who was outstanding during the 1986 World Cup. Since then he has played in Spain for Logrones and is now with Real Madrid.

Yuri SAVICHEV (USSR). Born 13 February 1965, he has just come into the senior Soviet side after playing most creditably in the 1988 Olympic Games in which he scored the final goal in the 2–1 victory against Brazil.

Enzo SCIFO (Belgium). Born 19 February 1966, the gifted Scifo moved from Anderlecht to Internazionale Milan for the 1987–88 season. Like many others, he failed to adapt to the passion of the Italian game, and now is playmaker for Bordeaux.

Peter SHILTON (England). Born 18 September 1949, as Dino Zoff triumphed in the World Cup of 1982 and Pat Jennings shone in that of 1986, Peter Shilton will be set to prove that certain goalkeepers, like good claret, improve with age. He was first selected in November 1970, will be playing in his third World Cup and during this tournament will break the world record for caps received – a figure which surely would have been much larger but for his omission from international teams while Don Revie was the manager.

Paulo SILAS do Prado Pereira (Brazil). Born 27 August 1965, he was the most exciting player when Brazil won the 1985 World Youth Cup. He came on as a substitute twice during the 1986 World Cup, but now is an authoritative provider on the right side of Brazil's midfield, is very industrious, and has an excellent touch.

Haris SKORO (Yugoslavia). Born 2 September 1962, Skoro is a tall and agile forward who played for six seasons with Zeljeznicar, and moved from Dinamo Zagreb to Torino in June 1988. He ran through England's defence to score a memorable goal when Yugoslavia played at Wembley in December 1989.

Ruben SOSA (Uruguay). Born 25 April 1964 as Sosa Ardaiz Ruben, this quick-thinking stocky player moved from Danubio in Uruguay to Real Zaragoza in Spain during 1985 before joining the Roman club of Lazio in 1988. Was on incisive form in the Group games against Bolivia and Peru, scoring 5 goals in the 4 games.

Dragan STOJKOVIC (Yugoslavia) will be one of the most skilful midfield players on view. Born 12 November 1965 and selected on more than 40 occasions, Stojkovic has a clear vision of any game, is an excellent runner with the ball, an imaginative and precise passer, and also possesses a fierce shot.

Glenn STROMBERG (Sweden). Born 5 January 1960, the tall and well-built Stromberg has the appearance of a Nordic god, and performs like one, making daunting runs from midfield and scoring important goals. Formerly with Gothenburg and then Benfica in Portugal, in 1985 he moved to play for Atalanta of Bergamo.

Claudio TAFFAREL (Brazil). Born 8 May 1966, Taffarel was among the stars when Brazil reached the final of the Olympic Games, and made some dramatic saves during the penalty shoot-out with West Germany at the semi-final stage. Descended

## Leading players in the tournament

from German ancestry, with the former Uruguayan goalkeeper Ladislao Mazurkiewicz as his hero, he has an excellent long throw, is always calm and not given to histrionics.

Alveiro 'Palomo' UZURIAGA (Colombia). Born 12 September 1966, he is a tall player who formerly used to play basketball. Uzuriaga is still an unknown quantity, but he has the instincts of a poacher, has scored some important goals (such as that in the home game against Israel), and could blossom in this tournament.

Carlos VALDERRAMA (Colombia). Born 2 September 1961, Valderrama is a most elegant and constructive midfield player. Technically perfect, he dribbles with mastery and is an excellent passer of the ball. Elected South American Footballer of the Year for 1987, he was transferred during 1988 to play in France for Montpellier, took some time to settle, but now that he has joined Marseilles has rediscovered his drive.

Candido Filho VALDO (Brazil). Born 12 January 1964 and an incisive midfield player, Valdo was in Brazil's squad for the 1986 World Cup although he did not play. He was transferred to Benfica in 1987.

Marco VAN BASTEN (Holland). Born 31 October 1964, Van Basten is an instinctive predator who together with Ruud Gullit was transferred from Ajax to A.C. Milan in 1987. An electric finisher who scored the most goals in Europe 1985–6, he scored decisive goals in the 1988 European Championship and the 1989 European Cup Final, and has been European Footballer of the Year for both those two years.

Hans VAN BREUKELEN (Holland). Born 4 October 1956, Van Breuklen broke a bone in his left hand while training for the start of the 1989/90 season but recovered and will certainly be one of the best goalkeepers in the competition. He made his debut in October 1977, since when he has played more than 50 times, and was excellent in the 1988 European Championships.

Marc VAN DER LINDEN (Belgium). Born 4 February 1964, he is an incisive striker who plays for the leading club side of

Anderlecht, and has the distinction of having scored most goals (7) in the Qualifying competition.

Rudi VOLLER (West Germany). Born 13 April 1960, Voller burst on the football scene during his first season with Werder Bremen in 1982. Selected for the 1984 and 1988 European Championships and for the 1986 World Cup, he is a player of incisive skills who moved to Roma in 1987.

Chris WADDLE (England). Born 14 December 1960, Waddle played in the last World Cup when he was with Newcastle, was soon after transferred to Tottenham Hotspur, and now plays for Marseilles. His great strength is beating opponents with his running, and lately he has been on truly inspirational form.

Des WALKER (England). Born 26 November 1965 and brought into the side in the past two seasons, he is an exceptionally fast central defender whose speed has been vitally important for England's defence.

Ronnie WHELAN (Republic of Ireland). Born 25 September 1961, Whelan is an inspiring midfield player. Recruited by Liverpool from Dublin's famous soccer nursery of Home Farm, he has gone on to play more than 300 games. First selected by his country in 1981, he has become a mainstay in recent seasons, and has played more than 40 times.

Mike WINDISCHMANN (United States). Born 24 April 1965, Windschmann is an authoritative sweeper who has been a regular member of the side for the past three years, and was outstanding in that 1–0 victory against Trinidad and Tobago in November 1989.

Alexandr ZAVAROV (USSR). Born 26 April 1961, Zavarov was transferred by Dinamo Kiev to Juventus during August 1988. He took some time to settle into the regimen of Italian football, but now playing alongside his compatriot Sergei Aleinikov he has been on outstanding form.

# 10 ITALY – THE RECORD, THE MANAGER AND THE PLAYERS

Italy's record in the World Cup is most distinguished. The country acted as Hosts in 1934 when it won the tournament, and was victorious again in 1938 when the final stages took place in neighbouring France. After the war it qualified in 1950 and 1954, was eliminated by Northern Ireland in 1958, but then came a run of SIX successive qualifications in 1962, 1966, 1970 (when it reached the Final), 1974, 1978 (Fourth), 1982 (Winners on the third occasion), prior to it competing in 1986. Those eleven appearances produced the following results:

| P | W | D | L | F | A |
|---|---|---|---|---|---|
| 47 | 25 | 11 | 11 | 79 | 52 |

The urbane AZEGLIO VICINI was promoted from administering the Under-21 side on the resignation of ENZO BEARZOT after the 1986 World Cup. He has recently guided the national team in friendly matches against several countries of stature competing during June and July such as AUSTRIA (1–0), RUMANIA (0–1), URUGUAY (1–1), then followed games against three other seeds in BRAZIL (0–1), ENGLAND (0–0) and ARGENTINA (0–0), with a game in February against the 1988 European Champions, HOLLAND (0–0). Although Italy scored handsome 4–0 victories against HUNGARY and BULGARIA (both of whom qualified in 1986), he must be profoundly concerned by the goal famine that has struck his team.

The players he will call upon could be these:

Carlo ANCELOTTI. Born 10 June 1959, Ancelotti is an experienced midfield player who in 1988 moved from Roma to A.C. Milan. In October 1981 injured his right knee and was out for a year; he came back but in December 1983 injured his other knee and was forced to be away from the game for another eleven months.

Roberto BAGGIO. Born 18 February 1967, one of his best games this season must have been the 4–0 victory against Bulgaria last September, in which he scored twice and throughout the game showed himself to be a midfield player of outstanding gifts. He is a regular scorer at club level, which talent could become influential in the thinking of his manager.

Franco BARESI. Born 8 May 1960, Baresi showed himself to be a central defender of infinite class on his first appearance for A.C. Milan when he was only 17, and in 1978–79 he helped the club to win its tenth championship, playing in every match. He gained his first national selection in December 1982, but has been a regular member of the side only since October 1987. Although he lacks a spectacular shot, he compensates for this by reading the game with intelligence, tackling bravely and distributing astutely, often starting moves that conclude in an Italian goal. An inspiration.

Giuseppe BERGOMI. Born 22 December 1963 and the only player still selected from the side that was victorious in the 1982 World Cup, the hard-tackling Bergomi was the youngest Italian player to have been selected 60 times when he was chosen for the game against Brazil in October 1989 at only '25 anni, 9 mesi, 20 giorni'.

Nicola BERTI. Born 14 April 1967, Berti is an attacking midfield player who was transferred from Fiorentina to Internazionale at the start of the 1988–89 season, and promptly helped it to win the League championship.

Andrea CARNEVALE. Born 12 January 1961, Carnevale was transferred from Udinese to Napoli before the 1986–87 season and straightaway helped it to win its first League championship.

Massimo CRIPPA. Born 17 May 1965, Crippa is a busy midfield player who in 1988 moved from Torino to Napoli, whom he

## Italy – record, manager and players

helped to win the 1988-9 UEFA Cup. He missed the 1988 European Games because of injury but took part in the 1988 Olympic Games.

Luigi DE AGOSTINI. Born 7 April 1961 in Udine, De Agostini is a hard-tackling defender who also played for Verona before moving on three years ago to his present club, Juventus.

Fernando DE NAPOLI. Born near Avellino 15 March 1964, De Napoli first played for that town before being transferred to Napoli after the 1986 World Cup in which he played as a defensive midfield player.

Roberto DONADONI. Born 9 September 1963, he is most effective on the right side of the attack, making lengthy, sinuous runs from midfield. He plays his club football for A.C. Milan.

Ciro FERRARA. Born 11 February 1967, he is a young central defender who can play either at left-back or stopper.

Riccardo FERRI. Born 20 August 1963, Ferri is a strong stopper who was first selected in December 1986 and played in all Italy's games in the 1988 European Championship. After carrying a shoulder injury for most of the season, he finally had it operated on in late November and only started playing again in March.

Luca FUSI. Born 7 June 1963, Fusi is a tireless midfield player with Napoli, whom he helped to win the UEFA Cup in May 1989.

Giuseppe GIANNINI. Born 20 August 1964, captain of Roma, he gave a most impressive performance in November 1989 when Italy came to Wembley and gained a 0-0 draw.

Paulo MALDINI. Born 26 June 1968, an attacking fullback of great potential, he was first selected in March 1988 and played in the 1988 European Championships. However, his weakness in defence has let him down on several occasions, and he will want to tighten up that aspect of his game.

Roberto MANCINI. Born 27 November 1964, he was first selected in May 1984, and for several years he has been a club partner at Sampdoria to the outstanding Gianluca Vialli following his transfer from Bologna, for whom he appeared when only 16.

Giancarlo MAROCCHI. Born 4 July 1965 and a tireless worker on the right side of midfield, he now plays for Juventus, whom he joined from Bologna in 1988.

Gianluca PAGLIUCA. Born 18 December 1966, a young goalkeeper of immense promise, the tall Pagliuca joined Sampdoria from Bologna during 1986.

Salvatore SCHILLACI. Born in Palermo 1 December 1964, and filling a role with Juventus taken popularly by another famous son of Sicily in Pietro Anastasi, Schillaci joined Messina in the lower divisions but has scored regularly in his first season in the top division, many from free-kicks of frightening power.

Aldo SERENA. Born 25 June 1960, and an often-transferred player (Inter, Como, Bari, Milan, Torino, Juventus), Serena is now back with Inter scoring important goals. He was in the Italian party for the 1986 World Cup.

Stefano TACCONI. Born 13 May 1957, he is the deputy to Walter Zenga. He gained his first selection in June 1987, the 3-1 victory against Argentina in Zurich.

Gianluca VIALLI. Born 9 July 1964, he was first selected as a substitute in November 1985, but although he played in all four of Italy's matches in the 1986 World Cup, he did not gain his first outright selection until October 1986, since when he has become Italy's principal attacker. He broke a bone in his foot in late 1989, which might have affected his form.

Walter ZENGA. Born 28 April 1960, Zenga is a most accomplished goalkeeper who has been a first choice since October 1986, and bears comparison with recent internationals such as Dino Zoff and Enrico Albertosi.

# 11 COMPLETE FIRST ROUND DRAW

On December 7 the top seeds were announced as being ITALY, ARGENTINA, BRAZIL, WEST GERMANY, BELGIUM and ENGLAND. The remaining 18 teams were drawn into three pools so as to avoid the strongest playing each other. In pool 1 were SPAIN, SOVIET UNION, SCOTLAND, AUSTRIA, YUGOSLAVIA, and HOLLAND; in pool 2 were COLOMBIA, URUGUAY, CZECHOSLOVAKIA, REPUBLIC OF IRELAND, RUMANIA and SWEDEN; while in pool 3 were CAMEROON, EGYPT, SOUTH KOREA, UNITED ARAB EMIRATES, COSTA RICA and the UNITED STATES. The Draw took place in Rome on 9th December. Although it will play its other two Group games in Napoli, as Holders, Argentina will play the Opening Match of the tournament in Milan at 6 p.m. on Friday 8th June, with the Final being played in Rome a month and two hours later.

### GROUP A
*Olympico, Rome; Communale, Florence*

| | | | | |
|---|---|---|---|---|
| JUNE 9 | Italy | Austria | Rome | 9 p.m. |
| JUNE 10 | Czechoslovakia | United States | Florence | 5 p.m. |
| JUNE 14 | Italy | United States | Rome | 9 p.m. |
| JUNE 15 | Austria | Czechoslavakia | Florence | 5 p.m. |
| JUNE 19 | Italy | Czechoslovakia | Rome | 9 p.m. |
| JUNE 19 | Austria | United States | Florence | 9 p.m. |

### GROUP B
*Opening Game at Meazza, Milan; Sao Paolo, Naples; Della Vittoria, Bari*

| | | | | |
|---|---|---|---|---|
| JUNE 8 | Argentina | Cameroon | Milan | 6 p.m. |
| JUNE 9 | Soviet Union | Rumania | Bari | 5 p.m. |
| JUNE 13 | Argentina | Soviet Union | Naples | 9 p.m. |
| JUNE 14 | Cameroon | Rumania | Bari | 9 p.m. |
| JUNE 18 | Argentina | Rumania | Naples | 9 p.m. |
| JUNE 18 | Soviet Union | Cameroon | Bari | 9 p.m. |

## GROUP C
*Communale, Turin; Luigi Ferraris, Genoa*

| JUNE 10 | Brazil | Sweden | Turin | 9 p.m. |
| JUNE 11 | Scotland | Costa Rica | Genoa | 5 p.m. |
| JUNE 16 | Brazil | Costa Rica | Turin | 5 p.m. |
| JUNE 16 | Scotland | Sweden | Genoa | 9 p.m. |
| JUNE 20 | Brazil | Scotland | Turin | 9 p.m. |
| JUNE 20 | Sweden | Costa Rica | Genoa | 9 p.m. |

## GROUP D
*Meazza, Milan; Renato Dell'Ara, Bologna*

| JUNE 9 | Colombia | United Arab Emirates | Bologna | 9 p.m. |
| JUNE 10 | West Germany | Yugoslavia | Milan | 9 p.m. |
| JUNE 14 | Yugoslavia | Colombia | Bologna | 5 p.m. |
| JUNE 15 | West Germany | United Arab Emirates | Milan | 9 p.m. |
| JUNE 19 | West Germany | Colombia | Milan | 5 p.m. |
| JUNE 19 | Yugoslavia | United Arab Emirates | Bologna | 5 p.m. |

## GROUP E
*Communale, Verona; Friuli, Udine*

| JUNE 12 | Belgium | South Korea | Verona | 5 p.m. |
| JUNE 13 | Spain | Uruguay | Udine | 5 p.m. |
| JUNE 17 | Belgium | Uruguay | Verona | 9 p.m. |
| JUNE 17 | Spain | South Korea | Udine | 9 p.m. |
| JUNE 21 | Belgium | Spain | Verona | 5 p.m. |
| JUNE 21 | Uruguay | South Korea | Udine | 5 p.m. |

## GROUP F
*Sant'Elia, Cagliari; Della Favorita, Palermo*

| JUNE 11 | England | Republic of Ireland | Cagliari | 9 p.m. |
| JUNE 12 | Holland | Egypt | Palermo | 9 p.m. |
| JUNE 16 | England | Holland | Cagliari | 9 p.m. |
| JUNE 17 | Republic of Ireland | Egypt | Palermo | 5 p.m. |
| JUNE 21 | England | Egypt | Cagliari | 9 p.m. |
| JUNE 21 | Holland | Republic of Ireland | Palermo | 9 p.m. |

## SECOND ROUND

| JUNE 23 | B1 | v | A3/C3/D3 | Naples | 5 p.m. |
| JUNE 23 | A2 | v | C2 | Bari | 9 p.m. |
| JUNE 24 | C1 | v | A3/B3/F3 | Turin | 5 p.m. |
| JUNE 24 | D1 | v | B3/E3/F3 | Milan | 9 p.m. |
| JUNE 25 | A1 | v | C3/D3/E3 | Rome | 9 p.m. |
| JUNE 25 | F2 | v | B2 | Genoa | 5 p.m. |
| JUNE 26 | F1 | v | E2 | Bologna | 9 p.m. |
| JUNE 26 | E1 | v | D2 | Verona | 5 p.m. |

# Complete First Round Draw

### QUARTER-FINALS

| | | | | | |
|---|---|---|---|---|---|
| JUNE 30 | W/TURIN | v | W/VERONA | *Florence* | *5 p.m.* |
| JUNE 30 | W/GENOA | v | W/ROME | *Rome* | *9 p.m.* |
| JULY 1 | W/BARI | v | W/MILAN | *Milan* | *9 p.m.* |
| JULY 1 | W/NAPLES | v | W/BOLOGNA | *Naples* | *9 p.m.* |

### SEMI-FINALS

| | | | | | |
|---|---|---|---|---|---|
| JULY 3 | W/FLORENCE | v | W/ROME | *Naples* | *8 p.m.* |
| JULY 4 | W/MILAN | v | W/NAPLES | *Turin* | *8 p.m.* |

### THIRD PLACE MATCH

JULY 7                                                                  *Bari*      *8 p.m.*

The competing countries are: —

.................................. v ..................................

### FINAL

JULY 8                                                                   *Rome*      *8 p.m.*

The competing countries are:

.................................. v ..................................

The players are:

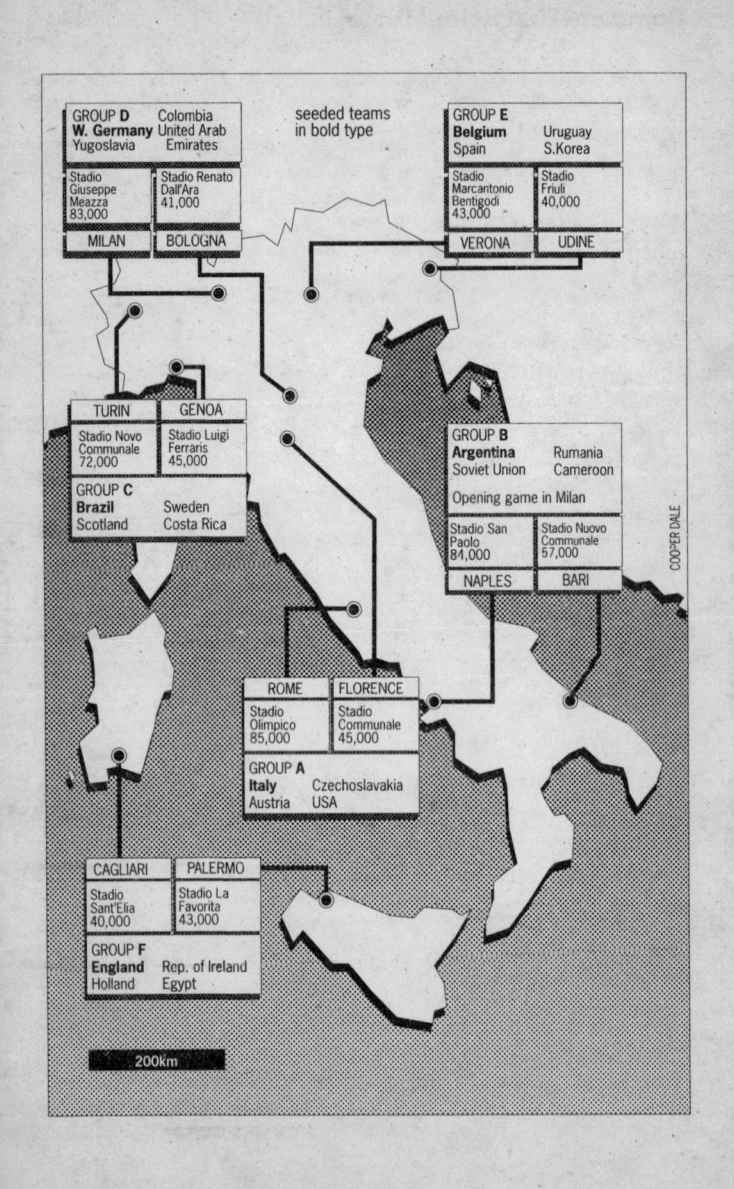

## GROUP D
**W. Germany** Colombia
Yugoslavia United Arab Emirates

| Stadio Giuseppe Meazza 83,000 | Stadio Renato Dall'Ara 41,000 |
|---|---|
| MILAN | BOLOGNA |

seeded teams in bold type

## GROUP E
**Belgium** Uruguay
Spain S.Korea

| Stadio Marcantonio Bentigodi 43,000 | Stadio Friuli 40,000 |
|---|---|
| VERONA | UDINE |

| TURIN | GENOA |
|---|---|
| Stadio Novo Communale 72,000 | Stadio Luigi Ferraris 45,000 |

## GROUP C
**Brazil** Sweden
Scotland Costa Rica

## GROUP B
**Argentina** Rumania
Soviet Union Cameroon

Opening game in Milan

| Stadio San Paolo 84,000 | Stadio Nuovo Communale 57,000 |
|---|---|
| NAPLES | BARI |

· COOPER DALE ·

| ROME | FLORENCE |
|---|---|
| Stadio Olimpico 85,000 | Stadio Communale 45,000 |

## GROUP A
**Italy** Czechoslovakia
Austria USA

| CAGLIARI | PALERMO |
|---|---|
| Stadio Sant'Elia 40,000 | Stadio La Favorita 43,000 |

## GROUP F
**England** Rep. of Ireland
Holland Egypt

200km